Indelible Big Blue Memories

Life in the THINK Tank

Winston C. Fraser

Foreword by John M. Thompson

1225 rue Bellevue
Saint-Lazare, QC J7T 2L9
438-969-2510
wcfraser@sympatico.ca

Layout and production: Jim Fraser

Front cover photo: Fraser family archives

Back cover photos:
    Top row: punch card and UPC code: Author's collection
              PC: Courtesy of Steven Stengel, oldcomputers.net
    Bottom: Fraser family archives

Printed and bound in Canada by:

Katari Imaging
282 Elgin St.
Ottawa, ON K2P 1M3
613-233-1999
www.katariimaging.com

ISBN: 978-0-9950842-3-0

Contents

Dedication

This book is lovingly dedicated to my family: To my late dad, Donald Fraser, who taught me binary arithmetic. To my late mom, Alice Hood, who nurtured and encouraged me. To my late wife, Rebecca (Becky) Humphrey, who unconditionally loved me and supported me throughout my career. And to our children, Andrea, Charles, Elaine and Elizabeth, who have always been and continue to be a source of great pride and much joy.

In a love letter from April 1967, my fiancée (and bride-to-be) wrote: "Whatever you decide to do. . . I will be with you 100% and will support you at all times." And that she did for the next 25 years.

My parents, Donald Fraser and Alice Hood; my wife, Becky Humphrey; our children Andrea, Charles, Elaine and Elizabeth; 1983 (Photo by author)

Foreword

It was at least 25 years ago that I last heard the name Winston Fraser, so you can imagine my surprise when I unexpectedly received his note asking if I would write a Foreword to his book, *Indelible Big Blue Memories*.

I remember Winston from working together at IBM in Montreal where he was a talented, young Systems Engineer and I was his Branch Manager. We worked together on the world's first pilot of scanning systems for grocery store checkouts. I also recall his later reputation across IBM for being an expert consultant in all types of computerized store systems and for the many software applications that he created for our customers.

Winston's story is about how he developed from his humble beginnings growing up on a farm in the Eastern Townships of Quebec and attending a small rural school to becoming one of IBM's technical geniuses.

IBM is a company where anyone can aspire to a career in a multiple of disciplines: technical, sales, marketing, finance, manufacturing, R&D and so on. Many of us took advantage of this and followed various paths. Winston, however, stayed true to his love of systems engineering and programming throughout his career and earned the reputation of becoming a master at finding solutions to challenging customer problems.

Reading Winston's story is a trip down memory lane for those of us who lived through the dawn of the computer age. We experienced the exponential growth, challenges and excitement of the first four decades of an industry that changed the world. Commitment, passion and hard work flowed in our veins.

Winston walks us through his descriptions of what life at IBM was like in those days by relating a myriad of interesting anecdotes, many of them seen through the eyes of his friends and colleagues and even including a few of my own. His long list of contributors from the Montreal Datacentre, the Montreal Branch and elsewhere in IBM Canada, U.S.A. and Europe brings back many fond memories of those who were there and their numerous experiences. As expected, many of the stories are hilarious, particularly when seen through the culture of the day and of IBM.

In each chapter Winston has also incorporated some charming exhibits of memorabilia that he collected and preserved over the years. Included as well are some of his excellent photographs. Who knew, for instance, that Winston was accredited by National Geographic, National Wildlife Federation and Encyclopedia Britannica, and had his photographs featured in Hallmark's annual calendars?

One of the messages that will resonate with IBM readers is Winston's descriptions of IBM being a special place to work. The focus on serving customers, the esprit de corps, the importance of making a contribution, and the respect we all had for families and colleagues comes through loud and clear.

I am honoured to write this Foreword and hope you enjoy reading *Indelible Big Blue Memories* as much as I did.

—John M. Thompson, retired Executive Vice-Chairman, IBM Corporation

Preface

Outside the horse barn at Pine Hill Farm, Cookshire,
Que., ca. 1956 (Photo by Malcolm Fraser)

This is the unlikely story of a shy farm boy who hated school but ended up working more than 25 years for one of the world's most successful companies of the 20th century. It chronicles my 27-year IBM career that ironically began – of all places – in the classroom!

Before I joined IBM Canada in May 1965 I had never even seen a computer. So it was with equal amounts of excitement and trepidation that I became an employee of the company that would become known as "Big Blue." Hired as a programmer trainee, I somehow managed to remain in a technical role throughout my career, resisting the pressure to move into marketing or management roles. This was no meagre achievement, especially in a company that was known, first and foremost, as a marketing juggernaut. However, it gave me the unique opportunity to work on software development projects that stretched the limits of both the available technology and my cognitive capabilities.

This book is a candid collection of recollections, more than 25 years later, of what life was like working in the world's premier THINK tank. It highlights both the deep demands and the rich rewards of working at IBM, a company whose main motto was "THINK." It relates challenges we faced and hilarious incidents that occurred. And it even contains some personal confessions revealed for the first time. Very importantly, it pays tribute to my contemporaries, many of whom have shared their own memories within these pages. As colleagues, managers and mentors (or in some cases tormentors!) during our IBM days, some became lifelong friends. To my fellow IBMers, with whom I shared both the trials and the triumphs, I owe an enormous debt of gratitude. Without them and their support, I could never have survived, not to mention succeeded.

These recollections are presented in the form of a trip down Memory Lane with frequent stops en route. The journey begins on Boyhood Backroad to learn about my early days, growing up on a farm in Quebec's Eastern Townships. It then continues to Classroom Cloister to take a look at my schooling. The trip resumes on Datacentre Drive to experience the technical achievements of the Scientific Services department of the Montreal Datacentre. We then spend a significant amount of time on Scanning Street to witness a world's-first implementation of UPC barcode scanning and its exciting aftermath. Our route leads us next across a variety of different pastures to Petroleum Place where we add a European flavour to our travels. After a pause to reflect on extracurricular projects, offsite adventures and the IBM company as I knew it, we finally end up on Afterlife Avenue where we discover, to our surprise, that there actually **is** life after IBM!

May you enjoy this journey back in time – whether to relive some of your own experiences, to learn something new about the IBM of my day, or just to be entertained and inspired.

Disclaimer: Every effort has been made to ensure the accuracy of the material presented. However, given that much of this book relies on the collective memories of septuagenarian and octogenarian colleagues of events that happened as long as 50 years ago, it is impossible to give an iron-clad guarantee!

Winston

Acknowledgements

Firstly, I wish to thank IBM for having given me more than 25 years of challenging, enjoyable and rewarding employment, upon which this book is based. Secondly, I would like to recognize the many IBM colleagues who responded to my reach out and kindly shared their memories, photographs and other memorabilia. The list is very long and I apologize in advance to anyone who may have been inadvertently omitted. To all of the following, I extend my sincere thanks. Your contributions have made this book what it is – an inside look at a great company in its heyday.

Adele Berenstein, Alex Klopfer, André Erian, André Gauthier, André Joubert, Bill Selmeier, Bill Tyrrell, Bob Kostiuck, Bob McLachlan, Bruce Marshall, Bruce Singleton, Carmelo Tillona, Claude Huot, Cliff Carrie, Colin James, Dainius Lukosevicius, Dan Hopping, Dave Mordecai, Dave Moxley, Dave Shonerd, David Antebi, David Dolman, David Gussow, Debbie Rourke, Don Heys, Ed Streich, Eilish Kelly McCallum, Eric Moss, Frank Hall, Gabor Fabian, Garth Durrell, Gary Mohr, George Dunbar, George Galambos, Giorgio Toso, Gord Kelsey, Gord Wishart, Harry Berglas, Harvey Bergman, Jack Sams, Jacques Crépeau, Joe Kern, Joe Major, John Sailors, John Thompson, Jonas Bacher, Kathy Stivin, Khalil Barsoum, Larry Diamond, Lee Fesperman, Margaret Eastwood, Mary Biedermann, Michel Parent, Norm Ullock, Paul Biron, Paul Morrison, Peter Bedoukian, Peter Benda, Phil Lester, Pierre Allaire, Pierre Lussier, Ray Hession, Reg Emery, Richard Wilding, Robbie Kemeny, Robert Dionne, Roger Archambault, Sally Harmer, Stan Albert, Stan Marchand, Sue Pidoux Carlisle and Wayne Giroux.

As well, I extend my appreciation to several non-IBMers who have assisted in various ways: Anna Grant, Bob Simon, Claudette Jacks-Nancoo, Denise Richard, Dr. Charlie Carman, Durwood Fincher, Eric Major, Gordon Beck, Jim MacKinnon, Louise James, Monika Fabian, Peter Gurd, Phil Norton, Phil Scheuer, Selby Shanley, Ted Warn, and my children: Andrea, Charles, Elaine and Elizabeth.

I would be remiss not to mention the very helpful cooperation of Amy Bradley of IBM Corporation in obtaining permission to use IBM copyrighted material in this book. I also wish to thank Pat and Bill Ivy, who encouraged me to write the book; artist James Harvey for the excellent sketches that he created to illustrate scenes and situations for which no photographic evidence was available; my son-in-law Greg Beck for his photo retouching services; and Dr. Derek Booth, Barbara Challies and Brian Jenkins for their book reviews. Finally, a special word of appreciation to my brother Jim for his expert proofreading, layout and production services.

Chapter 1   Binary Beginnings

The obvious place to begin a story would be at the beginning. But in my case, when was the real "beginning"? Was it being born as the fifth of 12 children to a poor farming family in the Eastern Townships of Quebec? Perhaps. Or was it learning how to do math before I started school? Maybe. Was it being convinced by my high school teachers to attend university instead of immediately getting a job? Possibly. Or was it deciding to attend an on-campus IBM recruitment interview during my final year of university, even though I had already lined up a job? Could be. In fact, each of the above circumstances, in its own way, could be considered as the beginning. So I will briefly cover each of them in turn.

My first family photo, Pine Hill Farm, 1944 (Fraser family archives)

The family farm

My dad was a fourth-generation farmer in the small town (approximately 1000 residents) of Cookshire, Quebec, located between the larger centres of Sherbrooke and Lac Mégantic. He made a meagre living tilling the same land as his paternal grandfather's father-in-law, who had emigrated from the United States in 1796. Dad's paternal great-grandfather had emigrated from Scotland to Quebec in 1790 as part of the Highland Clearances.

Ever since the late 1790s and up until a few years ago, Pine Hill Farm (as it came to be known) was the site of an active agricultural operation that involved almost every species of farm animal and food crop known to man. In addition to the cattle, horses and swine, there were silver foxes and turkeys. In addition to the world's best turnips and strawberries, crops have included sugar beets, popcorn, hops and horseradish. And let's not forget the maple products – syrup, sugar and wax. Dad was an excellent farmer who worked very hard in the fields, the forests and the barns. Mom was the quintessential farm housewife, who not only cared for us kids and her invalid mother-in-law, but also tended to every aspect of running the household. She also kept a daily diary – perhaps I inherited some of her writing skills!

No less than six generations of our family have tilled the fields, pampered the animals and toiled night and day to eke out a hard but honourable living on this land. Around 1960, as Dad began to slow down, my older brother Malcolm (we call him "Moose") became the latest Fraser to take on this responsibility. He enthusiastically embraced farming and was the initiator of many advances in the farming methods used. In fact, it is safe to say that Moose introduced more changes during his tenure than did all his ancestor predecessors combined. Among the machinery, tools and techniques that he brought to Pine Hill Farm for the first time: the tractor, the pickup truck, the hay baler, the chainsaw, barn ventilators and purebred livestock – to name but a few. Truly he singlehandedly

My birthplace, Pine Hill Farm, Cookshire, Que. (Photo by author)

With my 'Fraser 12" siblings, ca. 1965 (Photo by Dick Tracy)

brought Pine Hill Farm into the age of modern agriculture.

But Moose's farming advancements did not happen without difficulties and, indeed, opposition. Dad's feeling was that if four-legged horsepower was good enough for him and three previous generations, it should be good enough for his son. Dad used a pair of heavy Belgian draft horses for every aspect of farm work: plowing, harrowing, mowing, hay loading, hauling wood and gathering maple sap. He loved his horses and cared for them like children. After a hard day's work he would unharness them and rub down their sweaty backs with fresh straw.

My siblings and I worked very hard on the farm. We were probably seen by some as unpaid hired hands. Personally, I never felt that way. It was the only life that I knew as a youngster, so I considered it normal. Doing the haying took all summer because of the outdated methods we used. We were fortunate to finish haying in time to attend the County Fair in late August, but in rainy summers, haying might last right up to Labour Day and the return to school. In addition to our full-time summer farm work, we had daily farm chores throughout the year. My duties began at 5 a.m. when I headed to the woods to find the cows and bring them to the barn for milking. Next I would clean out the horse stable – hopefully without being kicked by the old grey mare. Then I would sit on a three-legged wooden stool to milk four or five cows before eating breakfast and getting ready for

Dad haying with horses, Pine Hill Farm, Cookshire, Que.:
Mowing (top) and hauling a load (above) (Photos by author)

Top: Dad's maple sugar camp (cabane à sucre), 1958;
Above: Hauling wood for the furnace and cookstove, 1957 (Photos by author)

Fraser family outhouse at Pine Hill Farm, Cookshire, Que. (Photo by author)

Baking bread in woodstove oven at Pine Hill Farm, 1957 (Photo by author)

school. On the way to school I delivered milk to neighbours and fetched the mail for my godparents (my godfather was the local Member of Provincial Parliament).

Although we lived in a large, solidly-built brick farmhouse, it lacked most modern conveniences. It had no flush toilet but it did have a large three-hole outhouse in the back of the attached woodshed. It had a wood furnace in the cellar and a wood cookstove in the kitchen where Mom baked bread and cooked all our meals. We had no bath or shower; a large oval-shaped washtub was brought into the kitchen for our weekly clean-up. We had no refrigerator; in summer food was kept cool in the giant icebox in the shed. Unsurprisingly, we had no automatic washer or dryer. But we did have an old-fashioned wringer-washer that Mom operated every Monday; the clothes were then hung out, even in winter, on the 100-yard clothesline to dry. Being the fifth child and having two older brothers, most of my clothes were hand-me-downs, except for the occasional new item from Sherbrooke's bargain store, Au Bon Marché. We had no TV, but we enjoyed the radio, listened to records on the hand-cranked gramophone, and played board games such as checkers, Monopoly and Snakes & Ladders. In retrospect, our way of life sounds quite primitive, but at the time it seemed quite normal to me.

My parents never owned a car, so we didn't travel far when I was a child. An occasional trip to Sherbrooke – a full 15 miles away – was a major adventure. The only long trip I can recall from my early years was a school trip to Montreal to see the famous Sun Life building. Little did I realize that one day I would work directly across the street, in the IBM Building at 5 Place Ville Marie.

As I reflect on how my life on the farm influenced my IBM career, I can identify several ways. Most importantly, it instilled in me a strong work ethic. It also provided ample experience in problem solving and crisis management. And it taught me to have humility and respect. Being part of a large family, I also learned the importance of teamwork. Finally, it taught me the ability to concentrate in the midst of constant noise and sometimes chaos.

Playing checkers with Dad, ca. 1954 (Fraser family archives)

School days

Let me begin by stating that I hated school. Perhaps it was because my academic career began on the wrong foot. But more likely it was due to my personality – I was painfully shy. Family legend has it that I would hide under the kitchen table whenever visitors would come to the door! I would emerge from my hiding-place only after they left.

But before I discuss my schooldays, I would like to share a special pre-school experience that ultimately impacted my IBM career. When I was about four years old, Dad taught me how to "figger." (That was how he pronounced "figure.") Yes, he taught me how to count (1-2-3-4-5-6-7-8-9-10, etc.) and to do simple arithmetic (1+1=2, etc.). But that was much too elementary. He also taught me the powers of 2: 2-4-8-16-32-64, etc. Years later, Mom tells the story about finding me still awake when she came upstairs to bed, and asking me, "Why are you still awake?" Apparently my response was, "I'm trying to figure out what 512 times 2 is." With these binary beginnings at the age of four, perhaps it is little wonder that I was destined for a career in computers!

In September 1949 Dad proudly walked me to the local Cookshire High School to

"Are they gone yet?" (Sketch by James Harvey)

"How much is 512 times 2?" (Sketch by James Harvey)

With my siblings and our Grade 1 teacher Louisa Elliott, 1964 (Photo by Dick Tracy)

My elementary and high school, Cookshire, Que. (Photo by author)

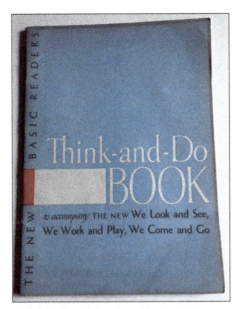

Think-and-Do school workbook, 1950s
(ebay.com)

register me for Grade 1 (there was no kindergarten in those days). But the school refused to accept me because I was too young (I was only five). Dad probably protested and told them that I already knew how to do math, but it was all to no avail. So I was taken back home and had to wait another full year before starting my unhappy years of formal education.

The next year I started school for real. For meek little me it was a most difficult experience. I think it was on the very first day when I peed in my pants because I didn't know how to use the flush toilet, and was afraid to ask. My Grade 1 teacher was Miss Louisa Elliott (or "Miss Ett," as we pronounced it), who was a primary grade teacher for more than 30 years at Cookshire school. For much of that time she taught grades 1-4 in the same classroom. From 1941 to 1965, every one of my 11 brothers and sisters, as well as myself, experienced the unique tutelage of this remarkable woman.

Miss Elliott taught me enough about discipline to last a lifetime. She possessed an impressive array of natural tools to accomplish the task: lungs of leather, the vision of an eagle, the hearing of a canine, the memory of an elephant, and the stature of a sergeant major. On top of this, she was a veritable mind reader. Even while this dear lady was busy teaching one of the other three grades in the classroom, we poor innocents couldn't get away with a single thing. For anyone who dared try, the punishment was immediate and unmerciful: that icy stare, with eyes practically popping from their sockets, was the first indication that you were in trouble. The scolding bellow from her built-in loudspeaker confirmed your worst fears, and the invitation to sit beside her at the front of the classroom represented the final humiliation. I am grateful that Miss Elliott taught me to respect authority, something that has proved invaluable in my later life. Unfortunately, though, this experience of discipline through fear caused me to develop an intense dislike for school, an attitude that persisted throughout my student life and even beyond.

One aspect of elementary school that I clearly remember were the "Think-and-Do" work books. The memory of these challenging exercise books that accompanied the "Dick and Jane" series of reading books came vividly back to mind when I first encountered THINK notepads at IBM.

During my high school years I became somewhat less shy, but still did not enjoy the classroom experience – I was always afraid of being asked a question to which I didn't know the answer. However, through the encouragement of some of my teachers, particularly Mrs. Hazel Burns and Mrs. Mary McGerrigle, I participated in public speaking contests. As a result, in Grade 10 I earned a trip to New York City as part of the United Nations Pilgrimage for Youth. The work of the interpreters in the Security Council and General Assembly fascinated me, and I aspired to become a translator.

The following year I graduated from high school first in my class. Although I did well academically, I had no interest in furthering my education. I was just very happy to be done with school. I was finally free – no more classes, no more books! It was time to get a job and start working like my older brothers had done. My two older sisters had both gone to college, but no one in my family had ever attended university. However, the two high school teachers mentioned earlier – whom I respected greatly – had other ideas for me. And somehow they succeeded in convincing me that I should go on to university.

University

But now, having acquiesced, I faced two very significant problems. Firstly, how would I pay for it? My parents didn't have the financial resources. Secondly, where

My alma mater, Bishop's University, Lennoxville, Que. (Photo by author)

Wearing frosh hat and name placard on my first day at university, 1961 (Fraser family archives)

would I stay? It would be very costly to live on campus. Almost miraculously, both problems were quickly solved. Our local Member of Parliament, Claude Gosselin, was able to arrange for a bursary to cover my tuition fees. And my eldest sister, who lived in the university town of Lennoxville, Quebec, invited me to live with her family for free. So in September 1961 I entered the four-year Bachelor of Science program at Bishop's University, a small (less than 1000 students) liberal arts institution founded in 1843 as a college for the training of Anglican priests. Here we were required to wear long, black made-in-England academic gowns to all classes. Although I was enrolled in the Physics-Mathematics program, I also took courses in religion (it was compulsory) and languages (English, French and Russian). My first year was particularly challenging – especially Calculus, which I failed the first term. As the years progressed, I became more confident and started to do things that would have been totally out of character for me only a few years earlier.

I joined the Literary and Debating Society and participated in debating tournaments as part of Bishop's "B" team. (I never made it to the "A" team that included such luminaries as former Globe and Mail Editor-in-chief Norman Webster and lawyer/politician David Marler.) This experience of "thinking on my feet" proved useful later at IBM when going on customer calls, making presentations or giving courses. Under the guidance of one of my Physics professors, Dr. Harry Dutton, I founded the Physics Society and organized a series of speakers on subjects ranging from atomic energy to new math, and arranged field trips to such places as the Satellite Field Station in Andover, Maine. Without realizing it, these organizational activities honed skills that I would put to good use at my future employer.

My only exposure to computers and data processing during my university years occurred during a summer job with the Meteorology Division of the Department

Debating at University of Vermont International Debating Tournament, 1963 (Author's collection)

of Transport in Toronto in 1964. I was assigned a project to study climactic conditions in Canada's far north. My mission was to extract wind and blowing snow data from the dusty old weather report archives of the remote northern outposts and to analyze the relationships. To do the analysis, the data was punched onto cards and processed through an IBM card sorter.

There you have it – the first 21 years of my life compressed into a few pages. On the one hand, it illustrates what an unlikely background I had to one day work for a company like IBM. On the other hand, it reveals a variety of indicators along the way that portended my ultimate employment destination.

Chapter 2   D-Days of 1965

The Cambridge English Dictionary provides the following secondary definition of the term "D-Day": "a day when something important will happen." For me, the year 1965 was replete with such days. In this chapter I will discuss my own personal D-Days and their impact on my IBM career.

ATTENTION

GRADUATING STUDENTS IN

COMMERCE

ENGINEERING

MATHEMATICS

IBM

Interviewing For Positions In The
Montreal Data Centre
Thursday, January 28, 1965

STUDENTS INTERESTED

Please Sign The Interviewing Schedule At The Placement Service

International Business Machines Company Limited

615 Dorchester Blvd. West, Montreal, Que.

IBM Datacentre recruitment ad in the McGill Daily newspaper, Jan. 27, 1965 (Courtesy of International Business Machines Corporation, © 1965 International Business Machines Corporation)

Decision days

In January 1965, only a few months before my graduation from Bishop's University, Professor Dutton called me into his office to deliver some good news. His friend and former colleague in British Columbia was prepared to offer me an associate professorship in the Physics department of the B.C. Institute of Technology. Naturally I felt very honoured to receive such an offer. Just imagine –

4. We find the complement of a number by subtracting each digit in the number from 9 and then adding 1 to the result. Thus the complement

of 1 3 9 5
is 8 6 0 4
+ 1
= 8 6 0 5

In the following computations, if the sum of two numbers exceeds four digits, omit the left-most digit and add 1 to the right-most digit. Thus

5 3 4 7
+ 7 1 2 5
equals → ①2 4 7 2
omit + 1
equals 2 4 7 3 Answer

Given that A = 9106, B = 4937 and C = 2859, perform the following computation in accordance with the above procedures.

Find the complement of the quantity [A plus the complement of (B+C)]

Answer: _8689_

B   4937
+ C +2859
7796
Complement of (B+C) 2203
+ 1
equals 2204
+ A 9106
1 3 1 0
$X_{any} = [A + Comp. (B+C)]$ equals 1 3 1 1
8688
Comp. of X equals + 1
8689

Part of my IBM interview Programming Aptitude Test, 1965 (Courtesy of International Business Machines Corporation, © 1965 International Business Machines Corporation)

going from being an undergraduate student to becoming an associate professor in one fell swoop! It almost seemed too good to be true. I thanked Dr. Dutton and gave him my verbal acceptance. He assured me that the paperwork would follow "in due course."

Around the same time, job interview notices were popping up on the bulletin boards of the Student Union building. Among the companies recruiting were several that were familiar to me, including Bell Telephone, Shell Oil and Imperial Oil. There were also some that I knew nothing about, including International Business Machines Company Limited. In any case, I wasn't particularly interested in signing up for interviews. When my friends asked me which companies I had selected for interviews, I replied, "None, because I already have a job." But they insisted, "Aw, c'mon, you should attend some interviews just for the heck of it." So I relented and signed up for a few.

My IBM interview with a Mr. Bartram was most interesting, in that it opened my eyes to a whole new world of which I was totally unaware. Shortly thereafter I received a letter from Mr. D. J. Lynn, Systems Engineering Manager, inviting me to go to Montreal for a second interview. On February 19 I had my interview at the IBM office on 1255 Laird Blvd. in Town of Mount Royal (TMR). While there I wrote the IBM Service Bureau's programming aptitude test. I remember thinking what an unusual test it was. I had never seen anything like it. (I learned many years later that I had scored 90%.) In any case, a few short days later, on February 22, I received in the mail IBM's job offer: Datacentre Systems Trainee, at a starting salary of $475 per month. The job description document that accompanied the employment offer included the following statements:

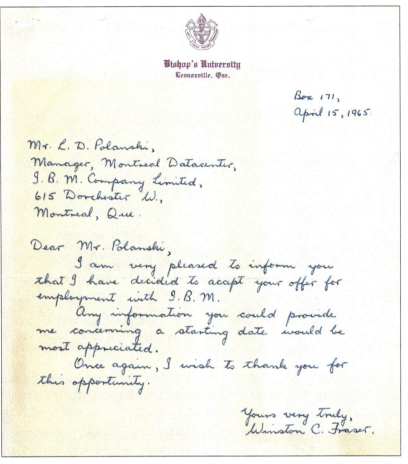

Letter of Acceptance of employment at IBM, 1965

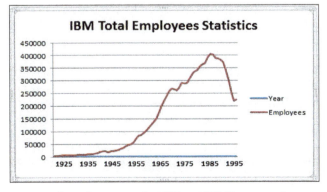

IBM Total Employees graph, 1925 to 1995 (Courtesy of
International Business Machines Corporation, ©
International Business Machines Corporation)

The IBM Systems Engineer is a professional man. As a problem solver rather than a theoretical scientist, he is concerned with intelligent, workable economical solutions to data processing problems. His technical support function will keep him in contact with the top levels of business, industry, and government. He performs such duties as:

- developing solutions to customer's problems
- selecting and recommending equipment
- training customers or IBM personnel in technical subjects or technical language
- developing new applications, systems, and short range plans for advanced applications
- coordinating total system studies and establishing long range plans for customers

The IBM Systems Engineer has a high level of analytical ability in using scientific methods and creativity in dealing with scientific and management problems as well as in analyzing business methods.[1]

In the Personal Traits section, the document specified:

A high moral character with a pleasant appearance, personality and speech is required. Mathematical aptitude and the ability to communicate ideas are important.[2]

As attractive as IBM's offer was, I did not accept it immediately, preferring to wait until I had received the results from my other interviews. However, I did send IBM a letter of conditional acceptance right away, because I was 99% certain that I would accept their offer. I made my final decision on April 15 – a decision that would have an enormous impact on the rest of my life. Although I didn't realize it at the time, I was a beneficiary of the beginning of IBM's massive recruitment program that would last for the following 20 years (see graph on preceding page).[3]

Compared to some of my contemporaries, my hiring process was relatively lengthy. My Datacentre colleagues, Gabor Fabian and Dainius Lukosevicius, describe their experiences:

I was all set to begin work at Air Canada, where my dad worked, when I received a call from the Datacentre manager's secretary, Carmella Di Lalla, asking me to come in for an interview. I told her that I already had a job lined up. A few minutes later she called back to say that Mr. Polanski absolutely wanted to see me right away, and that they would pay for a taxi. So I went down to IBM, wrote the test, and met with Mr. Polanski. He told me that I scored very well on the test (96% I think) and

---

[1, 2, 3] Courtesy of International Business Machines Corporation, © International Business Machines Corporation

offered me a job. I got hired on the spot and began work the next day!
–Gabor Fabian

I was playing bridge with someone who worked for IBM and he arranged for me to have an interview with the Datacentre manager, Lorne Polanski. So I went to the IBM office and wrote the various tests all morning. When the secretary told me that Mr. Polanski wanted to meet with me after lunch, I told her, "My time is too valuable to wait." Two minutes later, I was escorted into his office. He hired me on the spot and I started work the next day! –Dainius Lukosevicius

On the other hand, colleague André Joubert spent almost two years in his quest for employment at IBM before his perseverance landed him a job – one that would last for 25 years:

My road to IBM began in 1965 when I placed very high in a Canada-wide school mathematics competition, which led to my participation in a month-long mathematics camp that summer. The last week of the camp was an introduction to computers, in which we went from zero to a working program – and I was smitten. Anything and everything to do with computers fascinated me.

One day as I was passing through the Queen Elizabeth Hotel I noticed that IBM was demonstrating a new terminal to the public. When my turn came to try it, the IBMer remarked on how comfortable I was using it. He introduced himself as Gerry Claude. After completing an accelerated two-year diploma program at Montreal Institute of Technology I started to actively look for a job in the computer field. Without waiting for the on-campus recruitment days, I went directly to IBM to apply for a job, but without success. A month later, on the official recruitment day, I met with IBM's Bill McClay who gave me an application form to fill out. Shortly thereafter I was invited for a second interview in the IBM offices.

There I met the SE [Systems Engineering] manager who simply passed me on to the branch manager, Mr. Bastien. The latter just talked about his kids, his difficulties in learning French and other small talk. Finally I asked him, "And what about a job?" He replied, "Oh, they didn't tell you? You're hired!"

Degree day

The date was May 29, 1965. My mom's diary entry for that day reads as follows:

Cool breezy day. A little rain a few times. . . John took Dad, Mom, Winston, Meryl & Marilyn to Convocation then supper at Dr. Dougan's. [Author's note: John is my brother, Meryl my

My Bishop's University graduation photo (Photo by Studio Sears)

My degree from Bishop's University, 1965

Receiving awards from Cardinal Léger at Bishop's University convocation, 1965 (Photo by Dick Tracy)

sister-in-law, and Marilyn my sister. Dr. Dougan was the father of fellow Physics graduate Hayes Dougan.]

That simple entry documented the most significant event of my life up until that point. My university convocation was the culmination of four years of enduring the compulsory classes, the long nights of studying and the singular stress of final exams. But it was all worth it. The feeling of accomplishment as I walked across the stage to accept my degree and awards (including the Governor-General's medal for top graduate) from the hands of Cardinal Paul-Émile Léger was very special. Obviously it was a turning point in my life's journey – suddenly I was no longer a student. But it was not only my occupation designation that had changed. Later that day, when I unrolled my parchment degree certificate, I was surprised to discover that my very identity had also changed. Because the document was totally written in Latin, my given names had been transformed from "Winston Charles Bruce" to "Winston Carolum Brutum."

Departure day

My graduation day was a very short-lived moment of glory, as witnessed by Mom's diary entry for the following day. Her entry for May 30 reads:

> Cool, some sun, breezy. . . John and Meryl left at 4:45 p.m. for Montreal taking Winston.

Barely 24 hours after receiving my degree, I was on my way to Montreal where I would report to the IBM Education Centre for "work" at 8:30 a.m. the next morning. I really had no idea of what to expect. My brain was still saturated with the laws of Newton, Kirchoff and Coulomb, and the literature of Shakespeare, Molière and Tolstoy from my four-year feeding frenzy of formulae, facts and fiction. My grey matter was completely void of any knowledge of the new world to which I was headed. I couldn't even explain to my family what my job would be. As I would later hear a speaker say: "You know that you're in high tech if you can't describe your job to your mother!"

As mentioned earlier, I knew absolutely nothing about computers. My university didn't even have a computer during my time there. In fact, it was not until several years later that they installed their first computer, and several more years before a Computer Science course was offered. Retired computer science professor, Dr. Charlie Carman, summarizes the history of computers at Bishop's University:

> In the early 1970s an IBM 1130 was installed and shared with Champlain College (they had access in the morning and Bishop's used it in the afternoon). I was hired in July 1974 as a member of the Math department to teach FORTRAN and COBOL courses. There was no Computer Science department then. By the end of the 1970s, a major was offered by the new Computer Science department. I was the full-

time faculty member as well as director of the Computer Centre. We had replaced the IBM 1130 with a Xerox 530 by then. It was used for both administrative and academic tasks. Carol Bennett, my indispensable assistant, did the majority of the administrative programming (payroll, student records etc.). It was a busy and exciting time!

In fact, only a handful of Canadian universities had computers, and none of them had established Computer Science departments at that time. The University of Toronto, the University of Alberta and the University of British Columbia had computers as far back as the 1950s, but their Computer Science departments were only established in the 1964-1968 period. University of Waterloo and McGill University installed their first computers in the mid-1960s. The McGill School of Computer Science was formally created in 1969. It is not surprising, then, that a small university like my alma mater had no computer during my student days.

My brother and sister-in-law delivered me to my new abode in Montreal around 8 p.m. Sunday evening. I had arranged for room and board in the upscale neighbourhood of TMR. My landlady, Mrs. Jean Campbell (herself also an Eastern Townships native) lived in a third-floor apartment on "the circle," conveniently located beside the train station and quite close to the IBM office on Laird Blvd. She considered me almost as her grandson – a situation that would have very serious ramifications later on.

Discovery days

My first IBM employee badge, 1965

May 31, 1965, was the first of 80 consecutive days of intensive training for my twenty-some colleagues and me. The course was called BCT. It stood for "Basic Computer Training" but could as easily have stood for "Boot Camp Trials." The days were long and the teaching was fast-paced. Fellow classmate Serge Meilleur recalls:

Lectures, testimonials, case studies and simulations followed one another at a feverish pace. We frequently worked late into the evening.[4]

---

[4] DMR : La fin d'un rêve (p. 46; translation by author)

Above: Early IBM THINK sign (Courtesy of International Business Machines Corporation, © International Business Machines Corporation)

Right: The original THINK pad (Courtesy of International Business Machines Corporation, © International Business Machines Corporation)

Our class, probably the first of its type to be held in Montreal, was comprised of a very diverse group of new recruits hired in anticipation of the success of the newly announced IBM System /360. Some of us had science backgrounds, others were business graduates. Some were francophone but most were anglophone. Most were from the Montreal area, but there was a group from Ottawa that included Gary Mohr, who recalls:

> I remember being impressed by IBM putting the four of us (Ray Hession, Doug Begin, Jean-Pierre Kingsley and myself) from the Ottawa office into a lovely apartment on Crescent Street in downtown Montreal. We commuted daily by rail to Mount Royal and back.

The physical environment of the classroom was conducive to learning. On the table in front of each trainee was a tent-shaped cardboard with your name on the flap facing outward and the word THINK facing towards you. And there were also THINK signs on the walls. The word was being implanted in our minds to prepare us for life in the THINK tank. (THINK, of course, is the famous IBM slogan that was initially coined by long-time IBM Chairman, Thomas J. Watson Sr., in 1911 before he joined IBM.)[5]

The physical classroom environment was also conducive to sleeping. Because some of my classmates were chain smokers and because it was summer, the non air-conditioned room was always smoky, hot and stuffy. Often by mid-afternoon – and sometimes sooner – I found myself starting to doze off. (It would be several

---

[5] Courtesy of International Business Machines Corporation, © International Business Machines Corporation

BCT class homework: "Any questions?" (Sketch by James Harvey)

decades before society recognized the dangers of smoking and moved to ban smoking inside public buildings. Only starting in July 1989 did IBM ban smoking in its Ontario locations.) I wasn't the only person to experience drowsiness during BCT. Colleague Margaret Eastwood, who attended the next year's BCT class, was once told by her instructor, "You are the only person I've ever seen who could sleep with their eyes open!"

One of our instructors was Jim Low, a very friendly guy with a delightful Irish accent. We sometimes referred to him by the literal French translation of his name, "Jacques Bas." He was very knowledgeable and made good use of the audio-visual tools of the day – blackboard and flipcharts. This was before the days of the overhead foil projector or the whiteboard.

The course curriculum covered a wide range of technical and marketing subjects. We learned what a computer was and how it worked. The available models at that time were the 1620, the 1440 and the 1401 (System /360 had just been announced but was not yet installed). Had I joined IBM a few years sooner, I would have learned about some of the earlier technology that had now become obsolete. Margaret Eastwood, who joined IBM in 1963, remembers the control panels of the IBM 402 Accounting Machine:

> We learned how to wire panels. After the course only the female employees wired panels. We had a female supervisor, but of course the managers in the branch were all men. I liked wiring panels – it was a bit like doing puzzles.

IBM 402 Accounting Machine control panel (wikipedia.org)

I must confess that after 50 years of working with computers, I have never really comprehended exactly how a computer works. Until I came across an old 1967 Life magazine article while doing research for this book, I had attributed my lack of understanding to my limited "technical" skills. But after reading through Life's

12-page article that explained, in minute detail, how a computer adds 1+2 to come up with the answer 3, I felt somewhat exonerated!

During BCT we were exposed to the various computer accessories such as punched cards, paper tape, magnetic tape and continuous printer forms. These were all new to me. And then there was the computer lingo that consisted of old words with new meanings, as well as newly coined words and phrases that hadn't yet made it into mainline dictionaries. In 1968, an animated short film "A Computer Glossary" was produced for IBM which attempted to explain some of the terminology associated with the new computer age.[6] For example:

- Program – a set of instructions for performing computer operations
- Software – a computer's programs and the procedure for their use
- Flowchart – a graphic version of a program in which symbols are used to represent operations
- Simulation – the use of a computer program as a model of a real situation
- Linear programming – a popular method of arriving at a best strategy when the factors are proportionally related

We also learned about arrays, algorithms, abends and ASCII. Bits, bytes, bugs and buffers. Coding, compilers, characters and constants. Data, default, dumps and debugging. Et cetera and ad infinitum. This is but a small sample, but gives you an idea of the "computer speak" language that we gradually became familiar with. Several years later, newly hired colleague Pierre Lussier struggled with one of these words:

> During a break in my Basic Systems Training I returned to the Montreal office and met Paul Biron in the elevator. I asked him, "What is a bug?" He was very amused by my question.

The first programming language we learned was FORTRAN. I found this part of the course to be quite fascinating, especially when we began to write programs on coding sheets that would then be submitted for keypunching. We also learned to use the keypunch ourselves. The newly available 029 keypunch was the latest version of a device first developed 74 years earlier. The punch and its companion, the IBM 59 card verifier, were used to record and check information in punched cards. The cards were then read and processed by a computer or an accounting machine.[7] Although destined to eventually go the way of the dodo bird, these workhorse machines would still be in general use more than a decade later.

To test our newly acquired skills, we were required to write a program to calculate the current value of the $24 proceeds from the sale of Manhattan had the Native

---

[6,7] Courtesy of International Business Machines Corporation, © International Business Machines Corporation

Americans invested it at an annual rate of x%. We had to be extremely careful in how we coded the program statements. Everything had to be in block letters and we had to clearly distinguish between the letter "I" and the number "1," as well as between the letter "O" and the number "0." Failure to do so would have disastrous consequences (as I would learn later when I spent a week helping a customer track down an error caused by a letter O that should have been a digit 0). In 1964 IBM issued the following directive in this regard:

> The practice to be followed is:
> - the number, zero, will be slashed, i.e., Ø
> - the letter, oh, will not be slashed, i.e., O

I'm not sure how strictly this directive was followed, because I know for certain that in the Datacentre (where I was assigned upon graduation from BCT) we did the exact opposite. So much for standards!

We also learned about Job Control Language (JCL), that specified the various parameters related to a "job" for processing on the computer. One such parameter was SYSOUT, which specified the program output destination (e.g., printer, card punch, disk, etc.). Datacentre colleague Jonas Bacher recounts the consequences of an incorrect specification:

> One afternoon, just before leaving the office, I submitted a job that would produce hundreds of pages of printed output. That evening the computer operator phoned me in a panic to tell me that my job was punching out thousands of cards. It was the result of my having specified "SYSOUT = B" instead of "SYSOUT = A." What a difference a letter made!

BCT class photo, 1966 (Courtesy of Peter Bedoukian)

Naturally, we were taught a lot about the IBM product line and how to market it to customers. This very heavy emphasis on the marketing aspects I found especially challenging because I was not by nature a marketing type. However, to use today's vernacular, "I sucked it up"! One such activity was to make practice customer call presentations to experienced IBM managers or sales representatives posing as customers. Gary Mohr remembers two such role-playings in particular:

> In one case the student complimented the prospective client on his nice tan. The client responded that it was skin cancer. When the student said that he was sorry to hear it and that he hoped it wasn't too serious, the client informed him that it was terminal!

> In another session the student noticed on the desk a photo of the "client" posing with a large fish that he had presumably caught. The student mentioned it and then got into a somewhat detailed conversation about fishing. After a few minutes of "fish talk" the client looked at his watch and told the student that his time was up and that he (the client) had to rush off to another meeting. The student never did get around to giving his sales presentation.

Serge Meilleur recounts an equally embarrassing "customer" call:

> It was during one of these simulated interviews that I first met Bernard Côté, who was a rising star at IBM. . . A few days after the beginning of our training we were doing sales call simulations. On this particular afternoon I was the fourth to go, so I carefully prepared in order that the 20-minute torture would be the least painful possible. Taking advantage of the fact that my interviewer and I were both francophones, I was counting on obtaining a good mark and impressing my instructors. Very confidently, I began "Monsieur Côté..." but he immediately interrupted me: "Mr. Côté is sick. My name is John Smith and I don't speak French." Whispers and suppressed laughter could be heard in the room. Bernard Côté continued to torment me for the next 45 minutes. He would keep interrupting me to bring up new information, make an objection or to express an unexpected argument. Each time I got further stuck in my already incoherent remarks. When I left the room, still stunned by my pitiful performance, I hoped never again to meet this abominable marketing manager from the Montreal downtown office! [A few months later, Serge was hired by Monsieur Côté to be a sales representative in his branch.][8]

Although BCT was extremely demanding, it did include some lighter moments – like eating at nearby Nash's Restaurant, or going on an occasional field trip. Classmate Robert Dionne, the self-proclaimed class "vice president," remembers one such outing:

---

[8] DMR : La fin d'un rêve (pp. 46-47; translation by author)

As vice president of the BCT class (i.e., president of the vice), I was responsible for organizing the entertainment. One night we visited Molson's Breweries on Notre Dame Street. The beer flowed very freely. Because I had given them a generous tip to start with, they served us beer one after another all evening. At closing time at 11:00 p.m. we all sang "Alouette."

I usually brought a bag lunch that my landlady prepared for me. Practically filling a large Steinberg grocery bag, it contained several sandwiches, half a pan of date squares, a few apples and a pint of milk. No wonder that, in spite of the stresses of boot camp, I added at least 10 lb. to my "skinny 135-lb. weakling" physique (like the skinny guy in the Mr. Atlas ads on the back cover of comic books). Because my lunch bag contained much more than I could comfortably consume, I happily shared the contents with very appreciative classmates.

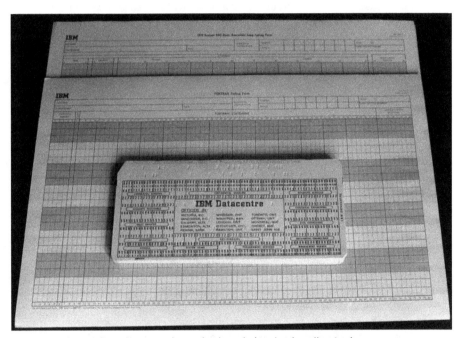

Programming coding sheets and punched cards (Author's collection)

Among my classmates one stood out above all the rest. His name was Ray Hession. Not only did he tower above us all physically, but he possessed a marked maturity compared to the rest of us, who were still green behind the ears. And there was something more that was hard to describe. An aura of care, concern and compassion surrounded him. No wonder I considered him like a father figure – even though he was only a few years my senior. Little did I realize the significant challenges, both personal and professional, that Ray faced during our BCT time together. Here is his story in his own words:

June 1965 was the key crossroad of my adult life when, as a young captain in the Canadian Army, after months of at times agonizing reflection, I decided to accept an offer to join the IBM Datacentre in Ottawa. Having spent the preceding 18 months as a system development team leader participating in the redesign of the army's logistics supply system, it seemed the most natural option to pursue. That said, I walked away from a good offer from the finance department at Imperial Oil in Toronto to do so. The dominant factor in that decision was the incipient birth of our second child and the shared desire with my French-Canadian spouse to live in a bilingual setting.

Early that month, while my family remained in Ottawa, I went off to Basic Computer Training (BCT) at the IBM Education Centre in the Town of Mount-Royal. There I met my classmates for the first time, and realized that I was in the unaccustomed role as the oldest guy in the group. All but me were university graduates that year, while I had graduated from the Royal Military College in 1962. In hindsight, the difference was trivial but nevertheless noticeable. One outcome of the age/experience difference was my early election by my classmates as class president. I was honoured and, thankfully, not burdened by it.

The coursework at BCT was demanding. It required homework every night and weekend to grasp the intricacies of 1440 Autocoder, FORTRAN and COBOL, along with the basics of computer systems architecture. Frankly, I loved it! The demanding work schedule included periodic presentations to the class by individuals and teams mainly focussed on computer applications and sales techniques. These latter activities played a key role months later in the trajectory of my early IBM career.

Notably, while teamwork played a big part in our day-to-day lives during BCT, I naturally became especially friendly with three classmates: Al Robinson (a Montrealer), Winston Fraser (a son of Quebec's Eastern Townships) and Jean-Pierre Kingsley (an Ottawa boy). Kingsley was my roommate at an apartment-hotel on notorious Crescent Street in downtown Montreal. Interestingly, to the left of the hotel entrance was a hot spot known as Chez Parée – complete with scantily clad dancing girls (so I'm told). Next door was an apartment building – a known bordello! Jean-Pierre and I tolerated each other as we worked late into the night doing our assignments. He was struggling, and indeed was one of the few people who failed the BCT course. Many years later, I met him in Ottawa in his new government appointment as Chief Electoral Officer of Canada!

Al Robinson was a big strapping mining engineer of proud Scottish origin married to a French Canadian, as was I. Winston Fraser was a product of a farming family with a unique mix of superior intellect and strong spiritual grounding which together formed a reserved and caring personality. These two gentlemen impacted my consciousness of what makes for a good man more than most. So, with that, our lives at BCT were made up of many shared experiences with little free time. As our lives progressed, however, enduring friendships shone through.

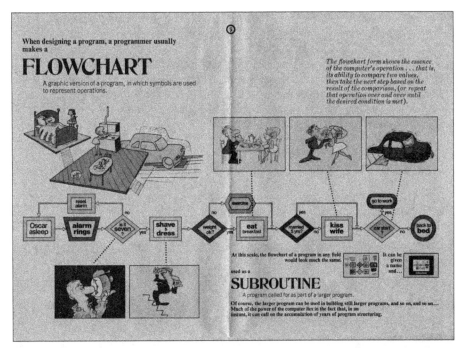

IBM Computer Glossary pamphlet explaining Flowchart, 1968 (Courtesy of International Business Machines Corporation, © 1968 International Business Machines Corporation)

Literally days after BCT got started I received an emergency call informing me that my spouse had been rushed to hospital to have our second baby. I, of course, took off for the hospital in record time, having been excused by my course managers, Jim McAlpine and Jim Low, for a few days. The baby was born shortly before my arrival! A boy and brother for his 14-month-old sister. Two days later I was back at BCT. About seven weeks into the 16-week course we were all dispatched back to our home branch offices for on-the-job training (OJT). For me that also meant quality time with my young family in Ottawa.

A week into OJT, my branch manager asked to see me. Apprehensively, I appeared in his office where he informed me of my exemplary performance at BCT thus far. And then he dropped a bomb. He said that he didn't think that I was the best fit for the Datacentre job for which I had been hired. Rather, said he, I was much better suited to be a marketing representative! My reaction was mixed. On the one hand, the marketing function was arguably the mainstream of the company with virtually all of its top managers/executives having risen from those ranks. On the other hand, it was a commissioned function, putting my family income at risk at a time when my family expenses were blossoming. So, after thinking about it for a few minutes, I agreed to give it a shot! During that same period, unexpectedly, the Ottawa office was visited by none other than the iconic Jack Brent, Chairman and CEO of IBM Canada Ltd. I was sitting at my desk in the "bullpen" when he and my branch manager approached me for introductions. I bolted up from my chair and said in a firm voice, "Good morning, SIR!" Mr. Brent replied, "Call me Jack" to which I replied, "Yes, SIR." That military-like reply drew a big laugh! Shortly thereafter I was back at BCT. The balance of the coursework emphasized presentation and communications skills including role-playing in sales situations. Frankly, I loved that too!

As the end of the course neared I was receiving increasing signs from my spouse that she was overburdened with her two babies. The home situation seemed increasingly threatening to her well-being – so much so that I approached Jim McAlpine, again seeking my release from the balance of the course to support her. He agreed and off I went back to Ottawa.

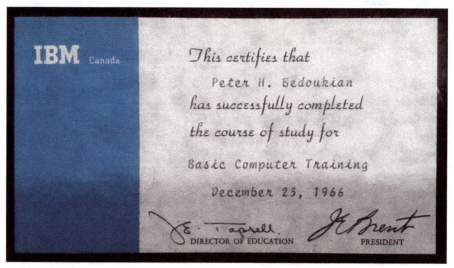

BCT completion certificate, 1966 (Courtesy of Peter Bedoukian)

At the end of September we quietly graduated and went our separate ways. I don't remember any special celebration – no graduation party, not even a class photo. But strong friendships had been forged – some that would continue and others that would be renewed many years later.

Datacentre days

My final D-Days of 1965 were spent in the IBM Datacentre, located in downtown Montreal at 615 Dorchester Blvd. (now called Boulevard René-Lévesque). That phase of my career is covered in the next chapter.

Chapter 3   Among Technical Giants

These IBM specialists make the IBM Datacentre your problem-solving department

Their special skills can provide a powerful management tool for you. Each man in each IBM Datacentre is expert in the art of conveying your data processing problems to an IBM computer, and arriving at the right answers to your problems, fast. IBM have screened and trained these specialists meticulously, providing more than two years of further schooling at IBM, to develop them to their present high competency. They know their applications well, and they know IBM systems. They are ready and able to apply the ever-increasing library of Programmed Applications to your business, scientific or engineering problems.

IBM Specialists in mathematics, engineering, accounting, science, and operations research are ready to solve your problems, big or small. The work is done fast, economically, efficiently.

Phone or visit your nearest IBM Datacentre for full information.

Datacentre

373 Broadway Avenue
Winnipeg — 942-2181

IBM Datacentre ad, Winnipeg Free Press, 1964 (Courtesy of International Business Machines Corporation, © 1964 International Business Machines Corporation)

My long-time Datacentre colleague and close friend, Gabor Fabian (who stood 6-foot-6 and weighed over 250 lb.), used to jokingly tell people that he and I were the technical giants of the Datacentre Scientific Services department – with me being technical and he being the giant! His characterization of my abilities was grossly exaggerated because I was probably one of the least technical IBMers ever to work in a technical capacity. In fact, technology in general and computer hardware in particular, actually frightened me.

But, be that as it may, upon graduation from BCT I was assigned to the Scientific Services department, managed by Joseph Kern. At that time, the Datacentre was composed of three main groups, of which my department was one. The Commercial group handled a large variety of business applications such as payroll, accounts receivable and sales analysis. The Brokerage section was responsible for processing brokers' daily transactions executed on the Montreal and Toronto stock exchanges. Customer projects that didn't fit into either Commercial or Brokerage were routed to Scientific Services. This meant that we got to work on some very unique and unusual types of jobs. It also meant that we sometimes had to reach beyond our group in order to deliver the best quality solutions to customer problems. In doing so, I had the privilege of meeting and working with a number of true technical giants, some of whom will be profiled later in this chapter.

My first assignment was a 1620 FORTRAN programming job for Imperial Oil to calculate the volume of oil remaining in each of their giant storage tanks at their refinery in Montreal's East End. Every day, refinery workers would take dip-stick

measurements and keypunch the readings data, which would then be processed by my program. Some days, if the punched cards were too greasy, they had to be re-punched on fresh card stock before being read into the computer. This program ran very successfully on a daily basis for several years.

With tools of the trade, ca. 1970: cards, tape, flowchart template, slide rule (Author's collection)

As I gained experience, I was assigned to handle more complex custom programming projects made possible by our newly installed and much more powerful IBM System /360 model 65. The System /360, announced in 1964[9], was, as IBM president Thomas J. Watson, Jr., said at the time, "the most significant product announcement in IBM history." It was the industry's first major "family" of compatible computers. Its processors, ranging from small to large, could use most of the same peripheral equipment and programs, making it easier for the user to move up to greater computing power.

---

[9] Courtesy of International Business Machines Corporation, © International Business Machines Corporation

This "fisheye" view shows a System /360 Model 40 processor with control panel, a string of eight IBM 2401 magnetic tape units and controller, and three IBM 2311 magnetic disk storage drives.[10]

1620 Data Processing System (Courtesy of International Business Machines Corporation, © International Business Machines Corporation)

In the following sections I will share some details of a few of the more interesting, unusual or challenging projects in which I participated during my eight years in the Datacentre.

Saving the whales

One of the biggest and most satisfying projects on which I worked was simply called "the whales project." My colleague, Gabor Fabian, aptly described it as "a project and a half."

In 1967, Dr. Edward Mitchell, marine biologist with the Fisheries

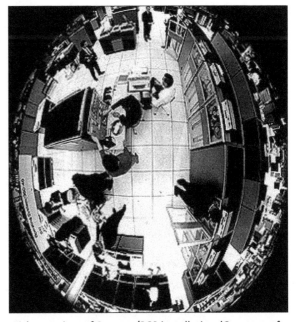

Fish-eye view of System /360 installation (Courtesy of International Business Machines Corporation, © International Business Machines Corporation)

Research Board of Canada in Ste-Anne-de-Bellevue (Quebec), approached IBM for assistance in analyzing the tons of whale-related data that his department had accumulated over the preceding years from its whale-tagging program. Their requirement was expressed very simply. They wanted to use the data to find out how many fin whales could be hunted each year without depleting the fin whale population.

But the solution was not immediately obvious. After examination of the nature

---

[10] Courtesy of International Business Machines Corporation, © International Business Machines Corporation

IBM helps determine safe whale quotas

Mrs. Elaine Sloan of the Fisheries Research Board takes a look at a "whale study" printout with Gabor Fabian, left, and Winston Fraser at the Montreal Datacentre.

MONTREAL — Back in 1967, Montreal Marketing Representative Pierre L'Esperance called on Scientific Services, a group of Montreal Datacentre specialists with scientific and engineering backgrounds. He had a new account with a unique problem. The Fisheries Research Board wanted to study the biological characteristics and migration habits of the fin whale. Dr. Edward Mitchell and Mrs. Elaine Sloan, in charge of the study, wanted to determine a safe quota for the annual kill, using DP methods.

Most of the programs were written in COBOL and run through the Datacentre on a System/360 Model 65.

"Now," says Mrs. Sloan, "we can receive instant information on any individual whale, or we can look at any one of 700 scatter diagrams, or at any one of hundreds of different categorized samples. The possibilities are practically limitless."

Gabor Fabian and Andrew Kelemen are the two Associate Systems Analysts assigned to the whale study this summer. Says Gabor: "The biggest challenge was not in programming the file-handling routines (even though there were over 20,000 cards), but in providing the Fisheries Board with the facility of requesting any one of the thousands of automatically scaled scatter diagrams possible. In addition, any point on the diagram must be identified as a particular whale."

This is the first such study attempted anywhere in the Northwest Atlantic. Some work has been done in Japan, the U.S.A. and the U.S.S.R. but not on the fin whale. "It's amazing how little is known about whales," says Elaine Sloan, "so it's necessary work. The government has already outlawed the killing of the famous blue whale because there are so few left and there may be other species in the same danger of extinction."

After the fin whale study has been completed, probably by the winter of 1971, other types of whales will be studied in the same way. "We'll probably

Whales project article, IBM Canadian News, 1969, pages 1 (above) and 2 (opposite). (Courtesy of International Business Machines Corporation, © 1969 International Business Machines Corporation)

be including dolphins in later years," says Mrs. Sloan.

The Fisheries Research Board has been sending out teams of men to tag whales off the eastern coast of Canada. When later caught by whalers, the numbered tags were sent back to Dr. Mitchell and Mrs. Sloan who compared the date and place tagged with the date and place caught. This gave them some idea about the whale's migration habits. It was at this point that the researchers, who had been filing their data manually, ran into problems. "It was an almost impossible job," says Elaine Sloan.

The real problem lay in co-ordinating the hundreds of pieces of data collected on each whale. Scientific Services worked jointly with Dr. Mitchell to develop a "whale master file" which now contains coded information on 2,200 fin whales. The information included such factors as year tagged and caught, number of whales caught at a particular whaling station, sex and size. In all, 275 different measurements were coded for each whale.

"Fisheries Research Board wanted to be able to plot 'scatter diagrams'," said Winston Fraser, Systems Analyst and co-ordinator of the project, "with the ordinate showing one set of data and abscissa another. For example, the distance out to sea when caught against the size of the whale; or the number of ovarian scars on a female against its age." For the moment, these diagrams are purely experimental, says Mrs. Sloan. Each one is an attempt to find significant relationships between any two given facts and to then draw a meaningful conclusion.

Tag numbers on captured whales are recorded by a member of the Fisheries Research Board field team.

Beached whale skeleton, Anticosti Island, Que. (photo by author)

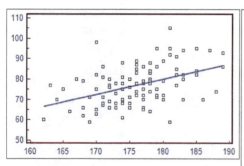

Above: Scatter diagram sample

Right: Whales project article, IBM World Trade News, July-Aug. 1970 (Courtesy of International Business Machines Corporation, © 1970 International Business Machines Corporation)

Whale of an Idea: To save the fin whale from the possibility of extinction, Canada's Fisheries Research Board has undertaken a computer study to determine safe quotas for the authorized annual kill.

When one of 2,200 whales that have been tagged for identification is caught, the tag is sent to the Board. At Montreal's Datacenter, a System/360 Model 65 plots various scatter diagrams which relate, for example, the distance at sea when caught and the whale's size.

Studies of other types of whales and dolphins are scheduled for the future. "The government has already outlawed the killing of the famous blue whale because there are so few left," says Mrs. Elaine Sloan of the Fisheries Research Board, "and there may be other species in the same danger of extinction."

and volume of the data and following discussions with Dr. Mitchell and his assistant, we decided to create a flexible database and a parameterized data extraction/analysis facility. As a result, the Fisheries Research Board was able to produce "scatter diagrams" that plotted the relationship between any two variables from the database.

Development and testing of the custom set of COBOL programs required several months of concentrated effort by a team of three. The project was described in detail in a 1969 article in the IBM Canadian News and in a 1970 article in the IBM World Trade News. As well, Dr. Mitchell references IBM's involvement in his paper "North Atlantic Whale Research," published in the 1969 Annual Report of the Fisheries Council of Canada. I found the project to be particularly satisfying because we were directly contributing to the effort to save whales from extinction.

Collection of data on North Atlantic right whales, Grand Manan, N.B. (Photo by author)

An interesting footnote to this project is that now, some 50 years later, the Canadian government is still collecting data on North Atlantic whales, as evidenced by a harbour sign recently seen posted on Grand Manan Island, N.B.

All about planes

This solo project was probably the most challenging one that I undertook in my entire IBM career. That represents a rather bold assertion because I faced many technical challenges during those 27 years. But this one was unique.

In the summer of 1971 the Datacentre received a request from ICAO (International Civil Aviation Organization), a United Nations agency headquartered in Montreal. The initial request seemed straightforward enough: ICAO just needed to produce a special report called "Table MET 2A – Exchange of Operational Meteorological Information" related to the provision of weather data. But, as the expression goes, the devil was in the details.

The project was assigned to me once it was determined that it wasn't quite so simple after all. A meeting was arranged with Mr. Mike Nancoo, ICAO's Senior Meteorologist, a soft-spoken gentleman from Trinidad. He explained to me the details of what was required. First he provided me some background. The ICAO member countries were required to provide weather reports to one another based on the flights that overflew their respective countries. For example, in the

FROM OR RELATED TO PROVENANT DE OU CONCERNANT DE O RELACIONADO CON	TO BE AVAILABLE AT DOIVENT ETRE DISPONIBLES A ESTARAN DISPONIBLES EN	INFORMATION REQUIRED RENSEIGNEMENTS REQUIS INFORMACION SOLICITADA				
		H	S	F	SI	A
	●STAVANGER				x	x
	●WARSZAWA				x	x
	●WIEN				x	x
	●ZAGREB				x	x
	●ZURICH				x	x
UPPER VOLTA						
BOBO DIOULASSO						
OUAGADOUGOU	MARSEILLES/MARIGNANE			x		
	●BORDEAUX			x		
	LYON			x		
	●MADRID			x		
	MARSEILLES/MARIGNANE			x		
	●PARIS			x		
URUGUAY						
MONTEVIDEO	●MADRID			x		
USSR						
EREVAN	●ANKARA	x	x	x		
	●BEIRUT	x	x	x		
	●TEHRAN	x	x	x		
KIEV	●BEOGRAD	x	x	x		
	BERLIN EAST	x	x	x		
	●BUCARESTI	x	x	x		
	●BUDAPEST	x	x	x		
	●PRAHA	x	x	x		
	●SOFIJA	x	x	x		
	●WARSZAWA	x	x	x		
	●WIEN	x	x	x		
	●ZURICH	x	x	x		
LENINGRAD	●BEOGRAD	x	x	x		
	BERLIN EAST	x	x	x		
	●BRATISLAVA	x	x	x		
	●BUDAPEST	x	x	x		
	●HANNOVER	x	x	x		
	●HELSINKI	x	x	x		
	●KOBENHAVN	x	x	x		
	LONDON			x		
	●MALMO/BULLTOFTA	x	x	x		
	●PARIS			x		
	●PRAHA			x		
	●STOCKHOLM	x	x	x		
	●WARSZAWA	x	x	x		
MINSK	●WARSZAWA	x	x	x		

IBM Canada Ltd.

Meteorological Data Exchange Table report, ICAO project, 1971 (Courtesy of International Business Machines Corporation, © 1971 International Business Machines Corporation)

case of a flight from Paris to Istanbul, all countries on the flight path were required to provide weather information to each other. Now, having understood the requirement, my challenge was how to program it. Apparently, until that time, it was all done manually. Using a large world globe, they simply stretched a piece of string between a given flight's origin and destination (e.g., Paris and Istanbul) and visually noted the countries over which it passed! However, given the rapidly increasing number of airports (and the flights between them), this manual approach was no longer feasible.

Without really knowing how, I assured Mr. Nancoo that we could meet his request in the required timeframe. (The reports were required for a special meeting to be held later in the year in the Philippines.) After a bit of head-scratching, I realized that this would involve "great circle route" calculations using the latitude and longitude coordinates of the origin and destination cities. But that was only the beginning. I also had to figure out a way to determine the country boundaries that were crossed en route. That would involve calculating the intersections of two spherical planes. Realizing that I was now out of my depth, I walked up to the McGill University science library and signed out a book on advanced spherical trigonometry. In it, I discovered the magic formula I needed. The next challenge was to code the formula in FORTRAN. And the final hurdle was how to test that the program was working correctly. That turned out to be the easy part. I needed only a world globe and a piece of string!

I delivered the final report to Mr. Nancoo, who was very satisfied. End of job, right? No, in fact it was not. There was another unexpected challenge yet to come. Mr. Nancoo explained to me that the program would need to be rerun at the

World globe with string (Photo by author)

Philippines meeting after member countries submitted their updates. However, at that time there was no computer in the Philippines powerful enough to run this program in a reasonable amount of time. Our solution: Mr. Nancoo would send us the modifications by telephone, we would rerun the program in Montreal and then hand-deliver the updated reports to a pilot at Dorval airport who was leaving for Manila. To borrow a line from Shakespeare, "All's well that ends well!"

Just in time for the Manila flight (Sketch by James Harvey)

Raising cane

Barbados Foursquare cane factory, 1980s (Courtesy William Burton, BajanThings.com)

In the spring of 1968 IBM was approached by Cane Commodities Caribbean Limited in connection with a reorganization of the sugar cane industry in Barbados. Because this project involved the use of optimization techniques, and because I had previous experience with such applications, the project was assigned to me.

The purpose of the study was to determine mathematically the optimal number, sizes and locations of sugar cane processing factories in Barbados so as to maximize the net industry revenue. Input data included cane transportation data, sugar and molasses yields, and investment data for existing and new factories. Among the constraints were factory locations and capacities and cane supply areas. The challenge was to formulate this information into an optimization model, though it was not obvious what the best method would be.

Initially formulated as a "zero-one integer programming" problem, this approach was abandoned because no acceptable solution was arrived at after running for several hours on the Datacentre's most powerful computer. Therefore we developed a customized program to determine the optimum allocation of cane from each supply area without exceeding the maximum capacity of any factory. A report was produced that showed optimal solutions for various scenarios in terms of the number of new and existing factories involved.

In July I travelled to Barbados to present my report to the leaders of their sugar industry and to visit the Foursquare cane processing factory. Upon my return, I implemented a number of requested changes and produced a final report. A letter of appreciation from the customer to my Datacentre manager read (in part):

Cane field and winding road, Barbados (Peter Gurd photo, courtesy of Peter Gurd)

> I would like to take the opportunity to express our appreciation of IBM's performance, and the confidence with which your company and the staff selected for this study has approached the project. I would particularly like to express our appreciation of the services provided by Mr. Winston Fraser whose competence in the subject and personal conduct while in Barbados was excellent.

It is interesting to note that the results of this study did have an important impact on the Barbados sugar industry. A November 28, 1969 article headlined "Barbados sugar industry to be turned into quasi-co-operative enterprise" in Kingston, Jamaica's *The Daily Gleaner* contains the following reference to our project:

> The new Sugar Producers Association plan results from recommendations for reorganization of the industry's manufacturing sector, made by a consulting firm named Cane Commodities Caribbean a year ago.

When all else fails . . .

One project I worked on deserves a special mention because of the unusual nature of its solution. A trucking transportation company wanted to equally allocate its many delivery routes to its fleet of trucks. Each delivery route had a number of characteristics (e.g., distance travelled, number of stops, volume of cargo, etc.) that were different for each route. The objective was to allocate the routes in such a way that each truck travelled the same total distance, had the same total number of stops, carried the same total volume of cargo, etc.

An initial test run on the IBM 1620 using a subset of the data resulted in an integer solution, which was what was needed. But when we ran the full model on the more powerful IBM 7044 at McGill University, the result was a continuous solution. This was clearly unacceptable since it allocated partial routes instead of whole routes. With no automated options left, we turned to the next best method – manual!

Yes, our solution was totally manual, giving credence (in this particular case) to the tongue-in-cheek assertion that I.B.M. stands for "It's Better Manually"! What we did was to cut narrow strips of multi-coloured poster board into varying lengths according to the "size" of the different characteristics. Each characteristic was

represented by a different colour. And each strip was labelled with the route number. The coloured, sized and labelled strips were then laid out on a large chart with one row per colour per truck. Repeated swaps were then made until a near-optimum distribution was achieved. During the process someone might say, "I need a short blue, together with a medium yellow and a long red."

Truck route assignment problem input data
(Photo by author)

Obviously it would have been more than a little embarrassing to deliver our solution to the customer in this format, so we fed our manual results into the computer and printed out the results. Needless to say, we never revealed our solution method. Nevertheless, the customer was very satisfied and that's all that really mattered.

Application packages

In addition to (and sometimes concurrently with) the custom programming projects, we also supported customers in their use of various IBM-provided scientific application packages, such as:

- Project Management System (critical path scheduling for large-scale projects)
- Mathematical Programming System (linear programming)
- General Purpose System Simulator (system modelling tool)
- Vehicle Scheduling System (delivery/pickup vehicle routing tool)
- Continuous Systems Modelling Program (simulation of complex

engineering and scientific systems)

- Numerical Control System (definition of continuous path machining contours)
- PRALINE (questionnaire survey processing)
- TRIM (paper roll cutting optimization)
- Steel Detailing System (calculation of rebar requirements for concrete structures)
- COGO (computer aided drafting and design)
- Cut-and-fill (construction of roads, railways, etc.)
- Regression Analysis (statistical process to estimate relationships among variables)

Our support of these application packages took many forms. Sometimes we worked very closely with the customer right from the preparation of input through to the analysis of results. At other times we would develop and conduct customized customer courses. We were always on call to provide customer support to answer questions and help debug problems. And in still other cases, where the customer was self-sufficient, the Datacentre simply provided the computer power.

One thing is certain: our days were never dull in Scientific Services! And, in the midst of all the work, we had some fun too. Sometimes at lunchtime we would play ring toss using the write-protect rings for magnetic tapes and the coat hooks on the wall. All went

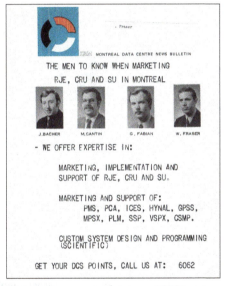

Datacentre promo sheet, ca. 1970 (Courtesy of International Business Machines Corporation, © 1970 International Business Machines Corporation)

well until we discovered one day that our manager was holding a meeting on the other side of the target wall! Occasionally, we played pranks on one another. Colleague David Gussow remembers a "tit-for-tat" situation that involved me:

> Once, when you were away from your desk, someone "decorated" your cubicle with miles of continuous forms sprocket feed tear-off edges. You were not amused and vowed revenge. Upon identifying the guilty party you obtained a boxful of keypunch chads and dumped them into the culprit's filing cabinet drawer. For months afterwards, he would still find these tiny reminders of your retribution!

"Hope they can't hear us!" (Sketch by James Harvey)

Brokerage department

Although I did not have any direct involvement with the Brokerage department per se, I did develop a stock analysis program for a Montreal brokerage firm. In any case, I would be remiss to not mention the miracles that this department performed each and every day. Long-time Datacentre employee and manager, Wayne Giroux, describes the operation:

> IBM Canada Datacentres in Montreal, Toronto and Vancouver handled most of the back-office processing for the brokerage and investment companies in the country because only one or two of the very biggest had their own computers. The schedule of activities to be performed between market closing at 4:00 p.m. and the next day's market opening was extremely tight. Brokers' trades for the entire Montreal market would be delivered by messenger each day soon after the markets closed. Confirmations of the day's stock market trades had to be ready for mailing by 8:00 p.m. in order to be delivered to trading clients the next day. During that less-than-four-hour window much had to be done very quickly.

All trades had to be first keypunched, then delivered to operations, and balanced (i.e., find keypunch errors and correct them). Meanwhile, name and address updates had to be keypunched and processed. Next the trades had to be sorted using the card sorter. Finally the confirmations had to be printed – on a different customized form for each broker. The confirmations would then go off to the collating, bursting and binding department. Individual confirmations were manually stuffed into envelopes that were different for each broker. The envelopes had to be sorted by mailing area (there were no postal codes at that time) and put through the postage machine. The stamped envelopes had to be stacked by area in order for the post office to accept them for next-day delivery. Before the clock struck eight, a staff member would then take the bundles to the post office several blocks away. If the deadline was missed, it was a major catastrophe.

Additional processing needed to be done on the second and third shifts. All the day's input from the brokers was processed and reports produced. By morning there was an individual package for each broker with every element needed for back office management: security inventories, bringing to market of bond and stock inventories, trades made, bookkeeping reports, etc. Each morning a courier for each broker would stop by on their way to work to pick up that broker's output. Each broker took it for granted that it would all be there when they arrived at their office that morning, and also that all their clients would receive their confirmations in the mail the same day.

Technical giants

During my time in the Datacentre, I came into contact with many exceptional IBMers whose creative and innovative thinking led to remarkable technical achievements. A few of them are profiled below.

Joseph Kern

Among the things I learned from my first boss was that nothing was impossible and that there was a solution to every problem. When I would accompany Joe on customer calls, I quickly realized that "No" was not part of his vocabulary. No matter how infeasible was the client's requirement, Joe's response was, "Yes,

Joe Kern, 1968 (Courtesy of Joe Kern)

we can do that." Only on the way back to the office would he confess that he didn't really know how the problem would be solved. But he was always confident that we would find a way. And we did! Perhaps unknowingly, Joe was heeding Thomas J. Watson Jr.'s remarks to a Columbia University audience in 1962:

> We believe an organization will stand out only if it is willing to take on seemingly impossible tasks . . . [Those] who set out to do what others say cannot be done are the ones who make the discoveries, produce the inventions, and move the world ahead.[11]

Innovation and the ability to quickly respond to the situation at hand were some of Joe's hallmarks. He reminded me of an incident that occurred in 1966 at the grand opening of the new IBM building at Place Ville Marie attended by Jacques Maisonrouge, president of IBM Americas/Far East Corporation. One of the feature demonstrations was QUIKTRAN, at which Joe was one of the presenters while I operated the keyboard. Joe recalls the event:

> I was the main English presenter and Alain Roy (who later co-founded DMR – Ducros Meilleur & Roy) was the main French presenter. Anyway, when things seemed to be quiet for a few minutes, Alain went downstairs to watch another graphics presentation that was happening concurrently. While he was absent my friend and Datacentre colleague Alain Pilon and his family arrived and asked me if I would do a presentation for them in French. I hadn't given it in French but I had listened to it in French a million times – so I said, "Yes, of course." Our demo was set up directly across from the elevators. I was halfway through the French presentation when the elevator doors suddenly opened and out stepped Jacques Maisonrouge, Jack Brent and Bill Moore. I didn't freeze – it would have been counterproductive to do so. I just continued my French presentation and said to myself, "Whatever you do, don't hesitate... just keep talking... it doesn't matter what you say, just say it like you mean it." So without losing a beat I continued the presentation. I think that Jacques Maisonrouge appreciated my European French accent. As for Jack Brent and Bill Moore, they probably didn't understand a word I said, so I had nothing to fear from my IBM Canada superiors. I managed to plow my way through the whole French presentation. At the end, they all applauded!

As for technical creativity and innovation, Joe was definitely ahead of his time. For example, in the mid-1960s he implemented a checkpoint-restart function for the TRIM program. This was years before such a facility became commonplace. Joe describes another technical breakthrough a few years later:

> One day I was looking at a PC Magazine article about printers, and read about a Toshiba 100 dots-per-inch model. I realized that such a printer

---

[11] Courtesy of International Business Machines Corporation, © International Business Machines Corporation

was almost plotter-quality and so wanted to try it out. But it was too expensive to buy personally, and I didn't want to ask management for the funds to buy one. However, I knew that Radio Shack had a 30-day return policy. So I went to Radio Shack and bought the printer with my own money. As soon as I got it home I started studying how to program it. After working steadily for three days I was able to print a huge "Z" with a perfectly formed non-jagged diagonal line. When I showed the result to management they were incredulous: "You did this on a printer?" With my mission achieved, I returned the printer for a refund, so it didn't cost me a cent!

Paul Morrison

During the late 1960s I was aware that some of my Datacentre colleagues were programming in something called "DOORMAT" that had been invented by Paul Morrison. Other than thinking, "What a strange name for a programming language!" I knew nothing at all about it. However, my colleague Jonas Bacher was someone who remembers using it. Little did I realize that this was the beginning of something hugely significant that would ultimately become known as Flow-Based Programming. Paul outlines the concept:

Paul Morrison (Courtesy of Paul Morrison)

> In computer programming, Flow-Based Programming (FBP) is a programming paradigm, discovered/invented by J. Paul Rodker Morrison in the late 1960s, that uses a "data processing factory" metaphor for designing and building applications. FBP defines applications as networks of "black box" processes, which communicate via data chunks (called Information Packets) travelling across predefined connections (think "conveyor belts"), where the connections are specified externally to the processes. These black box processes can be reconnected endlessly to form different applications without having to be changed internally. FBP is thus naturally component-oriented.[12]

Paul remembers his early use of the concept while working in the Montreal Datacentre:

> The first implementation of FBP was called DOORMAT (Data-Oriented Organization Running Multiple Asynchronous Tasks). But the name was judged to lack gravitas, so I gave it a new moniker AMPS (Advanced Modular Programming System). The neat thing about the Datacentre was

---

[12] J. Paul Morrison, *Flow-Based Programming, 2nd Edition: A New Approach to Application Development*

that we owned the code and ran the applications, thus allowing us to experiment with new technologies. So we started using AMPS to build customer applications, which proved to be more reliable, better-performing, faster to build, and most importantly, easier to maintain! This was followed by five years working on the Bank of Montreal's Mech project, where we used AMPS for almost all of the batch processes. At least one of those programs was still running every night 40 years later!

Paul recounts his most vivid memory of working in the Datacentre:

> I once had the dubious pleasure of having to modify an update program (not FBP, obviously!) whose author had written the client an explanation of why his enhancement request could not be satisfied, which started, "Owing to the limitations of data processing,..."! My clear recollection is that modifying that program (and, for a conventional program, it was really quite well-written) was only *almost* impossible!

Don Myles

As manager of the Brokerage department, the late Don Myles was the brains behind a number of programming and procedural innovations that significantly reduced the processing time required for the very time-constrained daily runs. Wayne Giroux remembers several of these:

> He did things like taking the card programs and loading the card images onto tape. It was revolutionary how he architected transferring from one program to the next in a job stream without having to manually reload it – just a series of programs on a tape for a particular sequence of jobs.

Don Myles (From 1966 BCT Class Photo, courtesy of Peter Bedoukian, retouching by Greg Beck)

> Before print spooling became available with the System /360, Don and his programmers wrote

their own spooling subroutine for the 1401 – and all Montreal programmers used it from that day forward. The idea was that writing to tape or disk was faster than printing (each print command involved wait time) and then printing could be done at full speed with no processing.

Don also led initiatives to increase productivity based on his prolific reading. He once said that he never had an original idea in his life, but he was able to recognize a good idea when he saw one. And he would try to figure how to use it. An example was binary searches. Don and his team devised the binary search subroutine that all our programmers used from that point on. One starts the search in the middle of the table/file instead of the beginning, and then the middle of the half identified, and so on, until a match was found. Brilliant! An item in a thousand entry table, for instance, could be found in about ten searches versus an average of five hundred using the sequential method. Slow updates suddenly became very fast.

Brokerage colleague Dave Mordecai also recalls Don's constant desire to improve system performance and efficiency:

> He would use a stopwatch to measure run times on the 1401 16K tape system. And I recall mentioning to him about the fill pages of the month-end statement. The next thing I knew Don had implemented an option to produce a short-length version.

Colleague David Antebi remembers Don's frequent reference to the "Rule of Seven": that a prospect needs to see or hear your marketing message at least seven times before they take action and buy from you.

Joe Major

It was early in my career that I met this brilliant man who would become my mentor throughout my time at IBM. Joe was giving a course at McGill University on linear programming and I was invited to attend. This experience not only opened my eyes to the fascinating world of operations research but marked the beginning of our professional and personal relationship.

Joe possessed an amazing mind and the ability to share his knowledge with both his peers and his students. Regardless of how busy he was with his own projects, he was always willing to assist me with mine. His expertise in the fields of operations research, benchmarking and capacity planning was well-known across IBM and far beyond.

Joe Major (Courtesy of Eric Major, retouching by Greg Beck)

When I recently visited Joe at a care facility in Montreal, he humbly recounted to me how he first got into the field of Operations Research:

> I noticed that more and more newspapers were talking about operations research, so I thought that I should find out something about it. So I looked for articles and read a few of them. It looked interesting, so I started reading more and more. I went to the McGill library to find out more about these new buzzwords. With my background in mathematics I was able to understand what it was about, and thought that it might be a good idea to develop some skills in the field. Eventually I acquired a little expertise – enough to talk about it. At that stage I only knew a little bit, but that was much more than others who knew nothing about the subject. Then I learned about an organization in Toronto called the Canadian Operational Research Society. I became the local expert even with my limited knowledge. Over the years I attended conferences and gradually increased my knowledge of the subject.

Jack Sams and Lee Fesperman

My 1966 Agenda Planner contains the following entry for November 24, 1966: "Endicott NY with Joe Kern." My manager and travel partner remembers that trip very well:

> We went to Endicott to meet with Jack Sams (manager of Industry Services) and Lee Fesperman to enact some changes that our customer, Dominion Steel, required in the Steel Detailing System, later known as 1130 PLAN (Problem Language Analyzer). They incorporated our suggestions and called them "The Canadian contribution."

Jack Sams, 1984 (Courtesy of Jack Sams)

> In retrospect we were in the presence of greatness. Jack later participated in the deal with Microsoft, making Bill Gates what he is today. Lee is the most brilliant programming mind I ever met. Lee was noticeable by his tee-shirt and a calculator on his belt – in the 1966 world of dark suits and ties.

Jack Sams' pivotal role in the introduction of IBM's Personal Computer deserves a special mention:

> Jack was the engineer in charge of software development for the prototype. He had worked on the IBM System /23, and had spent a year building the BASIC compiler for it, pushing the product behind schedule. He didn't want to repeat the same struggle with the new microcomputer, so he decided to license most of the software from an outside company. Sams met with Bill Gates to evaluate whether Microsoft could handle the task of writing a BASIC compiler for the IBM PC. This led to his recommendation to William Lowe that they use Microsoft software in the final product. In addition, when he was unable to make a deal with Digital Research Intergalactic for the operating system, Sams and his team turned to Microsoft. This led to the development of an operating system released by IBM as PC-DOS and by Microsoft as MS-DOS. The rest, as they say, is history.[13]

During the research for this book, some 52 years later, I contacted both these men to more clearly understand the context of our 1966 meeting. Jack described to me how the evolution of PLAN was tied to the Steel Detailing application:

> The steel detailing application at H.K. Porter in Birmingham, Alabama, first developed in 1963 for the IBM 1620, established the challenge of describing the geometry and reinforcement patterns of reinforced

---

[13] Courtesy of International Business Machines Corporation, © International Business Machines Corporation

concrete structures, after they were put on the market for bids. The premise was that the estimator could generate a shop bill of materials from their take-off rather than just the tonnage of straight, light bent and heavy bent bars. The devil was in the details. Did all (or part) of the steel in this bridge or building have 1–1/2" cover? Did each of the floors or spans replicate another? Et cetera.

As we tried to define an input scheme that captured all the relevant information for a succession of projects, we began to understand that we needed a formal, definable language with the ability to interpret nested descriptors. The grammar for defining commands, parsing the input offered, supplying context, defaults, and queuing executable modules became the PLAN interpreter specification. It was split out as a separate effort and re-implemented for the 1130 . . . The final 1130 version was released as a part of the 1130 Data Presentation System in 1965 and then as a separate product in 1967. PLAN eventually supported more than a dozen varied IBM application systems for graphics, optics, industrial, mechanical, and electrical engineering. UNIX, which was developed somewhat later, has some, but far from all of the capabilities of PLAN.

For me it felt good to know that, in some small way, Joe and I had contributed to their very revolutionary development.

Lee Fesperman worked for IBM Corporation for five years beginning in 1964 – mostly as a contractor but as a full-time employee from 1966 to 1967. He worked directly for Jack Sams for the entire time. Except for the last six months, he worked in Endicott, N.Y. on PLAN. Initially it was 1130 PLAN, which Lee then ported to System /360. During his final six months with IBM, Lee worked with Jack on LEOS (Low-End Operating System) for the System /370 in Boca Raton, Florida. LEOS had similar features to UNIX (though unknown to them at the time). IBM upper management cancelled LEOS while it was still in the Design Phase... otherwise IBM could have beaten AT&T to the punch!

Lee Fesperman (Courtesy of Lee Fesperman)

Quite apart from the technical giants profiled above, the Montreal Datacentre had a number of management "giants." Colleague Bruce Marshall remembers:

> My immediate manager, Jerry Laak, one of the other managers, Gerry McQuade, and their manager, Bill Tyrrell, were all well over 6 ft. tall. I remember a comment at a large meeting where an underling commented that they would never get ahead in the business because they weren't tall enough!

Supporting cast

In addition to its programmers, analysts and managers, the Datacentre was blessed with dedicated secretarial and administrative support staff. Of course, at that time, our secretaries typed all our letters, presentations and reports. Joe Kern remembered them with much appreciation:

> An often-neglected aspect of our work activities was our secretaries. In many ways they kept us out of trouble with a smile or with a baseball bat, but never with a frown. We owe them a lot for keeping us in line. Their competence became painfully obvious when I left IBM and was looking for someone like them – Carmella Di Lalla, Susan Lee, Beverly Gentry, to name just a few.

To Joe's honour list, I would add Karen Gélinas and Pat Kolosky, who joined us later. And who could forget dear Miss Jones – I never did know her first name – who manned the front reception desk? At that time, we didn't have our own separate telephone lines – all calls were answered by Miss Jones, who then summoned us over the intercom. Colleague Gabor Fabian recounts one such call:

> One time Miss Jones announced over the intercom, "Gabor Fabian – line 1." Because I was busy at that moment, I didn't pick up the line immediately. A few moments later, Miss Jones literally shouted over the intercom "Gabor Fabian – it's your mother on line 1!"

Another indispensable support service was the Art Room, staffed by Martha Shearer and her assistant. Martha recalls:

> I remember sales reps coming into the Art Room at the end of the day with huge presentations that they needed put on flip charts for the next morning. We would end up working all night on them. Usually the reps would appreciate our work and take us out to lunch (or give us boxes of cosmetics we didn't want!). The arrival of PCs eliminated the need of an art room.

And then there was Thelma Harding, whose meticulous management of expense accounts probably saved IBM many thousands of dollars a year. At her retirement event, she apologized for being so strict, but justified her penny-pinching because she was "taking care of the company's money."

Colleague Margaret Eastwood recalls that the office systems that replaced most secretaries were not universally embraced. "They were not that well received by anyone, but especially the managers. They were losing their secretaries and they didn't know how to type."

Another group of Datacentre employees that deserves special mention is the Keypunch department. Not only did they keypunch all our programs but they were a critical link in the Brokerage processing chain. Department manager Wayne

Giroux remembers them well:

> In the male-dominated world of Data Processing, keypunch operators were exclusively female. There were about 20 to 30 working the daytime shift, and 40 to 50 on evenings. The evening schedule was dictated by the requirements of the brokerage community, but they would also keypunch any jobs remaining from the day shift. These women, many quite young, would then be released onto Dorchester Blvd. around 11 p.m. to wait for husbands, boyfriends or taxis to come pick them up. Occasionally there was harassment, which would result in management issuing warnings to them about being careful when leaving the premises. Most worked part-time with little in the way of benefits. They were paid hourly between 40 and 80 cents an hour. I recall approving wage increases that eventually skyrocketed their hourly wage to over a dollar... wow! The daytime and evening supervisors would get together to decide who would be recommended for what raise. These were tough women who ran tight ships.

I cannot close this chapter without recognizing a small but indispensable group of "systems" experts, including David Gussow, Roger Archambault and the late Frank Carpenter. This trusty trio constantly came to our rescue when our programs didn't work properly. Also I pay tribute to the memory of two Datacentre colleagues who tragically died on the job: Yves Trudeau of a heart attack and Charles Cabana in a plane crash.

Over the course of my eight-plus years in the Datacentre, I declined opportunities to move into other areas of the company. I was content with where I was and had absolutely no desire to move into management or marketing. Then one day in late 1973, Montreal Manufacturing & Distribution branch manager Peter Glasheen came knocking. He was recruiting SEs for an exciting new project. I accepted and my career took a very significant turn. Goodbye Datacentre, hello Marketing!

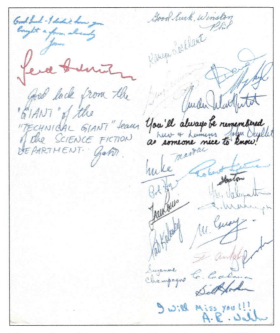

Farewell card upon leaving the Datacentre, 1973

Chapter 4   Daddy Bars

A sample Universal Product Code (UPC)

My kids always called them "Daddy bars" because they believed that I had invented the Universal Product Code (UPC). And I could never convince them otherwise, so, in their minds at least, the myth persists. As much as I would love to take credit for this development that changed the retailing landscape forever, it just ain't so. However, I did contribute, albeit in a modest way, to the UPC's use and acceptance. Dave Moxley describes my involvement this way:

> Winston was a key member of the technical team that implemented the first generation of point-of-sale scanners at Steinberg [originally known as Steinberg's] – the first store in the world . . . The implementation required 7/24 babysitting and the first generation of business benefits was limited to price accuracy, checkout speed and the elimination of item price marking.

But before talking about that experience, I would like to pay tribute to the real inventors of the UPC code and explain how IBM became involved in its development.

UPC history

The story of how the UPC code came to be is a most interesting one. Although many would be inclined to date its origins to the early 1970s, its invention actually occurred some 25 years before it finally saw the light of day. And there were many twists and turns along the way, as illustrated by the following historical summary by Bill Selmeier of IDhistory.com:

The first step towards the eventual UPC occurred around the end of the 1940s. A grocery executive approached the Engineering College at Drexel University [in Philadelphia, Pa.] requesting the development of automating product identification at checkout. The University did not accept the challenge, but a graduate student, Bernard Silver, overheard the request and related it to his friend Joe Woodland. Together they decided to take on the challenge.

Joe tells the story about dragging his hand through sand and realizing that varying the width of the lines could encode numbers much like a Morse Code. In October 1949 he and Bernard filed a Patent Application for a "Classifying Apparatus & Method." Patent 2612994 was issued in 1952, the original patent for a true barcode. It defined the characteristics of optical barcodes and went on to additionally make it circular or the bulls-eye shape. Eventually in 1992 Joe was awarded the National Medal of Technology by President George H. W. Bush for the invention of barcodes.

That same year, 1952, Joe created a "proof of concept" experimental system and installed it in the backroom of a Colonial Grocery Store in Atlanta, Ga. Joe and Bernard had created what was to become popularly known as the bulls-eye symbol but hardly anyone noticed. Eventually they were able to get $15,000 for their patent from Philco [which later sold it to RCA]. Joe went to work for IBM who was not interested in the patent at that time.

RCA then developed the technology and demonstrated it at a business show in 1971 using a working checkout scanner. The great excitement that was generated around the RCA booth did not go unnoticed by IBM. Shortly thereafter, Alex Jablonover was mandated to assemble an IBM team to investigate and exploit this new opportunity. One of his first actions was to find Joe Woodland (who was still with IBM in Armonk, N.Y.) and bring him down to Raleigh. (Both Jablonover and Woodland were later involved with our IBM Canada team.)

Around the same time that IBM's special team was being established, the grocery industry was looking for a standard barcode system, and issued an invitation for proposals from a number of technology companies, including IBM. In 1973 the industry group announced the winning bid by IBM's George Laurer, whose linear barcode design was accepted with only a few minor adjustments. The 12-digit code was made up of a 1-digit header, a 5-digit manufacturer number, a 5-digit product number and a 1-digit check digit. The IBM team's task now was to develop a scanner to read the newly adopted barcode. And that they did! On October 11, 1973, the IBM 3660 supermarket system with its high-speed laser scanner to read the Universal Product Code was announced.[14] Consisting of the IBM 3651 store

---

[14] Courtesy of International Business Machines Corporation, © International Business Machines Corporation

controller, the IBM 3663 checkout terminal and the 3666 scanner, this family of products was designed to perform normal checkout operations as well as to meet the data collection needs of the industry.[15] But it would be a full nine months later when the baby was born with the first installation of the scanning system at a Steinberg store in Dorval (Quebec) on July 26, 1974.

Steinberg scanning project

Steinberg store sign, 1960 (pinterest.ca)

Colleague André Gauthier explains how IBM Canada became involved in this historic project:

> In 1973 I became the marketing rep for Steinberg, one of the largest accounts in our branch. They were recognized as leaders in the supermarket arena and were constantly innovating. Their DP [Data Processing] director, Syd Passoff, was always looking for the latest and the best in technology. In my very first meeting with him after taking over the account he gave me an order for another System /360 – so I made my whole quota in one day! Anyway, Steinberg wanted to improve the front-end productivity in their stores and requested IBM's help to do so. The result was Project Vega, a comprehensive study of all aspects of the checkout process. Every individual action was precisely timed with stopwatches: ring time, bag time, pay time, idle time. At the end of the six-month study a detailed report was produced. At the same time, IBM in Raleigh, N.C., was developing the 3660 system to scan the newly introduced UPC code and were looking for potential field test sites.

---

[15] Courtesy of International Business Machines Corporation, © International Business Machines Corporation

IBM 3663 Supermarket scanning terminal (Courtesy of International Business Machines Corporation, © 1973 International Business Machines Corporation)

Grocery bagging timing study at Steinberg, 1973 (Author's collection)

Above: IBM-Steinberg Partners in Progress publication, 1978 (Courtesy of International Business Machines Corporation, © 1978 International Business Machines Corporation)

Right: Mechanical cash register timing study at Steinberg, 1973 (Author's collection)

Canadian industry marketing manager, John Thompson, learned of the Raleigh project through his U.S. counterparts. Together with Montreal branch manager, Peter Glasheen, and marketing manager, Ed Fudge, it was determined that Steinberg would be a good fit as a test site. So I proposed the idea to Syd Passoff and Vice-president Jack Levine, who were both very interested. The next step was to organize a visit to IBM in North Carolina for the Steinberg executives. We hired a private jet – money was no issue those days – and flew several of their executives including Passoff, Levine, Mitzi and Mel Dobrin and a few others down to Raleigh. The Steinberg contingent was very impressed with what they saw and heard during their time in the IBM development lab.

This trip confirmed their interest – indeed enthusiasm – to become partners in this most innovative of projects. Thus began a store systems partnership that would last for many years and later be documented in the Partners in Progress publication.

Now that customer commitment had been secured, the next step was to put together a multi-disciplinary project team consisting of marketing, systems engineering, customer engineering and administrative personnel. Steinberg, for its part, needed to assemble its own team and select a pilot store. They chose their store in Dorval, an upscale West Island community. Colleague Paul Biron considered it a wise choice. "There was a feeling that if scanning worked for the clientele in Dorval (known to be quite finicky), it would work anywhere."

Our IBM team worked closely with the Steinberg team on the many aspects of the project. Among them were checkstand redesign, item file creation, UPC source marking and consumer education. And of course, we worked very closely with Raleigh on everything related to the hardware, software and communications. As a result, there was a constant shuttling of resources among the initial centres of action: IBM offices at Place Ville Marie, the Steinberg Data Processing offices at 5400 Hochelaga St. and the Store Systems lab in Raleigh. IBMer Margaret Eastwood even had a Steinberg employee badge because she spent so much time at their Hochelaga location! As the project progressed, the Dorval store personnel would join the mix.

Steinberg access pass (Courtesy of Marg Eastwood)

The checkstand redesign was a major project in itself. Steinberg industrial engineer, Nabil Asswad, headed up this very critical aspect. The checkout lane had to be totally rethought in order to not only accommodate the integration of the scanner itself but to facilitate an entirely new checkout process.

Item file creation provided some major challenges in this new environment of scanning. Each of the more than 10,000 different items sold in a typical Steinberg grocery store required the addition of a receipt tape descriptor. This new product descriptor was limited to 12 characters and it needed to be bilingual. The following format was adopted: "MMMM FFF EEE" where MMMM is the product manufacturer, FFF is the French product descriptor and EEE is the English product descriptor. These criteria led to some very interesting results:

- KRAF CRA CRA (Kraft crackers)
- CAMP TOM TOM (Campbell tomato soup)
- AYLM LEG VEG (Aylmer vegetable soup)
- CATE SPA SPA (Catelli spaghetti)

Nevertheless, these contracted descriptors represented a significant step forward from the previous generic ones: GROC, MEAT and PROD. With a bit of interpretive ability, shoppers could now identify the items purchased by examining their customer receipt tape.

UPC source marking, or more accurately, the lack of it, proved to be one of the biggest difficulties encountered during the months leading up to the Dorval store installation date. Although the grocery industry had adopted the UPC code standard more than a year earlier, manufacturers were slow to apply the barcode to their products. Integrating the UPC code into the product packaging was a costly process that involved a total redesign. Very few were prepared to incur the expense with no immediate benefit in return. Steinberg contacted their major suppliers to encourage – even request – them to comply. Some responded positively, but in general, manufacturers were slow to come on board. This situation obviously posed a dilemma that could have put the entire scanning project in jeopardy. The solution was to supplement source marking with in-store UPC marking. Colleague Paul Biron describes the setup:

> There were two "production lines" located in the back-store at Dorval. Each had conveyors and a bar code printer that produced gummed UPC labels. These machines were used mostly by the night shifts as they were stocking the shelves. This was a very labour-intensive (and expensive) procedure that involved opening each case, printing the required labels, and applying one onto each individual item (e.g., can, box, bag, etc.) before moving the case to the appropriate aisle in the store. I remember that the labels did not stick well on frozen or even refrigerated products.

A Computerworld article on the Dorval installation in October 1974 (three months after the initial installation) stated that only 320 items were source-marked and that the store spent 200 employee-hours per week to print UPC labels for the many products not yet source-marked.[16]

These added costs were a major concern to Steinberg management. John Thompson recalls how IBM helped address that concern:

> Jack Levine, President of Steinberg's Grocery Division, was upset at the cost of manually labelling every product in the Dorval store with UPC labels. He wanted to accelerate the pace at which grocery manufacturers were pre-printing the codes on their labels. His idea was for IBM to host an afternoon cocktail party for his suppliers at the store to demonstrate the system and he would subtlety announce that pre-printing the code on labels was soon to be a criteria for Steinberg's Purchasing Department. The invitations were sent, food and drink were ordered and many IBMers helped clean the store and face up the shelves. The morning before the cocktail party, however, Larry Diamond, Marketing

---

[16] Computerworld, Oct. 30, 1974, p. 29 (Used with permission of Computerworld Online, Copyright © 2018. All rights reserved.)

Manager for Steinberg, came into my office and said that we had a huge problem. He had forgotten that it was a Jewish holiday and that no food or drink could be served before sundown! We fussed for a few hours, but then Larry, a very resourceful individual, shouted "I've got it! Bring me the Yellow Pages!" Half an hour later he came back with a grin, saying, "Problem solved!" He had hired three rabbis from the phone book, to be dressed in full regalia to be our waiters and bartender – an acceptable way to serve before sundown!

In spite of the challenges involved, in-store marking saved the day by allowing the scanning system to be properly tested in order to evaluate productivity improvements. Once the majority of items were source-marked, significant savings would ensue from the elimination of price marking in stores. But there was a small problem – actually, it was a big problem. Consumer activists had begun to complain that price removal could lead to consumers becoming victims of the new system in a number of ways – computer errors, on-the-fly price

Location of Scanning Systems		
Store Name	City, State	Date Operational
Pathmark Store	So. Plainfield, NJ	8/74
Ralph's Grocery	Lakewood, CA	9/74
Steinberg Store	Montreal CANADA	7/74
Wegmans Food Markets, Inc.	Rochester, NY	10/74
Shop-Rite (Piggly Wiggly)	Fort Worth, TX	11/74
Giant Food, Inc.	Severna Park, MD	1/75
Lucky Store	San Leandro, CA	2/75

Supermarket Institute summary of first scanning system installations, 1975

Vol. 8-4 · Distribution Codes, Inc. August 1, 1974

UGPCC BOARD CHAIRMAN JOHN L. STRUBBE REVIEWS TEN MONTHS OF ACCOMPLISHMENT BY STAC

UGPCC Board Chairman John L. Strubbe, in reviewing the outstanding accomplishments of the Symbol Technical Advisory Committee (STAC) during the July 17, 1974, Board of Governors meeting, recalled his challenge to committee and subcommittee members during the first meeting of STAC just ten months ago when he

TWO SUPERMARKETS "IN BUSINESS"

UPC STORE OPERATIONS BEGIN

A long-awaited milestone was reached last month when two grocery industry supermarkets, the Marsh store in Troy, Ohio, and the Steinberg store in Montreal, Canada, went operational using the Universal Product Code and symbol with production-line automated electronic and scanner point-of-sale equipment.

UPC Newsletter announcement of Steinberg scanning installation (Author's collection) changes while they were shopping or other ways that they might be ripped off. These fears also caused the government to sit up and take notice. In some jurisdictions this led to legislation. Steinberg confronted these concerns with an aggressive consumer education and awareness initiative. For several weeks prior to the Dorval store going live, shoppers received bag stuffers whose aim was to explain the benefits of the new system and to allay their fears. And, when the store did go live, shoppers were offered grease pencils to mark the shelf label prices on the items that they purchased. Interestingly enough, very few took advantage of the offer. IBM Industry Marketing manager, Frank Hall, explains the situation:

> Initially customers were sceptical. Were they being charged the right price for the item? But through government initiatives and corporate information and education programs, consumer concerns were gradually assuaged.

The lack of prices on items wasn't the only consumer issue. Conspiracy theorists, especially in the United States, claimed that the UPC code was "the mark of the beast" referred to in the Bible. In the Book of Revelation, it foretells an apocalypse in which a beast will rise from the earth, rain fire from the heavens, and lay his mark on all of humankind – a mark used to buy and sell:

> It also forced all people, great and small, rich and poor, free and slave, to receive a mark on their right hands or on their foreheads, so that they could not buy or sell unless they had the mark, which is the name of the beast or the number of its name. This calls for wisdom. Let the person who has insight calculate the number of the beast, for it is the number of a man. That number is 666. –Revelation 13: 16-18 (NIV)

Many challenges were confronted and conquered in the days leading up to the official launch of the revolutionary new scanning system in the Dorval store on July 26, 1974. All hands were on deck and there was excitement and anticipation in the air as UPC coded items, one after another, were successfully passed over the scanners. We didn't realize it then, but we were part of history in the making. For it was on that day in that place that a revolution in retailing was born, and we were midwives to the birth.

Visitors galore

That momentous event triggered an avalanche of visitors who descended on the city to see our newborn. First was our IBM Eastern Region Vice-president, Keith Johnston, who came, looked and liked so much what he saw, that he went back to his office and penned a congratulatory letter to our team:

> I was delighted to visit the Steinberg Dorval store on Monday July 29 and see the 3660 supermarket system in operation. As you know, this

installation is a world first, an event of which you and your team should be justly proud. I know your success is the result of extremely hard work by all members of the team and I'd like each to know how much this is appreciated by me as well as all IBM Canada senior management. Congratulations and best wishes for continued success with the project.

Next came the Head Office contingent, closely followed by foreign delegations from the U.S.A., France, Germany, Australia and elsewhere. The visitors included executives of major international retailers and IBMers wishing to acquire first-hand experience with the system. On September 24, 1974, Steinberg Vice-president Jack Levine proudly hosted an open house at the store.

Toronto sales rep Frank Hall recalls his visit to the store:

> MR. JACK LEVINE
> Executive Vice-President, Retail
> Steinberg's Limited
>
> cordially invites you to attend a demonstration
> of the IBM 3660 scanning system
> to be held in the first store in Canada
> to use the Universal Product Code.
>
> Steinberg's, Dorval Gardens Shopping Centre
> Tuesday, September 24th, 1974, 7:30 p.m.
>
> Qualified personnel will be on hand to answer
> any questions.
>
> R.S.V.P. by forwarding
> enclosed card or by
> telephoning 256-2611   Refreshments
> Mrs. Helen Claridge   will be served

Invitation to Steinberg Dorval scanning system demonstration, 1974

> A couple of Canadian Tire dealers wanted a tour, so we flew down to Montreal, me dressed in my blue suit IBM wardrobe. While my guests were wandering around the store, I was standing close to the ice cream freezer. An older woman approached and wanted to know the price of an item. I told her to look at the shelf label. She went away then returned and said, "You have a suit, you must be a Steinberg manager, now fix this!" I told her that I didn't work for Steinberg. She then loudly announced how (expletive deleted) stupid I was. Meanwhile, my CTC guests and Steinberg managers were laughing their heads off. I quickly moved to the canned soup section!

Monitoring

In the weeks that followed, the IBM team was omnipresent in the store to provide support and assistance as well as to detect small problems before they ballooned into big problems. We all took turns babysitting our newborn. This was a part that I really didn't like. Being quite non-technical in terms of hardware and telecommunications, I was petrified that the store might go down on my watch. Even my much more technical colleagues felt the pressure:

> I remember the pressure that I felt when a store would crash. Customers had very little patience and would abandon their carts in the aisle with

containers of ice cream melting onto the floor. Meanwhile, we would desperately try to bring the store back up. –Michel Parent

The 3660 system was somewhat unstable at the beginning and, as Murphy's Law would have it, it failed during the busiest periods. It was not unusual to see dozens of grocery carts being abandoned in front of the cash registers by customers who were tired of waiting for the system to come back up. –Paul Biron

I remember being in the Dorval store on a Saturday when the power went out. The store manager was in a panic. Unhappy customers, some already suspicious of the new system, were queued up at the checkouts while he tried to decipher hexadecimal codes on the controller, address the problem, then enter another hexadecimal code to restart it. –Sally Harmer

In addition to our store babysitting duties, we also continually monitored source marking progress. Paul Biron describes the process:

Every Tuesday morning we would do a complete store product survey to track the number of items source-marked with the UPC code. Winston included this statistic as part of his weekly "System for Highlighting Indicators and Trends" for Steinberg management. I recall that when I started a few months after installation, the number of items was just over 100 (maybe 110 or 115). At that time, it grew by 10 or 15 each week. As time passed we became tired of seeing many of the same items week after week, so we devised a shortcut to our counting process. We affixed a blue dot beside the shelf sticker of all source-marked items discovered to date. These items could then be skipped on our

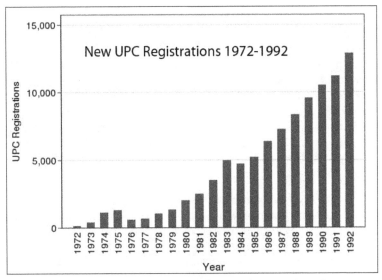

New UPC registrations ,1972-1992 (Uniform Code Council – reference
http://people.bu.edu/tsimcoe/documents/working/UPCv2)

subsequent Tuesday counts. Eventually we ended these weekly counts. Several years later, when visiting the store, I noticed some of these blue dots randomly scattered through the store. During the intervening years, of course, the shelves had been rearranged, so the blue dots did not correspond to anything logical. I nevertheless asked the grocery manager if he knew what the blue dots meant. He quickly answered, "Oh yes, they are part of a sophisticated shelf space allocation system." I replied, "Do you want to know what they **really** are?"

Troubleshooting

Very often our team came up with creative solutions to a variety of problems. For example, early on, cashiers complained that the "beep" to indicate a positive scan was too loud. The sound volume, although configurable, was already set to the lowest level. The solution? As would so often happen, it was a case of "Roger to the Rescue." Customer Engineer Roger Richard inserted layers of Kleenex in front of the speaker to lower the beep volume! Paul Biron recalls other home-grown fixes:

Roger (Mr. Fixit) Richard, 1983 (Courtesy of Denise Richard)

> The individual cash registers were connected two-by-two to TCUs (Terminal Control Units) that were rather bulky and located under the counter at every other lane. Sometimes, unexpectedly, two cash registers would lose power, which usually caused panic in the store. This happened until we found that kids had discovered the power switch, which was quite accessible on the back of each TCU. Kids being kids, they would play with the switch. Steinberg decided to install grilles to cover the TCU enclosure and prevent this from happening. Also, each TCU was connected to the store loop which allowed communication with the 3651 Store Controller located in the cash office. The store loop was a token ring network and the connection was made using a large four-pin connector. After a while the many vibrations present in such an environment (cash drawer closings, conveyor belt starting and stopping, etc.) caused the plug to become loose and fall out. This was fixed by Roger Richard's wife who crafted elastic bands to keep the store loop plugs in place.

> Scanner glass was also an issue. Repetitive scanning of glass and metal objects caused the scanner window to become scratched after only a few days of use. Of course this severely deteriorated the performance of the scanner, and store personnel typically had to change all scanner windows on a weekly basis. To make matters worse, Steinberg had found a cheaper supplier of scanner glass, which of course meant using glass that scratched even more quickly. We maintained constant pressure on

Raleigh to fix this issue. After a while, on one of my trips to Raleigh, I was handed a new experimental scanner window that had one side coated with a thin layer of sapphire. Of course I was instructed to install it the right way, as the other side, if facing up, would scratch just as another window would. I was expected to report back on the in-store test. The new glass was installed on lane 12 and the whole store management team was made aware of this special test. While the typical glass cost less than $5, the sapphire-covered glass was $400+. After a few days I went to the store to check the status, only to find that the sapphire glass was no longer there! It turned out that a cashier was told to change all the scanner glasses, which she did, and to throw the used glasses away. This was definitely most embarrassing for our team.

One Saturday afternoon there was a power failure in the Dorval store. The generator, which was usually verified on a regular basis, failed to start. Murphy again. And big lineups, of course. The store manager called IBM for help. Roger Richard literally "flew" from his home in Candiac to the store (luckily, he didn't get a speeding ticket). He entered the store by the front entrance, carrying a (heavy) car battery. When the customers and cashiers saw him, they all started applauding! Of course Roger was able to restart the generator, which was NOT an IBM product, and save the day. His clients praised him for his heroics.

Not all of our Roger Richard's interventions were to respond to customer complaints or problems. Sometimes it was the result of his own personal initiative. Paul Biron explains:

Roger had deep technical knowledge of computer hardware coupled with insatiable curiosity about how it operated. He enjoyed nothing more than getting inside the covers. So quite naturally when the IBM 3660 scanning system arrived on the scene he opened it up to examine the laser scanner. He found that by making certain adjustments he could improve the scanner's performance. As a result the scanners in the Dorval store were performing significantly better than elsewhere in the field, or even in the Raleigh development lab for that matter! This, of course, did not meet with the approval of Raleigh, who realized that most field customer engineers would not have the necessary expertise to make such adjustments.

Colleague Giorgio Toso remembers another of Roger's creative improvisations:

A store systems competitor came out with a customer receipt printer that cut the paper automatically, instead of the cashier having to rip it off. Realizing that Raleigh was unlikely to develop such a feature in the short term, Roger went to his basement and hand-built a prototype receipt tape guillotine. He used pieces of a hacksaw blade as the material for making the cutting blades and a solenoid for the actuation. I remember seeing the device work very well, but do not know whether it was ever installed in a store.

Although the 3660 scanning system hardware was very robust, one of the checkout terminals had a recurring problem with its keyboard. It had to be frequently replaced because of broken keys. Upon investigation, it was discovered that it was always the same terminal and the same cashier. Instead of using her finger to press the ENTER key, this cashier used whatever she had in her hand – like a large can of apple juice!

Although we were happy with the success of this first scanning installation, we realized that this was only the beginning and that there was much more to be done. We understood as well that this initial success was, in large part, due to all the hand-holding, jerry-rigging and babysitting that had been done. It was clear that this could not work as a modus operandi over the long term.

"They told me to hit ENTER!" (Sketch by James Harvey)

Nevertheless, during the months that followed IBM very actively marketed the system to Steinberg in hopes of landing an order for multiple stores. John Thompson describes his role and shares a most unexpected experience:

> After Steinberg agreed to be a pilot for the scanning system I was moved to Montreal to become the branch manager with hopes of turning the test into a chain-wide implementation. I bought a house in Westmount in February, but my family couldn't move until June when school was out. So I lived out of a suitcase in an empty house, had a rental car, and commuted to Toronto on the weekends. In April I was due to present our proposal for an extensive rollout to Steinberg's Board of Directors. I was up early that day, so I went for a walk around the block to take pictures of a nearby children's park so that my kids could see the neighbourhood. On my way back to the house, a car came racing down the street and forced me off the sidewalk. Two thugs jumped out, handcuffed me and tossed me into their car. I was convinced that the FLQ was back in business! However, after driving around the block, the car turned into a house's garage and I was chained to a radiator. Soon the RCMP showed up and I knew I was safe. The house was Brian Mulroney's, who had announced plans to run for Prime Minister, but was first finishing up an investigation into organized crime. His family had been threatened and the "thugs" were actually security guards who thought that I was photographing his home. The Mounties checked me out by taking me to my house, but I still looked suspicious because my house was empty and I was living out of a suitcase, so they asked me to name someone who could identify me. By this time I was late for the Steinberg Board meeting, so I told them to take me there. Two officers marched me into the Steinberg boardroom and asked if anyone could identify me. Sam Steinberg, the chairman, just glared, but after a moment of silence, Jack Levine, the president of Grocery, said, "So, Mr. Thompson, before I identify you, tell me again your best discount for the point-of-sale equipment!"

Frustrations

Over the next ten years the Steinberg success story gradually morphed into the Steinberg mañana saga. As IBM's store systems offerings evolved, we would come to discover that, no matter what new hardware or software we offered this client, it was never quite enough. A number of major performance tests were done specifically for Steinberg. Paul Biron describes one of the earliest ones:

> The three-day test occurred in February 1975 in the back-store demo room at Dorval. Its purpose was to measure "scan and bag" vs. "scan with wrapper." Sally Harmer and Marg Eastwood had prepared six grocery orders of varying sizes, including meat and produce. Keeping the meat at room temperature over three days (we rolled the carts into the fridge at night) and containing the blood and the smell was a challenge, but Sally insisted on having a test that mirrored real life. We also had

orders with varying percentages of source-marked items to evaluate the productivity impact. We had six different cashiers (one per half-day), and we repeatedly rotated each order (six carts) again and again, while taking measurements using a stopwatch. The idea was to see the impact of order size and wrapper/no wrapper on cashier productivity. Cashier Nicole Labelle (later to become my wife, but we were not yet dating) was scheduled on the Tuesday afternoon. I remember that for one of the orders, for which the other cashiers doing "scan and bag" required four bags, Nicole used only three bags, neatly packed. Everyone was impressed. And I learned later that it was her birthday, that very day! The conclusion of that test, if I remember correctly, was that wrappers (baggers) should be used, but only on Thursday night, Friday night and Saturday, when order sizes were typically larger. During the week "scan and bag" was appropriate.

Later tests included a major system stress test held at the Steinberg Training Centre. Positive results failed to be rewarded with a major sales order. Frustration was felt by both the local account team and IBM head office.

Colleague Michel Parent remembers his frustrations:

> I remember the various retail projects with Steinberg − a lot of development and lots of validation tests − but no purchase commitments on their part (3650 PSS and 4680). They made IBM work very hard to meet their requirements, but once they were met, the price was too high. I refer to the PSS task force that spent two years developing custom modifications followed by the 4680 pilot for which we reproduced the same changes − all to no avail.

Colleague Sally Harmer recalls being responsible for managing Steinberg's long list of requirements:

> I remember being the messenger for Arnold Sobrian (Steinberg project manager) in those Raleigh lab dealings, and of course everything needed to be fixed immediately. So when it came near the time for my maternity leave I thoroughly documented everything that was in progress with the lab, dotting all the i's and crossing all the t's. I entrusted this lengthy document to the most reliable and capable member of the team, resting in the knowledge that all would be done perfectly when I returned in 17 weeks. What a shock when I returned to discover that nothing had moved a centimeter since I left! And Arnold hadn't pulled out the equipment!

To be fair to Steinberg, some of their many requirements were very legitimate. One that I remember very distinctly − because I designed and programmed the solution − involved the "hold-up key." At that time, in the 1970s, Montreal experienced a rash of armed robberies, especially in supermarkets. Steinberg suffered, on average, one hold-up a week somewhere in its network of stores. Cashiers were instructed that, in such an event, they should immediately open the cash drawer and hand over the contents. However, with the added security features of the new cash register terminals, the cashier was prevented from opening the cash drawer except at end-of-transaction. If an armed robber were to demand cash in the middle of a 100-item transaction, the cashier would have to say, "Sorry sir, you'll need to wait until I finish this transaction!" Clearly a solution to this potential life-and-death problem was urgently needed. One of the existing keys on the keyboard was designated to be the "hold-up key." It was custom programmed so that when pressed three or more times consecutively, the cash drawer would immediately pop open, regardless of whether it was during or outside of a transaction.

Over the years I was frequently called on to make small ad hoc modifications to the checkout application. My manager, Stan Albert, recalls my unique method for estimating the effort involved to program such changes: "When I would ask you how long a certain modification would take to develop, your stock answer was always 'two weeks.' But I knew that you could probably code it overnight! I will always remember you as 'Winston two-week Fraser.'"

Although it was widely recognized that the hardware produced by IBM Store Systems was of excellent quality, the associated software definitely had problems. The architecture was unstable, the system was complex and the applications had bugs. David Dolman recalls:

> I was asked to give a foil presentation to Carl Corcoran to update him on the to-do list of Steinberg requirements – there were some 20 items on the list. My colleague Tom had already ticked off half the items (e.g., need a manual) but mine were things like "need to rewrite the application." I turned on the foil projector and saw smoke coming from it but just kept talking. When I was finished Carl simply asked: "Would you sell this to your mother?" I responded, "Only if I didn't love her!"

Paul Biron remembers some of the challenges related to the overall store systems architecture:

> At the time the 3660 architecture relied on the "Sister Store Backup" concept when a store controller failed. The idea was that the store with the failed controller would set its modem on "Backup" and physically dial the phone number of its assigned sister store which had a copy of its item prices and its cashier IDs and passwords. (This was a challenge in itself.) Early on, backup was unstable and it has happened that the manager of store 030 (Queen Mary) put the switch on his modem to "Talk" so that when store 038 (Dorval) called to go into backup, it would not work. He was simply protecting his own store, because accepting another store in backup mode usually caused his own store system to slow down or even crash. This was eventually fixed.

Michel Parent remembers similar difficulties with the later 4680 supermarket system: "With regard to the redundancy feature of the 4680 supermarket system, the system would often crash when the two controllers attempted to synchronize."

Even Raleigh recognized some of the shortcomings of its store systems. IBM executive Marvin Mann, in a speech to the Smithsonian on the 25th anniversary of the UPC in 1999, noted:

> Bob Martin, [President and CEO] of Wal-Mart, who is here tonight, was often on the telephone to me, and at times I wished I could turn the volume down. He was telling me in every way imaginable that it was unacceptable to have a Wal-Mart store out of business. I want to tell Bobby now that I knew that, I just didn't know how to fix it. I couldn't argue the point at all. Those were some dark days. . .[17]

In parallel with the never-ending preoccupation with Steinberg, some very innovative marketing techniques were used in Montreal in an effort to broaden the 3660 supermarket customer base. Paul Biron recalls one such initiative:

> The primary target of this initiative was Provigo, a chain made up mostly of franchisees/independent store owners. This meant that they had to be individually visited and shown something very convincing. So a project was funded to equip a "Store System Truck" with a fully functional scanning system as well as a projection facility for presentations. Pierre Lussier was one of the marketing reps working on this. I was involved a bit on the software side, but Jocelyne Charron-Boutin did most of the systems engineering work. The physical and technical aspects were

IBM Store System demo truck, June 1981 (Courtesy of Denise Richard)

---

[17] http://idhistory.com/ibm/UPCMannatSmithsonian1999.pdf. Courtesy Bill Selmeier, idhistory.com

handled by Roger Richard. I remember going to his house to see the finished trailer (and being very impressed). He was very proud of it, but his wife Denise was less enthusiastic because she could not use her car for an entire month while the huge van was parked in the driveway! The trailer even had a generator to allow it to function when parked in the parking lot of a Provigo supermarket. Many locations were visited, including at a shopping centre in Blainville, a northern suburb of Montreal. I also remember that Larry Diamond had the trailer parked on Atwater Avenue, next to the Steinberg head office, where he hosted a visit by Jack Levine, then president of Steinberg. I was part of the demonstration to Mr. Levine. In that demonstration Mr. Levine leaned on the flexible projection screen at one end of the trailer and Larry caught him just in time, otherwise his elbow would probably have perforated the screen.

Pierre Lussier making a presentation in the Store Systems demo truck, 1981 (Courtesy of Pierre Lussier)

Success at last

After suffering growing pains for well over a decade, the IBM Store Systems eventually enjoyed outstanding success as it became the world leader. And it all began at a Steinberg supermarket some 15 years earlier. By that time, the Steinberg chain was no more, but the legacy of its bold vision lived on in the retail industry with the universal adoption of the barcode.

An important element of IBM's ultimate success was the involvement of business partner MGV, under the leadership of its president, Bob Simon, a former IBMer. Bob explains his role:

> Our involvement with IBM began after the 1986 NRF IBM 4680 announcement. In 1988 MGV became one of the first IBM Canada POS (Point of Sale) business partners. I recall that when the University of

At their 4680 Open House, the Montreal SLAM Marketing Unit brought in a professional engraver to personally engrave the name of each customer on 4680 digital desk clocks which were presented at the end of the session.

Montreal Demonstrates "La Touche Personnelle"

Article and photo by Winston Fraser

Customers attending a gala 4680 Open House in Montreal, in February, experienced the real meaning of "the personal touch".

For starters, they were sent individual personal invitations to attend this exciting event at the beautiful downtown Four Seasons Hotel. Upon arrival, they were greeted with orange juice, coffee, muffins, and croissants.

IBM Canada's Eastern Region Vice President, George Khoury, was there to formally welcome the customers. In the presentations which followed, the assembled executives were shown the many personal touches which IBM has added to this new generation of Store Systems. Following the formal sessions, the customers were given an opportunity to touch, feel and operate the 4680 components.

A catered dinner allowed the customers to share impressions with their colleagues and pose questions of the IBMers. Finally, upon leaving the hotel, each attendee was presented with a handsome 4680 digital desk clock personally engraved with his/her name.

In Quebec, this is what we mean when we say that the 4680 system offers "la touche personnelle"!

This very successful event was the result of a brainstorming meeting organized no time in getting the wheels turning.

Plans were developed for 2 major events. It was decided to hold an internal Open House for IBMers within 10 days and a customer Open House within 3 weeks. Obviously, these targets were very aggressive. Especially when you consider the fact that we had no software, only part of the required hardware, and no French-language promotional material. But for folks who are used to performing store systems miracles, nothing is impossible.

This group of marketing dynamos sprang into action. Marketing reps Jocelyne Carreau and Jean Belanger developed writer's cramp keying all those invitation letters into PROFS. Michel Parent travelled all the way to Toronto to steal hardware, software, and documentation. Pierre Marchand practiced the put-together demo until he could do it blindfolded. And Debbie Rourke spent hours talking to the mirror, perfecting her French pronunciation.

The results speak for themselves. More than 50 customers attended the Open House and their reaction was positive and enthusiastic. In addition, close to 100 IBMers came to the internal Open House.

Marketing Manager Nabil Tabet expects this early momentum to lead to outstanding results in 1986. With a team like his, who can question his expectations?

4680 Open House, Montreal-Raleigh Review, June 1986 (Courtesy of International Business Machines Corporation, © 1986 International Business Machines Corporation)

Toronto Bookstore (our first implementation) opened, there with 22 Severity-1 issues. As you know, the early 4680 software was really very unstable. IBM and MGV together won accounts across Canada and around the world: The Bay, Woolworths, SDM, Longo's, Beaver Lumber, Price Club and Costco, to mention a few.

By 1990 IBM had become the world's leading provider of POS Systems. MGV's Remote Operator product offering was an important and exclusive component of IBM POS installations. Later MGV would become responsible for all development and maintenance of IBM's flagship sales applications: General Sales Application (GSA), Supermarket and Chain Sales. An MGV office was established in Raleigh with 80 personnel. Subsequently IBM and MGV signed an SDA (Software Development Agreement) that allowed MGV to develop the ACE POS product that has been very successful for both IBM and, later, Toshiba.

The announcement of the 4680 store system in 1986[18] generated a lot of excitement and spurred some very creative marketing initiatives. One such program, organized by the Montreal Store Level Account Marketing (SLAM) unit, was featured in the June 1986 issue of The Review published by IBM Raleigh Store Systems.[19] Called the IBM 4680 Open House, it included presentations, demonstrations and a catered meal. To top it off, each attendee received a 4680 digital clock personally inscribed onsite with their name.

The increasing acceptance of the 4680 system meant that some of the previous generation point-of-sale systems were becoming obsolete. MGV's Selby Shanley recounts a humorous story about obsolescence:

> In the early days of the 4680 we were replacing an older-generation IBM POS system with the new 4680 system at a Co-op in western Canada. The older IBM gear was now essentially worthless, and the general manager of the Co-op had been unable to find a buyer for it. It had these massive cables – reminded me of old mainframe cables. Recycling had not caught on yet. One Saturday night we began to "uninstall" the old system. I remember that they used huge bolt cutters to simply cut the cables as needed. All the old gear was rounded up and placed outside in a heap.

> The general manager was extremely worried that Co-op members would give him hell for not getting something for the old gear, so he didn't want to leave it sitting out back for them to see. When we left, after installing the new 4680 system, the old equipment was still there in a pile. As the story goes (although we didn't see this happen ourselves) that night they loaded it all onto a truck, drove to a friend's farm and buried it there!

Hats off!

Before closing this chapter I want to recognize an extremely talented trio of POS systems engineers whose outstanding contributions were key to the success of IBM Store Systems, not only in Canada but world-wide. As a direct beneficiary of their technical expertise and constant support, I was very privileged to have worked with each of them.

[18, 19] Courtesy of International Business Machines Corporation, © International Business Machines Corporation

Michel Parent

Michel Parent was one of the most brilliant store systems programmers to have ever worked for IBM. His quiet, calm personality and his methodical manner masked an enormous technical talent. He approached every challenge – whether small or large – with the same professionalism and dedication. Regardless of the nature of their requests, he always treated customers with the utmost respect. He was a master at developing creative solutions to difficult problems. And he could always be counted on to continue working on a problem until it was solved. It is no wonder that Michel was presented with the Bob James Memorial Award because he emulated so many of the legendary Bob's qualities. Félicitations, Michel!

Michel Parent (Courtesy of Michel Parent)

Paul Biron

Paul Biron's contribution to the success of IBM Store Systems cannot be overstated. From the time he joined the Steinberg scanning project as an SE trainee until he completed his IBM career as an SE manager, he consistently demonstrated an exceptional technical ability. Not only was he a very prolific software developer, but he also had excellent marketing skills. Paul's mind was in constant motion – always thinking

Paul Biron (Courtesy of Paul Biron)

about how to solve some problem or how to improve some process. Even as he moved into management roles, he couldn't resist the urge to code another utility program. And, like Michel, he was someone who stayed on the job right to the end. Even on the morning of his wedding day, Paul was seen in a Miracle Mart store solving a technical problem!

Bob James

Last but certainly not least, I pay tribute to the late Bob James, a remarkable technical talent and an outstanding individual. Although Bob was based in Toronto and I in Montreal, we often collaborated on projects and attended meetings, conferences and trade shows together. I knew him as an intelligent, hard-working and friendly SE whose creativity and dedication seemed to know no bounds. He understood his customers' needs and was always willing to go the extra mile for them.

From his CV, kindly sent to me by his son Colin, I learned that Bob was a World

War II veteran, having served in Europe with the Canadian Artillery from 1943 to 1945. Upon his return from the war, he attended the University of Toronto. Prior to joining IBM in 1964 he worked for an American advertising firm as a travelling sales representative in the western United States.

Following his passing in 1988, IBM instituted the Bob James Memorial Award, to be given annually to the Store Systems IBMer who best exemplified Bob's qualities. I had the honour of designing the award plaque on which the winners' names would be inscribed. The bilingual plaque reads as follows:

Bob James Memorial Plaque (Courtesy of Louise James, retouching by Greg Beck)

> This plaque has been created to honour the memory of Bob James, a truly unique IBMer, who devoted himself to the development and support of the Store Systems marketplace. Bob's human qualities, combined with his professional competence, earned him the respect and love of both IBMers and customers. This plaque is awarded annually to an IBMer working in Store Systems who most exemplifies those characteristics.

> Cette plaque a été créée à la mémoire d'un IBMiste remarquable, Bob James, qui s'est consacré au développement et au soutien du marché des systèmes de magasin. Les qualités humaines de Bob, ainsi que ses compétences professionnelles et son profond dévouement, lui ont valu le respect et l'estime à la fois des IBMistes et des clients. Cette plaque est décernée annuellement à un IBMiste qui réunit toutes ces qualités dans le secteur des systèmes de magasin.

Obviously, Bob's Toronto colleagues knew him much better than I did. Kathy Stivin shares some of her memories of this remarkable man and unique IBMer:

> Bob was a self-taught techie. One time we asked him how he knows things, and his answer was: "It's easy. I just take things apart, then I have fun putting them back together." He knew about small motors and large engines. He usually fixed his own car. He took small radios apart and put them together. One day he told me that his wife had been unhappy with

him for a few days. Upon further probing, he offered up the details of the story. Their washing machine failed. Bob thought that he could fix it, but he needed more space than your average basement offers, and he needed daylight and a bit of time. So he put the washing machine in his driveway, and bit by bit, took it apart, carefully laying out the parts in a logical order, in the order that he removed them. Once the washing machine was reduced to its components it took a bit of thinking and a bit of tinkering before he found the faulty part. Now he had to reassemble it, which also took a while. All this time he had his car in the garage, explaining his wife's unhappiness.

As newly-hired SEs coming off BST (Basic Systems Training) we were given a tour of the branch office to which I was assigned. Then they ushered us into a locked room full of equipment, POS cash registers all lined up, a controller computer, a meat and cheese slicer with an IBM manufacturing logo on it, and some memorabilia. In the middle of this room was a large table where a large man sat, with a ruddy complexion, and the biggest smile welcoming us. He was a big bear, a big lovable teddy bear. In front of him were stacks and stacks of computer printouts, folded in sheets, several inches high. It turned out that these were software "dumps" of failing 3651 controllers, printed in hexadecimal (hex) language that was all A's, B's and C's and numbers from 0 to 9 in what seemed random order. Bob taught me how to read hex. It's not for the faint of heart. I had a business degree and did not enjoy reading hex. Soon after my introduction to hex code I switched to sales because it meant not having to read hex any longer!

Bob James became our coach, mentor, teacher, friend, technical support and grandmaster of scotch drinking. Every day we went into this room where Bob would give us orientation while teaching basic problem-solving skills. First he introduced us to the silly design concept of the very first IBM in-store cash register system. Why silly? It was designed to operate in a continuous loop, without interruptions. If a cashier or a janitor unplugged one cash terminal, all the others downstream from it failed, since the continuous loop of the signal was interrupted. Or if an electrical wire was faltering due to bad connection, or a loose plug, it could break the signal. It was a nightmare to locate exactly which location broke the loop, yet it had to be found. The entire store was disabled from completing any sales until the problem was found. The skills required to do this were a mix of electrical signal knowledge, a bit of sleuthing under mice-ridden cash counters, and skilled questioning of the store personnel. Sometimes a cashier who shoved her purse a bit too energetically under her counter could knock out the plug and break the store system loop. In subsequent POS systems the continuous loop concept was abandoned and replaced with the daisy flower pattern, much to our relief. Now only one flower petal had to be isolated and the store was back in business of selling merchandise.

To help isolate the problem Bob James invented a little device for us all to carry with us to the store. It was a pocket-size electrical probe that you attached to either side of the store loop, one on the incoming side, one on the outgoing side. With a little ear piece you sat and listened to the 3651 computer chirp away. It had a musical pattern. Bob would sing the right sequence of chirps for us, had us listen to it, then he would break the loop, and had us listen to the silence, or the change in chirp. If you heard the chirp on the incoming side, but heard nothing going out, voila, you found the location of the break. This meant a lot of crawling around and a lot of cashiers giggling behind our backs. Imagine, young men and women, dressed in impeccable office clothes, blue suits, skirts, latest shirts, nice shoes, suddenly under your in-store cabinetry, plugging and unplugging and carrying an electrical listening device.

Bob was especially good at teaching the thinking process for problem determination. For example, in a problem situation you know there are many possible causes. Isolate the causes, one by one, then stop and think. Each time change only one thing. Eventually you will find the failing part. I used this skill all my life, on things that I know nothing about, and it works wonderfully.

We had a large contract to install new IBM POS systems for the Canadian Sears stores. There were dedicated systems engineers working with Sears employees, side by side, at its head office, and travelling to every store. I was sent to Calgary and Lethbridge, while Peter Large was sent to Calgary and Red Deer. Since we were rookies they sent Bob James with us. He carried a black briefcase with him everywhere. We assumed that it contained technical trade secrets, because we never saw it open at the client site. After many a full day in a Sears store we went out for dinner, most often the traditional Calgary steak or roast beef dinner, which Bob was especially fond of and nicknamed "roast beast." Back at the hotel he invited us to his room for a drink. Now the secret of the black briefcase was revealed! It was a travelling bar! It was fully stocked with two mickeys of old scotch, four shot glasses, cups for ice and other drink paraphernalia. I had a feeling that this was a remnant of Bob's former life on the road as a travelling salesman. The items inside the case were very well worn.

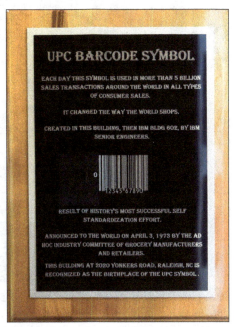

UPC Day 2017 plaque, IBM Raleigh Building 602 (Courtesy Bill Selmeier, IDhistory.com)

The Steinberg scanning project and the various subsequent point-of-sale projects were an awesome experience that those of us who were involved will never forget. Colleague Paul Biron sums it up best:

> My time as part of the POS team at IBM with such wonderful mentors was absolutely unique. So many fond memories! We had the opportunity to work in an environment that encouraged (or sometimes tolerated) our initiatives. The early days of POS were certainly not overly profitable for IBM, but they laid the foundation for the future, when IBM Store Systems effectively became the industry norm.

In 2017 a special plaque was installed at the IBM building in Raleigh, N.C., where the UPC barcode originated – a building that my colleagues and I visited so often. The plaque reads in part:

> Each day this symbol is used in more than 5 billion sales transactions around the world in all types of consumer sales. It changed the way the world shops.

And to think that we helped to make this all happen!

IBM implementation team for Steinberg and Miracle Mart, 1978. Front: Franklin Amzallag, Bob Engelberg. Back: Benoit Nadeau-Dostie, Ralph Foley, Marg Eastwood, Winston Fraser, Sally Harmer, Paul Biron. (Author's collection)

Chapter 5   Data Overflow

Data mining (Courtesy of indiadataentryhelp.com)

As a Datacentre programmer, I was very familiar with problems related to data overflow. Apart from the dreaded "address exception" and "divide by zero" errors, they probably gave software developers the most grief. Data overflow errors could be caused by such things as a data field being too short, a buffer being overrun or a data file's capacity being exceeded. But before getting lost in the technobabble of another era, I hasten to assure you that in this chapter we are talking about something quite different.

The previous chapter described the advent of store systems technology from an operational standpoint. Now we will look at it from a data viewpoint.

The problem

The introduction of scanning and the proliferation of point-of-sale systems brought with them a very major problem. Retailers were in dire danger of drowning in the massive amount of data being generated by their stores on a daily basis. They were totally unprepared for this sudden deluge of data. And so was IBM. Recognizing this problem early on, I made it my personal mission to design and develop applications to exploit this suddenly available goldmine of information. Today it would be referred to as "data mining." But back in the 1970s and the early 1980s the term had not yet been invented. Colleague Dave Moxley, who would later become a data mining expert, recognized the potential of my initiatives:

> Winston understood that the scanner data collected free as a byproduct would eventually revolutionize retail by implementing new category management techniques and advanced analytics for promotional analysis, item movement forecasting and inventory management based on historical sell-through. And maybe, some day, it would support a loyalty program that captured household-level purchases, thus enabling household retention, cross-sell and upsell programs to gain share of pantry. Winston played a pivotal role in transforming retail from an intuitive art to a blend of art and advanced analytical science.

I was extremely fortunate that my IBM management strongly supported my mission from the outset of the Steinberg scanning project and for years afterwards. To John Thompson, Ed Fudge, Larry Diamond, Stan Albert, Paul Biron, David Dolman and Frank Hall (among others), I owe an enormous debt of gratitude for allowing me to "do my own thing" while my colleagues were toiling in the trenches. Of course, not all my ideas or initiatives were feasible, practical or timely. As my manager, Larry Diamond, once told me, "Fraser, some of your ideas are crazy. . . but keep them coming!"

Through the years, others shared in this mission, and our team in Montreal built a reputation as a world leader in the intelligent processing of POS data. Following the release of one of the applications that we developed, we received the following letter of appreciation from Paul Balle, In-store Applications Manager, IBM Corporation, Research Triangle Park, North Carolina:

> Congratulations on completing a field developed program. In recognition of this accomplishment a plaque is enclosed documenting your contribution to store systems in developing the IBM 3650 Programmable Store System POS application Resource Management program. It is only with the kind of commitment and dedication demonstrated by you that store systems can create the inventory of useful programs that we all need to grow in the business.

Customer applications

Among the applications we developed in Montreal that IBM made available to the retail industry worldwide were:
- ELPS – Exception Log Processing System
- CAS – Cashier Assignment System
- IFAR – Inbound File Analysis and Retrieval

- SPARC – Store Produced Accounting Report Customizer
- SPOT – Simultaneous Printing of Observed Transactions

The first application to make use of 3660 scanning system data was the Exception Log Processing System (ELPS). The exception log was a sequential file on the store controller to which "exception" type events were recorded during the store's

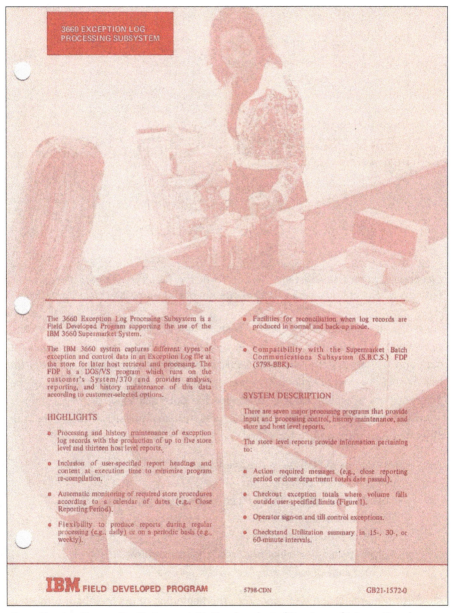

Exception Log Processing System application brochure (Courtesy of International Business Machines Corporation, © 1974 International Business Machines Corporation)

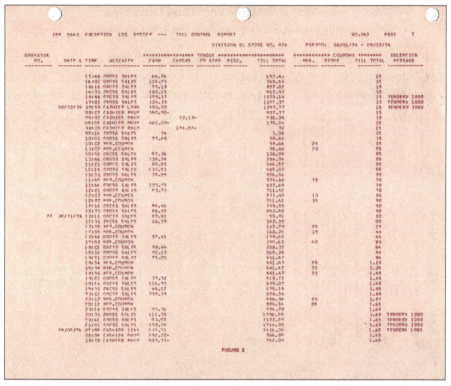

Exception Log Processing System – Till Control Report (Courtesy of International Business Machines Corporation, © 1974 International Business Machines Corporation)

operation. It included such data as cashier sign-on/sign-off, manufacturer and store coupon acceptance, item cancellations and refunds, transaction payment data and various system-related data. Its intended use was mainly as a tool for tracing security-related events. However, upon studying the characteristics of the different data available, I began to realize the potential value of this seemingly mundane mixture. Thus was born the idea for an application to format the disjointed data into useful information.

Among the features of ELPS were the following:

- Host and store level reporting
- Checkout exceptions that exceeded threshold values
- Checkstand utilization summary
- Operator productivity report
- Automatic monitoring of required store procedures
- Maintenance of log history

Although the application was used from the beginning of the Steinberg project, it was only announced as an official IBM licensed product several months later, in November 1974.

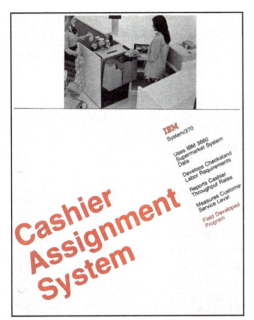

Cashier Assignment System application brochure (Courtesy of International Business Machines Corporation, © 1976 International Business Machines Corporation)

The next customer application to be developed was the Cashier Assignment System (CAS). It is interesting to note that all the applications that our team developed were given names – always short, and usually pronounceable. After all, they were our "babies."

Completed in 1976, CAS was instrumental in helping stores realize one of the most immediate and significant hard benefits of electronic point of sale systems – improved front-end productivity. CAS presented the data captured by the 3660 in a meaningful way to help store personnel project checkstand requirements and to schedule cashiers to handle the expected workload. Its functions included:

- Provide front-end staffing requirements
- Report the throughput rates of individual cashiers
- Report customer service levels (queue lengths)
- Allow store management to evaluate bagger assistance scenarios
- Allow comparison of active hours versus paid hours

Because of its practical application to the everyday challenges of operating a supermarket, CAS was widely accepted, not only in Canada but across the U.S.A. and internationally as well. Among the major American supermarket chains that installed CAS were Kroger, Wegman's, Roundy's, Price Chopper and H.E. Butt.

A July 1978 article in Computerworld by Michael D. McGee, Manager of Retail Operations for Roundy's, documented some of the benefits experienced by Pick 'n Save Warehouses (a division of the Roundy's chain):[20]
- Sales per employee-hour increase of 23%
- Checker productivity increase of 17%
- Waiting lines reduction
- Schedule creation time reduced by 67%

---

[20] Computerworld, July 31, 1978, p. 39

The worldwide interest in CAS meant frequent travel to make customer calls, hold classes and give seminars. In one 1977 Cashier Assignment System roadshow I visited six European countries. Such travel, though exhausting, was satisfying, knowing the broad interest shown in our locally developed application.

Industry Marketing Manager Frank Hall puts the CAS development into perspective as follows:

> In the early 1970s UPCs started to appear on some products we bought in our grocery stores. Today it is hard to find a product that doesn't have a UPC. Supermarkets commenced installing flatbed scanning systems. They liked them, they didn't have to individually price-mark items, and they could check out customers faster, saving money.
>
> Meanwhile, a small southern discount retailer thought: If I know what I am selling, know how much and when to order more, turn my inventory over faster than the time I have to pay for it so my inventory doesn't cost me anything, and make customers happy with low prices, I will grow big and get rich. The retailer's name: Walmart. The concept: supply chain management.
>
> Creative people found other profitable uses of scanning equipment, not thought of by the inventors of UPC and scanning equipment. Like figuring out the optimal number of lanes to open by day and by hour to provide fast, friendly check out. Winston created such a system, Cashier

CHECKOUT REQUIREMENTS

STORE 0038 ABC STORE --- MAIN STREET

| Time | Average Order Size | Group | Checkout Requirements | | | | | |
| | | | 0% Baggers | | 50% Baggers | | 100% Baggers | |
			Cashiers	Baggers	Cashiers	Baggers	Cashiers	Baggers
9:15	14	2	0.1	0	0.1	0	0.0	0
9:30	21	2	1.1	0	1.0	1	1.0	1
9:45	25	3	2.1	0	1.9	1	1.7	2
10:00	39	4	4.1	0	3.7	2	3.4	3
10:00	24	2	1.9	0	1.7	1	1.5	2
10:15	36	3	6.0	0	5.4	3	4.9	5
10:30	33	3	4.0	0	4.4	2	4.0	4
10:45	29	3	5.4	0	4.9	2	4.4	4
11:00	28	3	6.5	0	5.8	3	5.3	5
11:00	31	3	5.7	0	5.1	3	4.7	5

Figure 2. Checkout Requirements. This figure is an extraction of the significant data contained in the actual Checkout Requirements report.

Cashier Assignment System: Checkout Requirements report (Courtesy of International Business Machines Corporation, © 1976 International Business Machines Corporation)

Assignment System, saving labour costs and providing better customer service.

As illustrated above, our first two customer applications were specifically targeted to the supermarket sector. But from then on we changed our focus to the retail sector in general. For us this was a natural progression because we were becoming very involved with Miracle Mart, Steinberg's retail store division. The first retail customer application we developed was Store Produced Accounting Report Customizer (SPARC). The unique design of this application was in direct response to the customer constantly changing their report requirements.

SPARC provided the 3650 user with a flexible facility for implementing in-store accounting applications on the 3651 controller. A major challenge in the development of application software for the 3650 retail store system was to design a package that could cover a wide range of user requirements without becoming heavily burdened with overhead. This system was designed with those two often incompatible objectives – flexibility and efficiency – in mind.

A high degree of flexibility was achieved by allowing user specification of all major elements of the system: accounting field definitions, transaction log processing specifications and report definition. Program size and execution overhead were

STORE ACTIVITY PROFILE

STORE 0038 ABC STORE --- MAIN STREET

Time	Checkouts Active	With Baggers	Average Queue Length	Maximum Queue Length	Number of Customers	Average Order Size
15:45	5	0	1	2	18	33
16:00	5	0	1	3	13	46
16:00	5	0	2	6 *	68	35
16:15	6	0	2	4 *	22	35
16:30	8	1	3	6 *	34	27
16:45	6	1	3	6 *	22	36
17:00	6	1	3	9 *	22	31
17:00	7	1	3	9 *	100	31
17:15	7	3	1	3	35	29
17:30	8	2	1	2	31	40
17:45	7	1	2	4 *	31	32
18:00	8	1	1	3	30	33
18:00	8	2	1	4 *	127	33

Figure 1. **Store Activity Profile.** This figure is an extraction of the significant data contained in the actual Store Activity Profile report.

Cashier Assignment System: Store Activity Profile report (Courtesy of International Business Machines Corporation, © 1976 International Business Machines Corporation)

minimized due to the fact that the system contained a System /370 program that processed the user specifications to generate customized 3650 controller code for the major processing program. In addition, all programs were written as structured programs using the SPPS program structured macros. The system provided a framework for creating, updating, and reporting 70 individual units of data, such as accounting fields for each operator or each terminal, as well as an equal amount of data for the store office.

SPARC application brochure (Courtesy of International Business Machines Corporation, © 1977 International Business Machines Corporation)

The meaning of each of the 70 accounting fields was specified by the user. Further, the user defined their own reports to print out the contents of individual accounting fields or derived values. Transaction log processing was performed as a background job that could run concurrently with sales mode, or run after store hours in a special IML (initial machine load). While processing the transaction log the user could specify conditions under which a record could be selected and written together with logically related data to the selected exceptions file for further processing.

The major functions of SPARC were:
- Balancing of sales figures to till contents
- Maintenance of separate back office and front-end accounting
- Tracking of operator productivity
- Provision of sales audit figures by media type
- Selection of transaction log records for further processing

SPARC's revolutionary design philosophy attracted international attention. Following a customer call at J.M. Fields in Philadelphia, the account SE (systems engineering representative), Diana Gail DiMeo, specifically mentioned it in her thank you letter:

> My compliments to you on the design philosophy that you chose for SPARC. Its flexibility and ability to react quickly to changes via the

parameters coding technique makes it very suitable for the J.M. Fields environment.

The application also earned recognition from IBM Canada management in a January 16, 1978 letter:

> Congratulations on your outstanding technical support of Miracle Mart throughout 1977. The hard work and creativity that you displayed in developing the sophisticated accounting package program on the 3650 controller has been responsible for the overwhelming success at this account. The extensive inquiries from all over the world to make this package available as a licensed product are an excellent indication of your high level of performance. It is my pleasure to recognize your fine efforts with a marketing excellence award, and to invite you to the 1977 DPD convention which will be held in Montego Bay, Jamaica, April 2 to 5, 1978.
> - (Signed) Andy Sokol, Manager Field Support and Systems Engineering, IBM Canada

As a footnote, my management, my colleagues and I shared a development bonus of $2500 for SPARC. Some years later we were flattered that IBM Store Systems in Raleigh borrowed some of SPARC's design characteristics for their IBM 3650 Application Report Customizer (ARC).

Another customer application that I designed and developed in parallel with SPARC was the IBM 3650 Simultaneous Printing of Observed Transactions (SPOT). This flexible facility for terminal monitoring allowed management to follow the activity at another terminal – for security reasons, to analyze productivity, to evaluate training, or for problem analysis. Among the features of this application that executed on the 3651 store controller were the following:

- Real time monitoring of any terminal
- Custom formatted output on the 3653 receipt printer
- Selective scanning of the transaction log

SPOT proved to be a widely accepted program, with installations at several major retailers, including Macy's, Richway, Venture, Federated, Altman's and Target.

We also developed the Document Online Control (DOC) system as an extension to SPARC to facilitate the store-level control of tender documents. Among the benefits of this application were:

- Better control of tender documents
- Easier correction of errors
- Elimination of redundant data entry
- Faster entry of cash pickups
- Reduction of clerical effort
- Identification of potential fraud

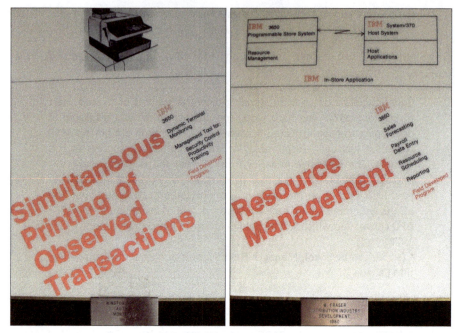

Application recognition plaques: SPOT, 1978; Resource Management, 1980 (Photos by author)

Implementation enhancements

While I was developing customer use-of-data applications, my colleague Paul Biron was busy designing and programming various management-of-data programs and procedures. Management of the masses of data collected by the IBM 3650 and 3660 store systems was complex and prone to error. Paul's first such program, which was announced as an International Program Offering in 1984, was Inbound File Analysis and Retrieval (IFAR).

IFAR was designed to work with the IBM Advanced Data Communication for Stores (ADCS) to enable the host user of IBM Store Systems to efficiently and reliably retrieve and route the data gathered by in-store controllers. It simplified the standard ADCS process by copying, under user control, selected data from the inbound (INBD) dataset to other VSAM datasets and to report on the operation. This copy process allowed the output VSAM file to contain only the data that was required by a host application, in the proper format and with the proper key.

IFAR's functional features included:
- Copy INBD data to VSAM dataset (key sequenced or entry sequenced)
- Custom formatting of data copied to OTBD
- Copy "as is" or unblock into logical records

- Optionally process data via user exit before copying
- Generate report of INBD or OTBD contents without copying
- Use of keyword-driven command input
- Support of all INBD data types

IFAR provided a number of important benefits:

- Faster implementation of host applications
- Improved host control of data
- Quicker recovery from store malfunctions
- Easier migration to new IBM store systems
- Improved availability of system information

Inbound File Analysis and Retrieval

Simplified Interface
for
Host Processing of IBM POS Data

IFAR application brochure (Courtesy of International Business Machines Corporation, © 1984 International Business Machines Corporation)

Another complexity reduction tool that Paul conceived and developed was the Programmable Store System Installation Productivity Option (PSS IPO). He describes its background, function and benefits:

When IBM announced the 3650 Programmable Store System in 1978, it answered a long-time request for greater flexibility. But it also introduced a level of change and complexity that most Systems Engineering teams were unprepared to tackle. Especially complex were the customization capabilities of the Supermarket Environment Program Product called "Extended Functions."

After considerable discussion with Industry Marketing in Toronto, a project was approved to develop the PSS Installation Aid. It was primarily intended to help the Canadian SE teams to more productively install PSS for their supermarket clients. Ed Streich from Toronto and Pierre Marchand from Montreal also participated in this project. Raleigh did not initially endorse this initiative.

The IPO concept had been invented in Canada several years earlier in order to help clients easily, quickly and successfully install DOS/VSE on small mainframes. The same concepts were applied to the PSS Installation Aid, where a single magnetic tape contained all the necessary software, microcode and initial data files pre-installed. The Aid also contained a facility to easily select and apply Extended Functions and "compile" the Supermarket Environment on VM/CMS. Finally, as PSS did not natively produce accounting reports, a facility was provided to create reports emulating the previous 3660 Supermarket environment for ease of migration. This facility was inspired by SPARC (Store-Produced Accounting Report Customizer), an IBM application also developed in Montreal by Winston Fraser.

With the Installation Aid, an SE team could achieve an operational PSS setup (i.e., be able to scan a first item) within one or two days, whereas it could easily take two to three months without the Aid. The PSS Installation Aid was announced in Canada on February 22, 1980. Some months later, it was announced in the U.S.A.

Colleague Giorgio Toso recounts a story that clearly illustrates the benefits of using the PSS IPO:

> I was sent to Vancouver to install a pilot store for Safeway who had placed an order for five stores. Within a week I had the store up and running, then I left on my vacation. When I returned home after my vacation I learned that Safeway had cancelled the order for five stores and replaced it with an order for 25! However, very soon thereafter I received a call from the IBM U.S. marketing team for Safeway. They were very upset because we made them look bad – they had a team of nine people working for a month and still hadn't got the system working!

Paul also developed other tools that enhanced the efficiency of store systems SEs. One of them was FLAME (File Listing and Application Maintenance Editor). This SPPS II application allowed the SE to use a POS terminal to view/modify various system files. Its function was similar to what was possible with the UPVF facility available on a 3270 display (that not every installation had).

Disappearing data debugging

In one case that we experienced during a Steinberg performance test, data didn't just overflow its buffers – it literally disappeared into thin air! Colleagues Michel Parent and Giorgio Toso tell the story of the famous GAG (Give Away Groceries) problem:

Bug in hexadecimal memory dump (Photo by author)

> When Steinberg was testing the 3650 PSS system they had a very reproducible scenario whereby multiple cashiers would scan an identical group of products as quickly as possible, in order to determine if the POS system could handle many lanes scanning at least 30 items per minute. If

the target was not reached, we had to make changes to improve the performance (sometimes over many weeks) then repeat the test. The tests also served as benchmarks to see if the accounting was keeping pace with the volume of transactions and stayed in balance. Since the number of items per shopping cart was fixed (e.g., 50 items costing a total of $75), they knew that the total item count and the total amount should always be exact multiples of 50 and $75 respectively.

In one of the tests a rogue product (i.e., not on file) was introduced, either intentionally (to see how the system would react) or inadvertently. When a cashier would scan the erroneous item, the scanner would beep (because the item had a readable UPC) but the POS terminal would then issue an error message (not on file) and the cashier would press CLEAR before scanning the next product. This meant that the known items counted as 49 (out of the 50 since the erroneous item did not sell). When validating the accounting, Steinberg noticed that the number of items accounted for was not an exact multiple of 49 (it was lower) and insisted that the system had lost track of some sales. By observing the video of the cashier on the problem lane, we realized that she was quick enough to scan two items (two valid scan beeps) before the first one issued the "not on file" error. When the cashier pressed the CLEAR key to acknowledge and clear the message, the system also cleared the second item.

The issue was reported to Raleigh, who said it was unreproducible. Being unsatisfied with that answer, we dug deep into the code ourselves and saw that both scanned items were correctly placed into a FIFO OS buffer to be eventually processed in sequence. While the first item was being processed, the second was just waiting in the buffer. The application eventually found that the first item was not on file, and issued the error message, waiting for the CLEAR key to be pressed by the cashier to acknowledge the error. When opening the keyboard driver to accept the CLEAR key, the whole buffer was being cleared, effectively removing the second item for which we had received the appropriate BEEP. The cashiers were being trained not to check the receipt, but to simply ensure they got beeps for each item they scanned. They did not realize they needed to rescan the second item.

Armed with that information, we went to Raleigh and demonstrated the problem to a small group of engineers in the lab, who then invited more of their colleagues to observe our demo. Their eyes popped out of their sockets and they scratched their heads in disbelief! They eventually fixed the problem by creating a second "priority" buffer to be used in cases like this. Our persistence had finally paid off!

As it turned out, the data overflow problem became an opportunity for our team to provide industry-wide leadership in the development of applications and tools for the intelligent use and management of point-of-sale data.

Chapter 6   New Pastures

Cattle in pasture, Pine Hill Farm, Cookshire, Que. (Photo by author)

After eight years of service in the trenches fighting in the POS wars, it was time for a change. Or to use a farming idiom, it was time to move to new pastures. The grass there was not necessarily greener but it was certainly different.

A/FE Productivity Centre

In October 1980 I moved to the IBM A/FE (Americas/Far East) Productivity Centre where I worked under Norm Ullock. One of the Centre's missions was to develop applications for the newly announced IBM 4300 midrange series of computers. My first assignment was to design a BICARSA (Billing, Inventory Control, Accounts Receivable, Sales Analysis) application for the English- and Spanish-speaking countries of A/FE. Although I was very experienced in application development, the BICARSA domain was very new to me. But I really looked forward to this new challenge. After several months of concentrated nose-to-the-grindstone work, I completed the specifications document – a veritable brick of some 600 pages. I named the application "ABC System" (A Business Control System). It included detailed file formats, screen layouts, processing details and report layouts for each interactive and batch application component. The next steps would be to validate

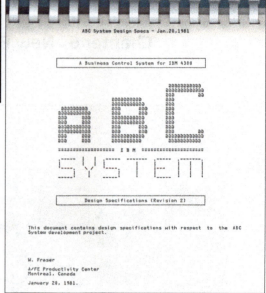

ABC 4300 BICARSA system specifications: Above: Vol. 1 of 2; Right: cover page (Both images courtesy of International Business Machines Corporation, © 1981 International Business Machines Corporation)

the specifications document with the member countries, integrate any required modifications and proceed to the development phase. But alas, fate intervened. Before I had the opportunity to present my specs document, the A/FE Productivity Centre was shut down. So my newest application "baby" was stillborn. It was time to swallow my pride and move on.

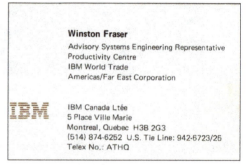

Winston Fraser

Advisory Systems Engineering Representative
Productivity Centre
IBM World Trade
Americas/Far East Corporation

IBM Canada Ltée
5 Place Ville Marie
Montreal, Quebec H3B 2G3
(514) 874-6252 U.S. Tie Line: 942-6723/26
Telex No.: ATHQ

My IBM A/FE business card

Back to retail

The next pasture to which I moved was a very familiar one – the retail industry! It was like coming back home, so I was not disappointed. In fact, I was very happy to rejoin some of my former colleagues in their ongoing store systems battles. As a member of the Retail Industry Support Centre, which had a national mission, I became involved with retail clients across the country. Not only did it broaden my perspective of the marketplace but it gave me the opportunity to work with a whole new team of retail specialists. One of them was Bruce Singleton, who remembers our shared mission:

> We worked together in 1981 and 1982. Under Carl Corcoran there was a special undertaking to capture more of the supermarket business to complement the increasing business on the retail side (e.g., Simpson's

and LCBO). I was the project manager of a group consisting of SEs from across Canada, including Gladys Daoud and yourself (Montreal), Bob Betts (Halifax), Ed Streich (Toronto) and Peter Large (Vancouver), as well as a number of sales reps. Among the target supermarket customers were Steinberg, Loblaws, Sobeys and Safeway. Our task was to demonstrate that they could program our programmable store system to do anything and everything they ever wanted to do! That, of course, was easier said than done due to the complexities of the system. Consequently, our efforts did not bear a lot of immediate fruit but did lay the groundwork for future successes.

Another retail expert under whose direction I worked during this phase of my career was Dave Moxley. He describes his group's mission and approach and my contribution:

I first met Winston when I was leading a team of IBM retail industry consulting experts. Winston was based in Montreal to address the significant retail presence in Quebec. Our national role was to study best practices in Canada and around the world, and to demonstrate in-store as well as head office opportunities for our clients to improve competitiveness, both for the chain and down to the local markets. We also collected Canadian market requirements and prioritized those into the various IBM labs for future products and software releases.

A key method we used was product briefings (in both official languages) under the banner of Integrated Retail Marketing Automation (IRMA). Briefly, the concept was to create a "future-proof" product scan to assure our IBM clients that by investing in IBM technology they would remain on the cutting edge of innovation in the retail industry – or a fast follower; the strategic choice was theirs. We even saw the potential for Artificial Intelligence (AI) algorithms to automate these approaches.

So tightly integrated and comprehensive was this strategy that we often joked that when a consumer purchased a steak in Provigo's Quebec store, a cow flinched in Alberta. We were building a tightly integrated supply chain from farm to fork. Winston's role in creating this marketing strategy was instrumental. It leveraged his extensive in-store technology experience, a keep-it-real discipline, and lessons learned as a pioneer of new POS scanner technology back in those early Steinberg days.

During our briefings, our clients would often challenge us with the "P" word – PRIVACY. Our solution was simple and well thought out based on "informed consent." We worked with federal legislators through the Retail Council of Canada on the first privacy laws that imbedded this principle of informed consent, including the right to be forgotten (opt out), the ability to review and correct information being collected, and restrictions on reselling data for other than the purpose for which it was collected. We believe that this is still the best legislation in the world, without the unnecessary overhead and administrative expense in the European Union and the free market approaches in the U.S.A.

One example of Winston's creativity was during a Canadian census. He approached Statistics Canada to request that specific questions be added about household level retailer consumption patterns. . . . Although we did not succeed in getting those questions added to the Census, they did form the framework for loyalty program sign-up questionnaires.

In 1984 I was part of the Store Level Account Marketing (SLAM) unit that specialized in Store Systems marketing and support.

P. Marchand, W. Fraser, *R. Faille,*
J. Carreau, A. Joubert, M. Parent,
J. Bélanger, (D. Gélinas)

IBM SLAM unit, December 1984 (Courtesy of Debbie Rourke)

Later on in my period of pasture hopping I found myself in Industry Marketing under the creative and inspired leadership of David Dolman and Frank Hall. During that time, I participated in a number of retail conferences and business shows.

Petroleum project

My nomadic wanderings in the retail world took another significant turn in September 1985 when I was asked to attend a meeting in Toronto about a totally new venture that IBM was considering. This pivotal meeting would launch my participation in a series of projects that would dominate most of the rest of my IBM career. Led by Mary Biedermann, it was known as the Petroleum POS project and was initiated in response to requests from Canada's oil companies. The objective was very simple and straightforward – to be able to directly connect gasoline pumps to IBM point-of-sale systems. But the solution was not nearly as simple. Technical challenges and regulatory requirements were among the hurdles that would have to be addressed.

The first objective was to do a proof of concept – that is, would it even be possible for a gas pump to talk to an IBM point-of-sale system? It had never been done before and the two devices had totally different communication protocols. Enter Terry Filby, a very talented developer from the IBM Canada lab in Toronto. His specialty was communications, so if anyone could make it happen, it would be him. After a period of trial and error, he was able to establish a very primitive connection between the two very different devices. He must have felt somewhat like Alexander Graham Bell in 1876 when he successfully sent the first telephone message: "Mr. Watson, come here. I want to see you." Or like Samuel Morse in 1844 upon transmitting the first telegraph message: "What hath God wrought!" Although perhaps not quite on the same scale, Terry's breakthrough achievement opened the doors to the automation of petroleum retailing and today's pay-at-the-pump technology that we all take for granted.

But Filby's successful proving of the concept was only the beginning. His jerry-rigged connection would need to be replaced with something much more robust, secure and elegant. Neither Terry nor any members of our team had experience working with gasoline pumps – other than my pumping gas at my uncle's service station! Therefore we needed to partner with someone having the necessary expertise. Enter Jerome Graham, president of Graham Electronics Inc. of Raleigh, N.C. His company manufactured a black box interface that connected the pumps

to a pump console inside the station where the attendant could follow the activity at the pumps. We felt that if Graham's black box (called the Graham Logic Module) was able to talk to the pumps, it would also be able to talk to our POS system. Furthermore, the GLM's communication protocol was more advanced

Business partner Jerome "Jerry" Graham at Provi-soir Petro pilot "war room," 1987 (Courtesy Jerry Graham)

than that of the gasoline pump. Graham agreed to partner with IBM for a pilot installation and to offer the services of his technical expert, Ted Warn. But before we could use the device with the IBM store system, we had to obtain regulatory approval from Consumer and Corporate Affairs Canada's Metrology Division.

For the IBM Petro development team, our manager Mary Biedermann recruited a

Above and right: Government approval for GLM gas pump interface (Author's collection)

SUMMARY DESCRIPTION:

The IBM 4680 store system is composed of an IBM personal computer (PC) AT store controller and the 4683 point of sale (POS) terminal interfaced to various makes of fuel dispensers through the Graham Logic Module (GLM).

team of experienced former IBM Canada Lab developers (Terry Filby and Claude Huot) and former customer engineers (Pierre Allaire, Jacques Crépeau and Roger Richard). Eilish Kelly also joined the team as marketing coordinator; she was based in Toronto but frequently came to Montreal to keep tabs on everything. Much younger than the rest of us, one morning she announced that she was engaged, and excitedly showed us old guys her ring. Immediately Pierre said, "My dog has died," to which Eilish comfortingly replied, "Oh, Pierre, I'm so sorry." But Pierre's dog hadn't died; what he said was the literal translation of the French expression "Mon chien est mort," which is the equivalent of the English expression "I've now lost all hope!"

Because of my previous experience in point-of-sale application development, I was assigned the role of project leader. It was a distinct privilege for me to work with such a talented, dedicated and compatible group of professionals. Without any doubt, this team worked together the most effectively of any team in my entire IBM career. Their different strengths complemented each other, which was the recipe for our success. Terry and Roger were hardware wizards, Claude and Pierre were exceptional developers, and Jacques and Eilish provided outstanding marketing and administrative support.

Piedmont pilot

Provi-soir IBM Petro pilot, Piedmont, Que. (Author's collection)

Because of the petroleum industry's interest in automating their retail operations, it was not difficult to find a pilot site. A Provi-soir dépanneur (convenience store) in Piedmont, Que, in the Laurentians north of Montreal was selected. The store's proximity to the Montreal-based development team was one of the factors in choosing this location. Another was the fact that this store operated 24 hours a day. For the following two years, it was the test bed and proving ground for the different phases of our development. Throughout that period there was close collaboration among Provi-soir personnel, Graham Electronics, the IBM Store Systems branch SEs and our development team. During the initial installation period we operated a "war room" in the nearby Auberge Mont Gabriel. At our weekly meetings we reviewed progress, identified problems and devised action plans. As a result, the pilot was very successful and a great

Store manager, Petro pilot at Provi-soir, Piedmont, Que., 1987 (Author's collection)

With colleague Terry Filby at Provi-soir Petro Pilot 'war room,' 1987 (Author's collection)

Examining the pumps at Petro pilot, Piedmont, Que. 1987 (Author's collection)

Jacques Crépeau (IBM) and Ted Warn (Graham Electronics) unload POS terminal (Author's collection)

closeness developed among the team. The comradery was so great that one day I arrived at the office to discover that the whole team had gone fishing!

The Piedmont pilot generated a lot of interest both on the national and international levels on the part of oil companies and IBMers alike. Finland, the United Kingdom, New Zealand and the U.S.A. all sent IBM systems engineers not only to observe the installation but also to participate in the ongoing development. Buoyed by the extent of the interest in our pilot solution and the announcement of the IBM 4680 Store System, IBM Canada decided to launch an international development project that would result in a more comprehensive petroleum retailing solution.

Piedmont Petro pilot IBM manager Mary Biedermann and store manager, 1987 (Author's collection)

"Looks like they've taken the day off!" (Sketch by James Harvey)

Petroleum Retailing Application

The Petroleum Retailing Application (PRA) was designed specifically for oil companies with retail outlets and convenience store chains with gas pumps to help them increase productivity and enhance customer service. It was made up of three major components:

- Pump Control
- Station Management
- Consumer Assistance Facility

The pump control module, which was fully integrated with the checkout application, provided functions to control electronic gasoline pumps via simple keying sequences and confirmation messages. Its features included:

- Single programmable device to control pumps, handle cash and credit sales and print receipts
- Consolidated receipt tape containing gas and other purchases
- Multiple manufacturers' electronic pumps supported through a compatible interface
- Up to 16 pumps can be controlled by a single POS terminal
- Graphic representation of the pumps on the terminal display
- Gasoline price changes can be programmed or implemented in real time
- Pump volumes can be read automatically
- Gas rationing can be automatically implemented

The Station Management module (Petroleum Retailer Integrated Information Manager – PRIIM) was an integrated information resource consisting of the station profile, an operational database and management tools. Among its menu-driven functions were:

- Shift turnover reports
- Shift reconciliation
- Fuel delivery reporting and tank management
- Remote or onsite price change control
- Customized reporting for audit control and performance analysis

The Consumer Assistance Facility was an interactive application that provided the gasoline retailer with innovative ways to attract new customers and increase customer satisfaction. Its features included:

- Information centre (news, weather, ski conditions, fishing conditions, lottery numbers, sports scores, etc.)
- Promotional vehicle (today's specials, hours of operation, etc.)
- Public relations medium (community events bulletin board, etc.)
- Classified advertising service for nearby businesses
- Customer feedback facility (online consumer surveys re: service quality, merchandise selection, etc.)

The official announcement of the IBM 4680 Petroleum Retailing Application in 1987 unleashed an avalanche of attention and activity. On the Canadian front, we prepared presentations and gave demonstrations to most of the major oil companies – Texaco, Shell, Husky, Petro Canada and Irving, to name a few. Colleague Eilish Kelly McCallum remembers the Irving demo:

> There was a demo at the Toronto-Dominion Centre for a member of the Irving family from New Brunswick. There was only one Irving but a multitude of other people, at least half of whom were IBMers. I remember that moving the pump simulator was always a worry because the wires did not always make a proper connection. That was Terry Filby's area of expertise. We set it all up in a very nice conference room. It was a bit nerve-wracking to prepare for these demos because you never knew until the last minute whether everything would work properly.

Point-of-sale SE Michel Parent has similar recollections:

> I remember moving the equipment for customer demos – especially the gas pumps. People in the elevator would be watching, their eyes practically popping out of their sockets!

A prime opportunity to expose our solution to a wider audience was the Petroleum Equipment Institute trade show in Toronto in October 1987. The elegant IBM booth was equipped with a 4680 store system running the Petroleum Retailing Application in a real-life service station environment, including gas pumps and a brand new late model car. Members of the PRA development team took turns demonstrating this avant-garde solution to potential clients.

In preparation for the show, Mary Biedermann arranged for a series of unique colour brochures that highlighted the different elements of the solution. These modern art renditions of the application components represented a refreshing departure from traditional brochures.

It was not only Canadian petroleum retailers that showed interest in our solution. Over the months and years that followed the product announcement we fielded inquiries and hosted visitors from several countries, including the United Kingdom, Finland, Austria, New Zealand and the United States. Some simply wanted to learn more about the solution, while others wanted to explore potential partnerships. These expressions of interest led to members of our team taking numerous trips abroad as well as to the IBM Store System lab in Raleigh, N.C.

Among the international contingent of IBMers that we hosted for varying periods of time were Phil Lester, Phil Schofield, Carol Buckingham, Timo Lainen and Brendan Pagett. Phil Lester in essence became a regular member of our team, as he often accompanied us on our travels. He absolutely loved coming to Montreal – perhaps mainly because of the Mmmuffins shop in Place Ville Marie!

IBM Petroleum Retailing Application

Overview

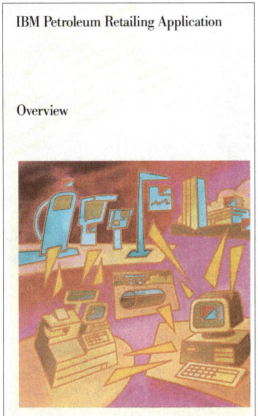

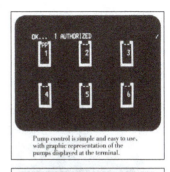

Pump control is simple and easy to use, with graphic representation of the pumps displayed at the terminal.

The Consumer Assistance Facility provides a unique opportunity to deliver added value to your customers.

You can, for example, allow nearby merchants to advertise their goods and services in your store, for a fee or as a special service to your customers.

A customer feedback facility can help you to further enhance customer satisfaction.

IBM Petroleum Retailing Application

Consumer Assistance Facility

Pump Control

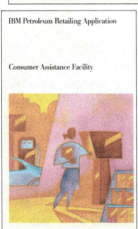

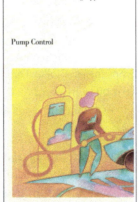

IBM Petroleum Retailing Application brochure covers: Overview, Consumer Assistance Facility, Pump Control (Courtesy of International Business Machines Corporation, © 1987 International Business Machines Corporation)

IBM Petroleum Retailing Application screens: Pump Control (top), Consumer Assistance (Courtesy of International Business Machines Corporation, © 1987 International Business Machines Corporation)

IBM Petroleum Retailing exhibit at PEI Business Show, Toronto, 1987 (Courtesy of International Business Machines Corporation, © 1987 International Business Machines Corporation)

On one of our trips to Austria we were given a diskette containing a copy of a potential business partner's software that we subsequently shared with our Raleigh colleagues. Unknown to all of us, the diskette contained a virus that had been propagated far and wide before it was detected. This led to strict new procedures concerning the transfer of diskettes and the reporting of viruses. Colleague Roger Richard was put in charge of virus detection and reporting for our team. One evening after Roger had left the office another colleague planted a fake virus on Roger's workstation computer as a joke. The next morning when Roger turned on his computer he freaked out when he saw the virus. He was just about to report it to IBM headquarters in Armonk, N.Y. when another colleague revealed the joke. Talk about a close call!

To say that our petroleum solution was slightly ahead of its time would be somewhat of an understatement. Although in terms of functionality it was even more than what the doctor ordered, the architecture upon which it was built was a bit too pricey for the target marketplace. But like UPC scanning a decade earlier, it laid the groundwork for the future. And for that, I am proud of what we accomplished. Colleague Michel Parent summarizes the situation well:

> The gas station solution was really a Research and Development (R&D) project in the 1980s but is very commonplace today. We were often at

Roger freaks out when he discovers the "virus" (Sketch by James Harvey)

the forefront of development without necessarily reaping the benefits. During the 1970s and 1980s we moved technology forward without financial justification for the branch offices. The store systems environment was a rarity in that it did much more than just sell hardware.

Petro project plaque, 1986-1987

One final pasture

I moved to one final pasture before being "put out to pasture" for good in 1992. During my final year at IBM I was asked to explore potential partnerships for Help Desk solutions. One of the companies we examined was Software Artistry, based in Indianapolis, Indiana. A visit to their offices more than 25 years ago remains etched in my memory – not for what was discussed with the principals, Don Brown and Joe Adams, but for the misdeed that I committed. As our meeting concluded, I pushed back my chair to stand up and leave. My chair hit the credenza and caused an antique glass Galilean thermometer to crash to the floor, breaking into a thousand pieces and releasing a toxic gas. Needless to say, my level of embarrassment was totally off the scale. It perhaps is not surprising that no partnership resulted from that visit! However, it is interesting to note that, five years later, IBM purchased the company for $200 million.

Galilean thermometer (wikipedia.org)

Chapter 7   Extracurricular Coding

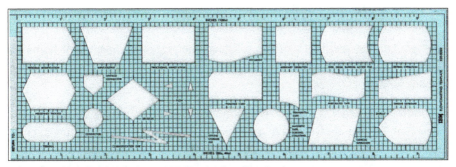

Flowcharting template, circa 1970 (Author's collection)

From my earliest days as a programmer I have been very fascinated by the power and the potential of computers. The blazing speed (20 microsecond cycle time) of the IBM 1620 was indeed something to behold. Never mind that today's most powerful computers are a thousand times faster. But what impressed me more than the speed was the limitless potential of these remarkable machines that had become such a big part of my life. I quickly became a believer that nothing was impossible for a computer.

Though it was always challenging and often frustrating, I really enjoyed programming. When in the midst of writing a program, I was oblivious to the passage of time. It could be 3 p.m. before I realized that I hadn't had lunch. Or the clock could strike 12 midnight before I would think about quietly crawling upstairs to bed. Of course it was "work" but, more than that, it was enjoyment. This may be difficult to understand for people who have never walked in my data processing shoes. However, for me, the incredible sense of satisfaction that followed the discovery of a bug buried deep within a 400-page core dump almost defies description. As does the eruption of euphoria that accompanied a program's successful arrival at end-of-job!

It is no wonder then that I spent such a large percentage of my waking hours programming. To adapt a few lines from the McGuire Sisters' 1958 hit song:

>Coding in the mornin'
>Coding in the evenin'
>Coding at suppertime.

In the early years of our marriage, my wife kept a diary. There were frequent references to late evenings at work as well as returns to the office on weekends. For example:

- April 13, 1969 (Sunday): Daddy dear had to go down to the office today.
- June 9, 1969: Daddy had to work late. Arrived home at 11:45 p.m.
- October 6, 1970: Daddy had to work late in Production, arrived home 12:30 a.m.

My son, Charles, recalls the program listings that I sometimes brought home to work on. "I remember you poring through those mega stacks of computer paper looking for bugs in the code."

Given the long hours that I worked on my assigned programming tasks, it would seem unthinkable that I would spend some of my spare time on unassigned personal programming projects. But that in fact is exactly what I did. Was I crazy? Was I a programaholic? Perhaps a bit of both. But more likely, it was a less serious character aberration. Sometimes it was to respond to a challenge. At other times, it was to fill a recognized client need. Or it might have been simply to develop an idea that popped into my head during my daily soak in the bathtub – my personal THINK tank. Whatever the motivation, I don't regret for a moment the unique experiences that these extracurricular projects afforded me.

Network plotting

The idea for this development was born out of a major customer need. Among the applications offered by Montreal's Datacentre was a program called "Project Management System" – a tool for the management of large-scale projects. PMS processed project data to provide comprehensive reports relating to cost, time, manpower, equipment and materials. Sometimes it was referred to as a critical path program because it was able to highlight the activities that had to be completed on time, otherwise the whole project would be delayed. My colleague, Gabor Fabian, was our resident PMS expert who helped customers debug their large project networks. Some client projects contained thousands of individual tasks or activities. Occasionally Gabor would ask me to help him find problems in a customer's network. Through this exposure to PMS, I became aware of a major shortcoming. Although the application produced a rich selection of reports, the customer was not able to see a visual representation of their network. So I decided to do something about it!

In November of 1972 I began to quietly work on this project at home in my spare time. In those days, I didn't have a lot of free time – what with helping care for our two babies, tutoring high school students in math and physics, and keeping the house roofs cleared of snow and ice. I didn't tell anybody at work that I was doing this. Only my wife knew. Perhaps I decided to keep it quiet in order not to create excessive expectations. Or it might have been a lack of confidence that I could actually achieve my goal.

As has always been my habit, before beginning this project, I gave it a name. I called it MAPNET – **M**ontreal **A**utomatic **P**lotting of **NET**works. (Its name would later change, but that will be discussed further on.) Although the concept was simple and straightforward – to graphically represent a network of activities and their dependencies – it was a case of "easier said than done." In a mid-February diary entry, I acknowledged this complexity:

> February 16, 1973: Very busy every spare minute these days working on MAPNET. It has turned out to be much more extensive than I first imagined.

Among the unanticipated complexities encountered were scaling for network size, adapting to different types of networks, and implementing horizontal and vertical page connectors. Nevertheless, I persevered, determined to bring my idea to fruition. By the time the snow had melted and the crocuses were emerging from their hibernation, I was ready to introduce my baby to the world (at least to the Montreal Datacentre world!). Fortunately, the large number of Datacentre PMS customers provided ample opportunity to test and refine the program. And I was happy and relieved that

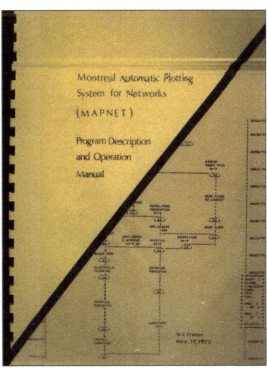

MAPNET application manual cover, 1973 (Author's collection)

customers reacted favourably to this new tool that was now at their disposal.

Before long, word began to spread across the country about MAPNET. But this increased visibility also posed a problem. How could IBM provide the program to a wider audience and ensure its support? After all, this program was the result of a one-man development and lacked any official status. In order for a program to be marketed, it had to fall into one of three categories: program product (PP), field developed program (FDP) or installed user program (IUP). The decision was made

Chapter 6: OUTPUT CHARTS   PAGE   43

```
M A P N E T  MONTREAL AUTOMATIC PLOTTING SYSTEM FOR NETWORKS

        PROJECT: PRODUCTION SCHEDULING - JUNE  CHART   1 OF 215
                                               DATE: 17MAY73

   IDENTIFICATION        STATISTICS              LEGEND
****************  ****************  ************************
*                *  *                *  *            * CRIT. *
* NET=DRILLS     *  * ACITEMS=    6  *  *  ************ *
* SUB=           *  * STARTS =    4  *  *  * NODE1      * *
* REF=K4         *  * ENDS   =    3  *  *  ************ *
* DPT=           *  * SIMCHNS=    5  *  *       |         *
* CYC=           *  * CMPCHNS=    3  *  *  ACTIV.DESCRIPT, *
*                *  *                *  *    DURATN   (QTY) *
* STOT=TUE-02    *  * LINES/WKDAY=2  *  *  NODE1 -> NODE2   *
* ENDT=MON-29    *  * CHNCOMBIN=ALL  *  *  STDATE  ENDATE   *
* I/P=OUTFILE3   *  * CHNORDER=C-MIC *  *  RES/ALT          *
* TYPE=RAP       *  * DOUBLEPRT=NO   *  *       |           *
* DATES=SCHED    *  * CALENDAR=SPECL *  *       |           *
*                *  *                *  *  ************     *
*                *  * PAGES(V)=   1  *  *  * NODE2      *   *
*                *  * PAGES(H)=   1  *  *  ************     *
****************  ****************  *       : FLOAT *
                                     ************************
```

```
MON-01 |                                                              | MON-01
TUE-02 |                          ************                        | TUE-02
WED-03 |                 |-------------------|                        | WED-03
THU-04 |                 :                   :          ************  | THU-04
                                                        * K4-01-S *
FRI-05 |                 :                   :          ************  | FRI-05
                               MFG. 617W 7/8"                |
SAT-06 |                 :      4/3  : (625)       SHIP 617W 7/8"      | SAT-06
                               TUE-02 : FRI-05     6/0  | (300)
MON-08 |                 :      K4*          :        -> K4-01-E       | MON-08
                                                   THU-04 | WED-10
TUE-09 |                 :                   |-------------------|     | TUE-09
WED-10 |                 :      ************                          | WED-10
                                * K4-01-E *
THU-11 |                 :      ************                          | THU-11
FRI-12 |                 :                                            | FRI-12
SAT-13 |                 :      ************                          | SAT-13
                                * K4-02-S *
MON-15 |                 MFG. 617W 7/8"      ************             | MON-15
                         4/1  | (1000)          |
TUE-16 |                 K4=MFG-S ->                                  | TUE-16
                              K4-03-E     SHIP 617W 7/8"
WED-17 |                 TUE-16 : SAT-20   5/2  * (250)               | WED-17
                         K4*    :          SAT-13 * FRI-19
THU-18 |                 :                   *                        | THU-18
FRI-19 |                 :      ************                          | FRI-19
                                * K4-02-E *
SAT-20 |                 :      ************                          | SAT-20
MON-22 |                 :                                            | MON-22
TUE-23 |                 :      ************                          | TUE-23
                                * K4-03-S *
WED-24 |                 :      ************                          | WED-24
THU-25 |                 :          |                                 | THU-25
                                SHIP 617W 7/8"
FRI-26 |                 :      4/1  | (550)                          | FRI-26
                                TUE-23 | MON-29
SAT-27 |                 |-------------------|                        | SAT-27
MON-29 |                        ************                          | MON-29
                                * K4-03-F *
TUE-30 |                        ************                          | TUE-30
```

Figure 6-2: Resource Plot (I-J Network)

MAPNET sample network plotting output chart (Author's collection)

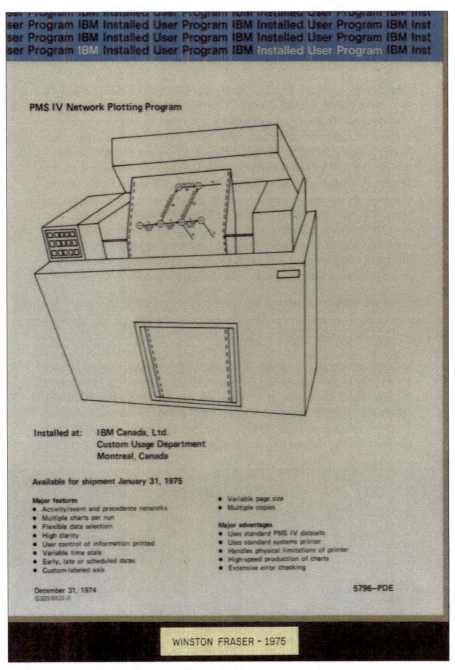

PMS IV Network Plotting Program plaque, 1975

to offer it as an IUP. However, to achieve this status, it would involve additional testing, enhanced documentation and a name change. More than a year later, the PMS IV Network Plotting Program was officially announced. The announcement letter's introduction explained the significance of this addition to the IBM product line:

> One picture is not worth 1000 words; it is worth much more. A picture can show what words cannot. This is especially true in project management. There is no substitute for a network diagram – a picture of the project. Network diagrams have been produced in the past, but primarily through laborious manual efforts. As a result of the difficulty to update them, they rarely corresponded to what was happening in the project. Available programs that could automatically produce diagrams required specialized plotting hardware, thus reducing user acceptance. Now IBM has a program, PMS IV Network Plotting Program, that overcomes both problems. By automating the drawing process, it enables the user to create a network diagram and keep it up to date. Since this program produces the diagram on the system printer, there is no additional hardware expense to automate the process.

Besides the satisfaction of having my creation recognized in this way, I was very honoured to receive an Outstanding Contribution Award for this development. The accompanying citation read in part:

> Winston designed and developed a generalized network plotting system called PMS IV Network Plotting Program. Six to nine months of effort on his own time and quite apart from his normal IBM responsibilities, resulted in the release of the program. The PMS IV Network Plotting Program, which consists of 40 PL/1 programs, uses input from PMS IV to generate project control network diagrams and is a significant functional

Left: Outstanding Contribution Award certificate for Network Plotting Application, May 1975
Right: Receiving OCA from Keith Johnston, Vice President, Eastern Region (Photo excerpted from IBM Canada News Service bulletin, author's collection)

enhancement to the PMS program product. The facility provided by this program reduces the man hours required for project planning and control. It has already been used by the Steinberg project team in Montreal for the installation of the first IBM 3660 supermarket system in the world.

Home and away

As a young kid growing up on the farm, there was little time for sports. Winter Saturdays were normally spent working in the woods cutting firewood for the furnace and logs and pulpwood for the mills. However, once I entered high school, my parents relented and did occasionally give me time off to go play hockey in one of the neighbouring towns. I loved hockey even though I did not excel – in fact, if the truth be known, I made the team only due to a lack of players! But I really enjoyed playing in spite of my limited talent.

My official hockey portrait, 1957 (Photo by Malcolm Fraser)

Cookshire High School intermediate hockey team, 1959 (I am leftmost in the back row.) (Author's collection)

I equally enjoyed following professional hockey, especially the Montreal Canadiens. My idols were Maurice Richard, Doug Harvey and Dickie Moore. Every Saturday night the old radio on the dining room sideboard would be tuned to Hockey Night in Canada on CBC. My dad, my brothers and I would excitedly experience the Habs' hometown heroics as described by play-by-play announcers Danny Gallivan and Foster Hewitt. Our

With Canadiens stars Ken Mosdell and Phil Goyette, Bury, Que., 1959 (Fraser family archives)

imaginations were in overdrive because we had no TV at that time. And of course, this was the era of the Original Six, so hockey was at its apex of quality. Only several years later did I finally get to see the Canadiens play at the Forum in Montreal. But in 1959 I had a chance to meet some of them at an exhibition baseball game at neighbouring town Bury's annual 1st of July Dominion Day celebrations.

Canadiens Don Marshall and Doug Harvey signing autographs, 1959 (Author's collection)

When I moved to Montreal in 1965 to begin working at IBM, I brought my love of hockey with me. As often as possible, a friend or colleague and I would purchase a pair of $10 standing-room tickets high in the rafters to cheer on Les Glorieux. I remember that we had to take turns going to the washroom or buying a hot dog, so as not to lose our elbow space on the rail. Play-off games were extra special but tickets were very hard to come by. A very limited number of tickets would go on sale at 10:00 a.m. and sell out within a few minutes. Since our IBM working hours were from 8:30 a.m. to 5:15 p.m., we occasionally had to play hooky to snag a pair of ducats. One day, my colleague Gabor Fabian and I decided at 9:45 a.m. that it would be worth the risk, so we took off for the Forum on foot. Bad decision! On our way, who did we meet but our second-level manager, who greeted us with, "Going for an early lunch today, boys?"

It is with this background in mind that I share another of my extracurricular coding adventures. One day, in the fall of 1981, while driving home I turned on the car radio. The first words I heard were, "It's impossible to do by computer." Naturally my curiosity was piqued, so I turned up the volume to listen to the rest of the interview. I soon learned that the person being interviewed was Phil Scheuer, the NHL schedule maker, and that the subject being discussed was the NHL schedule of games. As I pondered what I heard, I felt very offended that anyone would dare say that something was impossible to do by computer. At the same time, I felt challenged to prove this person wrong.

The next morning I telephoned the NHL head office (which just happened to be located in the Sun Life building directly across the street from the IBM building). A very pleasant secretary who answered put me through to Mr. Scheuer. I mentioned to him that I had heard him on the radio and that I was interested to know more about his schedule-making process. (I did not tell him how offended I was with his dismissal of the computer's capabilities!) He told me that he would be very willing to show me how he accomplished this critical annual scheduling exercise. So we set up a meeting for a few days later.

Upon arrival in the well-appointed, even opulent NHL head office on the ninth floor, I was greeted by a very friendly, smiling Mr. Scheuer ("Call me Phil"). He was the kind of person whom you felt would be a pleasure to work with – a down-to-earth guy and a straight shooter. Phil took me into his office; upon entry I was honestly quite unprepared for the sight that I would behold. In front of us, on a

Phil Scheuer's NHL business card (Author's collection)

wall that spanned the full length of his large office, in living colour, was the entire 840-game NHL schedule. Somewhat overwhelmed by his masterpiece, I humbly asked Phil to explain how he did it. I expected him to show me some documents to indicate the basic information required to create the schedule. But no such luck – he had everything in his head! However, when pressed, he did admit that he did have some underlying documentation but that it would take time to assemble it. I explained to him that in order to computerize the process, I would require every last detail of the source information that he used. Phil agreed to prepare it all for me. Although this first meeting raised a bit of doubt in my mind, I was still determined to proceed.

A couple of weeks later Phil called to say that he had all the information ready for me. At our second meeting he provided me with a truckload of data in terms of schedule constraints that were used to build the current season's schedule. The constraints were of three types: overall league constraints, general team constraints and individual team constraints. The league constraints were as follows:

Phil Scheuer (Courtesy of Phil Scheuer)

- 840 games to be scheduled over 26 weeks
- Even distribution of games
- Certain specified no-play dates (e.g., All-star Game weekend)
- Maximize the number of weekend games
- Only intra division games during the final 10 days

The general team constraints (applicable to all teams) included the following:

- Available home dates (according to the availability of their arena)
- Equal number of home and away games
- Maximum of two games in three days
- Minimum of two games in seven days
- Minimize the occurrence of four games in five days
- Minimum of "n" days between visits of the same team
- Maximum of 900 miles travelled between games on consecutive days
- Maximum of seven consecutive games "on the road"
- Minimum of "n" games at home on a specific day of the week
- Maximum of one home game on two consecutive days

The individual team constraints (applicable to specific teams):

- Team "a" must be scheduled at home every Saturday
- Team "b" must have at least 11 Thursday games (e.g., for TV contract)
- Team "c" must not have home games on consecutive dates
- Team "x" wants to play team "y" only on week dates (not on weekends)
- Team "z" must play home games on certain specific dates

Armed with this data, I embarked on my mission to computerize the process. Simply stated, my task was to "Create a schedule that respects all the constraints, minimizes travel and treats all teams fairly." Frankly, I had no real idea of how I was going to do it. But I was confident that after a few early morning soaks in my think tank, I would come up with a solution.

I initially considered a number of approaches that were found wanting, including "zero-one integer programming" and adapting conventional scheduling techniques. Therefore I opted for a "roll-your-own" solution. A parameter-driven iterative approach was used to schedule the games. The following sequence of steps was found to result in the best quality schedule.

- Schedule "long" road trips against teams in other divisions more than 900 miles away
- Schedule "medium" road trips against teams in other divisions more than 900 miles away
- Schedule "imposed" road trips (i.e., when the travelling team does have available home dates)
- Schedule any possible remaining road trips against teams within the same division or within 900 miles
- Schedule any remaining games on a one-by-one basis
- Swap some already scheduled games to allow remaining unscheduled games to be scheduled

A key component of the final solution was the Road Trip Simulator, whose main functions were:

- Determine the eligible host teams (H1, H2, . . . Hn) for the trip
- Start the road trip at H1 if possible
- Wait for up to "n" days if necessary
- Move to the next date
- Determine the best next stop
- Schedule a game there if possible
- Wait up to "n" days if necessary
- Repeat for all remaining possible stops until no teams left or road trip ends

The simulator analyzed hundreds of possible road trips in order to determine the "best" one (where "best" is based on a combination of factors including distance travelled, number of games on consecutive dates and number of home dates sacrificed).

After months of trial and error development, the computer program succeeded in scheduling 829 out of the required 840 games. Manual adjustments were needed to schedule the remaining 11 games. As indicated in the summary table below, my final schedule was of comparable quality to Scheuer's actual 1981-1982 NHL schedule. As a result, the National Hockey League made use of my program in building their 1982-1983 and 1983-1984 schedules, IBM received significant system usage revenue for the computer processing time, and I succeeded in demonstrating that scheduling could be done by computer.

Case Description	Games Sched.	Mileage Min Max Avg			4 in 5 Min Max Avg			Fairness Min Max Avg		
Initial Pgm	767	230	651	441	2	13	4	68	207	103
Simulator	829	269	610	389	1	7	3	39	103	69
1st Adjust.	840	274	589	374	0	8	3	34	117	68
2nd Adjust.	840	264	589	375	0	2	1	51	74	63
N.H.L.	840	269	542	379	0	6	1	33	113	57

NHL Schedule program results summary (Author's collection)

PRINTED SCHEDULE

	BOS	BUF	CAL	CHI	COL	DET	EDM	HAR	...
MON. OCT 5	..								...
TUE. OCT 6					4 >VAN	9 >WIN		7 >QUE	...
WED. OCT 7		8P HAR		9P PIT	9 >LOS	3 >EDM	3M DET	8 >BUF	...
THU. OCT 8	9P QUE		9M MIN	8 >MON					...
FRI. OCT 9			9 >EDM				9P CAL		...
SAT. OCT10	8 >HAR	8 >QUE			3P DET	3 >COL	P	8M BOS	...
SUN. OCT11	8P HAR			9P COL	9 >CHI		8P VAN	8 >BOS	...
MON. OCT12									...
TUE. OCT13			9A EDM	9 >STL		3 >LOS	9 >CAL		...
WED. OCT14	2 >CHI	9P COL	P	2P BOS	9 >BUF		6M MIN	2 >PIT	...
THU. OCT15						8P WIN		9P TOR	...
FRI. OCT16	2 >CAL		2P BOS		P		P		...
SAT. OCT17		8 >MON		9A MIN	9 >HAR	8 >PIT	9P >LOS	9M COL	...
SUN. OCT18	2 >EDM	9M TOR	9 >CHI	9P CAL	9 >PHI	2P VAN	2P BOS		...

NHL Schedule program – Printed Schedule by date (Author's collection)

SCHEDULE EVALUATION REPORT

Tm No.	Miles (00's)	Consec Games	4 Games 5 Dates	Rested H-team	Bad Spacing	Weekend Home Gms	Comp. Score
1	294	22	2	5	1	18	62
2	307	19	1	15	5	26	62
3	467	21	2	10	4	14	67
4	310	24	1	12	1	22	66
5	538	23	2	7	4	23	73
6	357	22	1	9	7	19	63
7	466	17	1	18	5	26	74
8	359	21	1	8	2	22	54
9	589	21	1	11	1	16	56
10	396	22	1	5	4	15	57
11	325	21	1	6	1	17	51
12	264	21	2	3	1	15	61
13	315	21	1	12	3	20	65
14	324	25	2	3	3	18	73
15	309	24	1	11	6	16	68
16	373	18	2	4	2	14	58
17	390	21	2	4	3	16	61
18	397	21	2	6	5	16	69
19	443	23	0	7	2	24	53
20	302	22	1	11	1	21	61
21	360	17	2	10	4	32	71
TOT	7885	446	29	177	65	410	1325
AVG	375	21	1	8	3	19	63
MIN	264	17	0	3	1	14	51
MAX	589	25	2	18	7	32	74

Above: NHL Schedule program – Schedule Evaluation Report by team (Author's collection)

Right: NHL 1983-84 Schedule booklet cover (Author's collection)

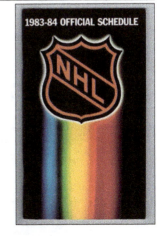

Although I received no monetary compensation for this development, it was the subject of a paper that I presented at the 1982 Summer Computer Simulation Conference in Denver, Colorado, in July 1982. And I was honoured to be invited by the NHL to attend their 1982 Awards Presentation at Place des Arts in Montreal.

Interestingly enough, I was not the first to try to build the NHL schedule by computer: The Ottawa Journal of January 17, 1968 reported:

> The 1968-69 schedule will open October 11 and finish April 7 and will be worked out by computer. "Of course, the computer schedule might not be satisfactory," [NHL President Clarence] Campbell said. "Other sports bodies have tried it and failed. If it doesn't work, we'll at least have a better idea about arranging a satisfactory schedule."

Recently, through the auspices of a common friend, Jim MacKinnon, I met with

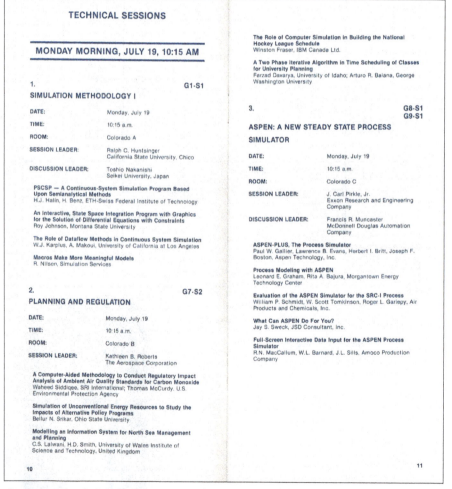

Computer Simulation Conference agenda, Denver, 1982 (Author's collection)

Phil Scheuer, now a scheduling consultant, to reminisce about our working together more than 35 years ago. Phil shared his recollections about the project as well as interesting details of his scheduling experience:

> Yes, I remember the project very well. The computer schedule that you made provided us with a good base for building upon. However, there were certain factors that the computer could not be expected to take into account. Therefore it could not adequately create the entire schedule. Normally it would take me about six months every year to create the schedule. And once created, I knew it all by heart. Ask me who played who on a specific date and I could tell you without even looking at my schedule board! One year – the year of the lockout – I made a new schedule almost every day. Speaking of the schedule board, it is now in the Hockey Hall of Fame in Toronto.

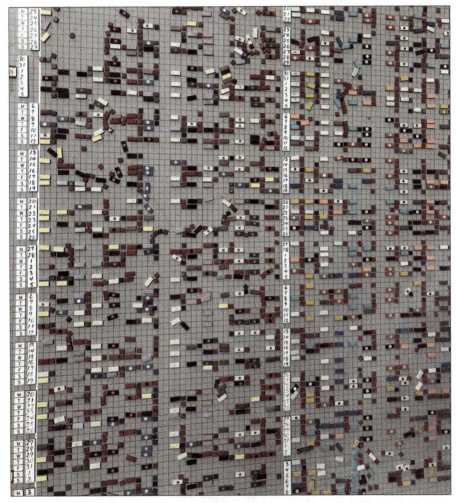

A section of Phil Scheuer's NHL schedule board (Photo © 2018, Bill Wellman, Hockey Hall of Fame)

Ya gavaryu po ruski

As you may have deduced, the header for this section is the English phonetical representation of the Russian translation of the phrase "I speak Russian." What, you may ask, does that have to do with extracurricular coding? Although not of the same scope as the other personally initiated projects presented in this chapter, it was nonetheless quite unique and is worthy of at least a mention. First, a bit of background.

During my university days I took two Russian language courses. There was no particular reason for doing so, except that the course was being newly offered and it sounded interesting. Indeed it was, as our professor, Dr. Sepp, brought the language to life with his teaching combined with his stories. By the end of the second year I had mastered the alphabet as well as the rules of grammar. In fact, with the help of the giant English-Russian dictionary – printed on toilet tissue-quality paper – I was able to read and comprehend articles in the Pravda newspaper. With the Cold War in full swing at the time, it is not unreasonable to suspect that my fellow Russian students and I were on an RCMP watch list.

Fast forward to 1970 when I was working as a programmer in the Datacentre. One day, I made a coding error that resulted in the printed output being garbled and illegible. I had mistakenly coded the printer carriage control character, causing two lines to be printed on top of each other (technically known as "overstrike" or "print and suppress spacing"). As I looked at the useless printout, my eye suddenly recognized a perfectly-formed Russian alphabet character that stood out from the otherwise unreadable mess. This was a Eureka moment. I thought to myself, "Maybe I'm onto something. What if I was able to print Russian text on a printer equipped with a standard English print chain?"

Anxious to test this exciting possibility, that evening I coded a Fortran program to print out every combination of up to three levels of overstrike of each character of the print chain with every other character. The next day, before leaving the office, I submitted the job in the overnight processing queue. Unfortunately, I had not warned the operator to expect an unusual printout. So, in the middle of the night, I received a panic call telling me, "Your job is making the printer go crazy! Do you want me to cancel it?" I assured the operator that it was "normal" and to let it complete!

The next morning I collected the printout and immediately began the meticulous search for Russian alphabet characters hidden among the garbage. Much to my surprise – and elation – I was able to find every last character of the Cyrillic alphabet. The implications of this discovery were quite significant. It meant that Russian text could now be printed on a 1403 printer using the standard English print chain. Up until then, the only way to print Russian text was to replace the

"The printer is going crazy!" / "It's OK, let it run." (Sketch by James Harvey)

English print chain with a Cyrillic print chain which was a time-consuming procedure. But even more importantly, it meant that English and Russian text could be combined in the same document. It is noted that my "discovery" occurred several years before the advent of laser printing and the introduction of the 3800 laser printer in 1976. Unfortunately no patent was ever applied for but I was content just knowing the possibilities that the idea afforded.

```
FORTRAN IV G LEVEL 1, MOD 4            MAIN            DATE = 70156          15/45/57

0001              DIMENSION B1(80),B2(80),B3(80),IN(40),P1(40),P2(40),P3(40),D(20)
0002              WRITE(6,6)
0003            6 FORMAT(//1H1,T20,'WRITING RUSSIAN TEXT BY COMPUTER')
0004              READ (5,1) B1,B2,B3
0005            1 FORMAT(80A1/80A1/80A1)
0006            2 FORMAT(40I2)
0007              WRITE(6,7) (B1(I),I=1,31),(B2(I),I=1,31),(B3(I),I=1,31)
0008            7 FORMAT(//1H0,'RUSSIAN ALPHABET :',T20,31(A1,1X)/1H+,T20,31(A1,1X)
                 1/1H+,T20,31(A1,1X)///)
0009           55 READ (5,2,END=99) IN
0010              DO 10 I=1,40
0011              J=IN(I)
0012              IF(J.EQ.0) J=80
0013              P1(I)=B1(J)
0014              P2(I)=B2(J)
0015           10 P3(I)=B3(J)
0016              WRITE (6,3) P1,P2,P3
0017            3 FORMAT(1H ,40A1/1H+,40A1/1H+,40A1)
0018              READ (5,4) D
0019            4 FORMAT (20A4)
0020              WRITE(6,5) D
0021            5 FORMAT(1H ,T50,20A4//)
0022              GO TO 55
0023           99 STOP
0024              END
```

Fortran program to print Russian text on 1403 printer with standard print chain, 1970 (Author's collection)

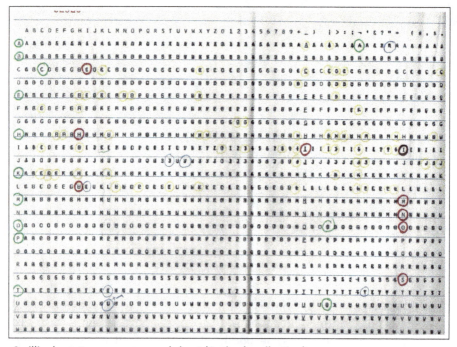

Cyrillic character generator worksheet (Author's collection)

```
                    WRITING RUSSIAN TEXT BY COMPUTER


RUSSIAN ALPHABET :А Б В Т Я Е Ж З И К Л М Н О Ь Р С Т У Ф Х Ц Ч Ш Щ Ъ Ь Э Ю Я


    ОН ОЧЕНЬ ВСЕМИ ЛЮБИМ.
                                            (HE IS VERY MUCH LIKED BY EVERYBODY.)


    Я РОДИЛСЯ В ЛОНДОНЕ.
                                            (I WAS BORN IN LONDON)


    ЭТОТ ДОМ СТРОИТ МОЙ ХОРОШИЙ ЗНАКОМЫЙ.
                                            (THIS HOUSE IS BEING BUILT BY A GOOD FRIEND OF MINE.)


    ГОВОРЯТ, ЧТО ОН БОЛЕН.
                                            (THEY SAY HE IS ILL.)


    МОЯ СЕСТРА ПИСАЛА КАЖДУЮ НЕДЕЛЮ.
                                            (MY SISTER USED TO WRITE EVERY WEEK.)


    ЕГО ОТЕЦ БЫЛ РУССКИЙ.
                                            (HIS FATHER WAS RUSSIAN)


    ЕСТЬ КОФЕ?
                                            (IS THERE ANY COFFEE?)
```

Printing Russian text on 1403 printer with standard print chain (Author's collection)

CHATR box

In an earlier chapter I mentioned that computer hardware was not my forte but rather my fear. So it may come as somewhat of a surprise to learn that one of my extracurricular projects was related to hardware. But such was the case.

IBM's announcement of the 4680 store system opened up a plethora of opportunities for retailers. Its 4683 point-of-sale terminal was designed to handle all the checkout functions. While my colleagues were busy programming and installing the system, I was very occupied during the day in the development of use-of-data applications. But after hours I was envisioning another use for the 4683 terminal. I imagined the terminal being repackaged as a consumer kiosk. Thus was born my idea of the CHATR box (Consumer Help Application for TRavellers).

The first challenge that I faced was related to a reconfiguration of the 4683 hardware components. For example:
- Only a small portion of the keyboard was required
- The cash drawer was not required
- The printer was required but needed to be hidden
- The magnetic stripe reader was required
- The inter-component cables needed to be hidden

To implement these physical requirements, a new packaging of the components was required. A robust, secure and attractive casing was needed. My good friend

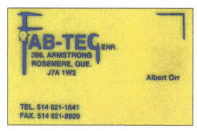

Albert Orr Fab-Tek business card
(Author's collection)

CHATR box at PEI Show, Toronto, 1987
(Courtesy of International Business
Machines Corporation, © 1987 International
Business Machines Corporation)

and neighbour, Albert Orr, was an experienced metal worker, so I solicited his assistance. He agreed to build a prototype based on my preliminary specifications. A couple of weeks later he delivered a durable and attractive CHATR box. The first implementation of the box was as part of Petroleum Retailing Application described in the previous chapter. For that use, its name was changed to Consumer Assistance Facility.

Only two CHATR boxes were ever produced – one for the Provi-soir pilot store in Piedmont, Que., and the other for demonstration purposes. Unfortunately, although the concept was well received, cost justification was lacking, so my dear CHATR box lived a very short life.

Chapter 8   Travellin' Man

Flying over Rockies, Calgary to Vancouver (Photo by author)

To say that IBM and travel go together like a horse and carriage would be something of an understatement. Datacentre colleague Sue Pidoux Carlisle reminded me of the longstanding joke amongst IBMers that I.B.M. stood for "I've Been Moved." In fact, most long-serving IBM employees have been moved at least once in their career, and some several times. American IBMer John Sailors recounts in his paper "A Retired IBMer's View and Experiences" that, during his 37 years with IBM, he moved his family no less than 17 times!

No travel, please

Certainly that was not my experience. In fact, I was never moved even once during my 27 years with Big Blue. However, even though I avoided a move of location, I was not able to avoid travelling. But it wasn't from a lack of trying. In October 1967, three months prior to my marriage to Becky, I met with my manager, Bill Vandersanden, to request an exemption from overnight travelling. His "Note to File" reads as follows:

Our wedding photo, January 6, 1968 (Fraser family archives)

> On October 23, 1967 Winston informed me that due to his forthcoming marriage, he would be unable to do any travelling that would require him to stay out of town overnight. He asked how this would affect his position and career with the company. I explained that the company would respect his wishes but that such a decision might affect his career with the company. Promotions, particularly to supervisory and managerial positions, would involve courses and his reluctance to attend out of town courses for periods of time exceeding one day could well jeopardize his future. Winston indicated however that he has no aspirations in this area, that he is quite happy in his present environment and would be pleased to progress in the technical area only. Although his development in this area may be hindered somewhat due to the fact that he cannot attend out-of-town courses, we feel that local training and self-study would adequately substitute such courses. Winston has in the past done an excellent job and has always improved his knowledge through self-study. I therefore explained to him that his decision would not affect his technical career or management's opinion of him. This decision in no way rules out a possible transfer to another center, should there be a need for his specialized knowledge.

Confident that our future marital bliss would not be interrupted by out-of-town overnight travel, we settled into our modest fixer-upper home in Rosemere (Quebec), a small bedroom community north of Montreal. My only travel would consist of a daily one-hour Buddcar commuter train ride to and from the office. This arrangement worked quite well for a few months. But then the wheels began

Rosemere to Montreal train commuters, 1979 (Photo by author)

to fall off. As I started to develop specialized expertise in certain areas, my services were in demand across the country and beyond. This developing situation posed a real problem for me. On the one hand, I had promised my wife that I would not go away overnight. On the other hand, I felt a strong obligation toward IBM. The initial solution to this dilemma was two-fold. Firstly, I would make every effort to minimize the frequency of travel. And secondly, when feasible, I would arrange to have Becky accompany me on some of the longer trips. Obviously the latter had significant financial implications, but I was willing to make the sacrifice in order to keep peace in the family.

This approach worked reasonably well for a while. However, as my travel requirements increased and as our children were born, both aspects of the "solution" took a hit. I was less able to minimize the frequency of trips and it became less feasible for Becky to join me. So we just had to live with it. We both realized the many benefits of my working for IBM and were willing to accept this sacrifice. But it was not easy. Although a woman of strong faith, Becky always worried greatly whenever I travelled. This is reflected in one of her diary entries:

> December 4, 1969: Up at 5:30 a.m. as Daddy left for airport. He called me when he arrived at 9:10 a.m. (he knows that I am a "worry wart"!) Back home at 11:10 p.m. as plane was 30 minutes late. He brought little Andrea a thick-leaved book of nursery rhymes and a lovely Christmas corsage for me.

It should be noted that my wife's worries were not without justification. During the 1970s and 1980s there was an unusually high number of plane crashes and hijackings. And, more often than not, they seemed to occur when I was away from home. I tried to do everything I could to alleviate Becky's anxieties, such as safe-arrival calls and notification of delays. And, whenever possible, I would bring home a little gift for her and trinkets for the kids. I know that she specially treasured a cross made of nails that I brought from Corpus Christi, Texas. Daughter Elaine (I call her "Fuzzy") remembers one of her trinkets:

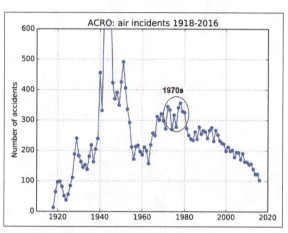

Aircraft incident statistics (wikipedia.org)

It was always very exciting when you arrived back home and opened your luggage and pulled out the special treat (usually wrapped in a plastic bag) for each of us. "Brown bear" and the stuffed animal horse "Horsey" are my two most prominent memories. Brown bear was (and is) a little fuzzy bear that has a plastic face and sucks his thumb. He was a

gift from one of your IBM trips that brought me years and years of comfort. He followed me through my childhood and eventually became a decorative feature in my bedroom as a teen. He was never tossed out or given to charity during any of my many decluttering and redesigning moments! He even appeared – as a surprise – on my wedding day when you included him in your speech. It was a touching moment that I will never forget. Brown bear continues to live on in a secure spot in my home. Perhaps one day he will be passed down to my kids' kids to be treasured as I have treasured him.

With my daughter Elaine's Brown Bear at her wedding (Fraser family archives)

Daughter Andrea recalls that there was an upside to my absence while on a trip. "When you went away we often went to the Ste-Rose Restaurant for Chinese food or ordered in pizza – foods that you didn't like."

Anyway, like it or not, I did become a "travellin' man." In fact, during the later years, I actually **requested** to go on certain trips to attend conferences to present papers. Altogether, I probably took more than 200 out-of-town trips – by air, by train and by car. Travel came in many flavours and every trip was different. There were customer calls, planning sessions, courses, conferences, forums, institutes, announcements and celebrations.

Destinations and connections

Aircraft at La Guardia Airport, New York, ca. 1974 (Photo by author)

My most frequent travel destination was Toronto. In the early years I usually took the midnight sleeper train from Montreal's Central Station, arriving at Toronto's downtown Union Station by 7:30 a.m. However, when that train fell victim to the government's rail cutbacks, it meant that I would have to get up at 5 a.m. to catch a 7 a.m. one-hour flight from Dorval to Canada's metropolis. Sometimes, especially if my wife was accompanying me, I would make the long six-hour evening drive on Highway 401, arriving at midnight. My first trip to Toronto was in 1967 to attend a course at the Datacentre on King Street. While there I stayed at the famous King Edward Hotel – we called it the "King Eddy"– and ate at Honest Ed's famous restaurants. In later years the quality of accommodation increased a notch or two, as we were most often booked at the Harbour Castle on the waterfront. This fine hotel, with its amazing breakfast buffet and its very talented lobby pianist, became a home-away-from-home for my wife and me even after my IBM days.

King Edward Hotel postcard, 1967 (Author's collection)

Streetcar, downtown Toronto (Photo by author)

Ed's Restaurants, Toronto (Photo by author)

Among other Canadian travel destinations were Halifax (Sobeys), Saint John (Irving Oil), Quebec City (Ville de Québec), Cornwall (Domtar), Kitchener-Waterloo (University of Waterloo), Winnipeg (CORS conference), Calgary (Texaco, Husky, etc.) and Vancouver (Safeway, Kelly-Douglas).

Upon joining the Steinberg project team in 1973, and during the years that followed, I travelled very often to the U.S.A. Raleigh, North Carolina, was by far my most frequent American destination due to the fact that the IBM Store Systems Lab and Marketing department were located in the nearby Research Triangle Park. I remember very clearly the first of my many trips to Raleigh in February 1974. When I left Montreal the temperature was -30 degrees F. and there was two feet of snow on ground. Three hours later, I stepped off the plane into late spring / early summer with the mercury showing 70 degrees F. and flowers blooming everywhere. What a shock to the system! That trip marked my introduction to one of the area's finest eateries – the Angus Barn steakhouse.

Colleague Paul Biron recalls a unique Raleigh menu item:

> On one of my early Raleigh visits I inquired about a local dish called "grits" that I had heard about. It seemed to be some kind of cereal. The two people who were with me offered very different views of how it should be eaten. One liked his grits with honey and while the other preferred theirs with mustard. This seemed so odd that I never did try grits!

My involvement in the development of various point-of-sale applications led to travels across the United States and beyond to make customer calls and to attend conferences. Among the American cities visited were Albany and Endicott, N.Y.; New York City; Montvale, N.J.; Cincinnati; Charlotte, N.C.; Atlanta; Miami; Chicago; Kansas City; Little Rock and Bentonville, Ark.; Dallas; Houston; Corpus Christi; New Orleans; Denver; San Diego; San Francisco; Los Angeles; and Seattle. We visited four of those cities on a single day, beginning with a morning meeting in Chicago, followed by a customer luncheon at Kansas City airport and a late afternoon workshop in Dallas before taking an evening flight to Los Angeles.

Many of my flights to the U.S.A., especially to Raleigh, involved a stop at New York's La Guardia Airport for a connecting flight to my final destination. In fact, I often spent more time waiting on the ground at La Guardia than I did in the air. Sometimes I had to spend several hours in their departure lounge cooling my heels, chewing vending machine peanuts and watching the world go by. On one such occasion, I took notes of what I observed:

> La Guardia Airport, December 4, 1988: An older man wearing a Mickey Mouse shirt is clipping stacks of coupons from newspapers. A middle-aged man, dressed in a camel hair coat, watches over three full seats of neatly arranged "junk." He shuffles his belongings from one pile to

Left: Bull-riding, Calgary
Stampede
Below: Rail yards and Canada
Place, Vancouver
(Photos by author)

Above: Anchor and lighthouse, Peggy's Cove, N.S.
Right: Fort Garry Hotel, Winnipeg
Below: Bonhomme Carnaval, Vieux-Québec
(Photos by author)

another. Among his possessions are cigarette butts, French fries, a piece of old lace material, a safety pin, a rubber band, a piece of string and half a box of raisins. He finds great joy in activating a little portable TV and playing with an 18-inch piece of broken snow fence slat. But his biggest prize seems to be a stainless steel table knife that he shuffles from one

pile to another before putting it in his pocket. He suddenly spots some money which he grabs. Then he takes off his coat, folds it neatly on the floor and takes out a thread and needle. He threads the needle quite easily, then throws the money from his clenched fist onto another pile of junk beside him. The regular garbage collector just looks at him and shakes his head. He tells me, "He moves his junk from one place to another all the time. I don't know why they don't move him out of here." Meanwhile the man continues organizing his junk as passersby mostly ignore him. A few seem amused and the occasional person looks a bit strangely at him, but nobody talks to him.

Top: Mardi Gras floats and Superdome, New Orleans
Middle: Peace Memorial, Old Town, San Diego, 1991
Above: Tornado damage, Raleigh, N.C., Nov. 1988
(Photos by author)

Most often, my trips were packed with business activities, leaving little free time. However, I usually managed to squeeze in a few hours to see the city and snap a few photos. My interest in photography meant that I almost always brought along my camera equipment – even with the airport security hassles to hand-check my film. However, for one particular two-day trip to Raleigh with a very full schedule, I decided not to bring my camera. On the morning of the second day, I awoke to the news that a major tornado overnight had devastated parts of the city. Determined to obtain photos of the disaster, I rented a Nikon from a camera shop and drove to the affected area before my meetings. Having learned my lesson, I never left my camera at home again!

Left: Eiffel Tower, Paris, 1977
Right: Tower of Big Ben and double-decker bus, London, 1988
(Photos by author)

My international travel included a one-week trip to the Caribbean and several extended trips to Europe. The former, to Barbados, was in connection with the sugar cane project described in Chapter 3. The latter trips, to various European countries, were in relation

Johann Strauss statue, Vienna (Photo by author)

to the point-of-sale applications we developed for supermarket, retail and petroleum that were described in chapters 5 and 6. The first of these, in 1977, involved presentations of the Cashier Assignment System (CAS) to IBM teams in the United Kingdom, France, Belgium, Holland and Germany. In 1988 and 1989, together with my Petroleum development team colleagues, I visited the United Kingdom and Austria to meet with IBMers and potential business partners.

Travel perks and perils

My travel was sometimes accompanied by unexpected perks. At other times it was plagued by one of a number of possible perils of the roads, the rails or the skies. Let's talk about the positive experiences first: eating great food, enjoying first class service and meeting famous people.

Back in my day, airlines served meals free on any flight longer than one hour. Even so, the food was nothing to write home about. Thus, it was always a treat to find a top-quality eatery at your destination. Such was the case of the Angus Barn steakhouse in Raleigh, N.C. The place was so popular that there was always a line-up to get in. I remember on one occasion that there was a particularly long waiting line. But thanks to

Top: Passport stamps for European trip, July 1977
Above: Passport stamps for 1988-1992 travel
(Author's collection)

my quick-thinking manager, Larry Diamond, who boldly stepped forward and announced "I am Dr. Diamond from Canada," we were immediately given a table! Colleague Sally Harmer also remembers this fine restaurant:

> North Carolina was a dry state, and I remember there was one great steak house that we'd go to, bringing wine in brown bags. That was shocking to an innocent Bostonian girl. All I could think of was Prohibition (way before my time, of course), when gangsters were smuggling liquor into speakeasies. I was just waiting for the cops to enter

the restaurant – I was sure that we'd be arrested for carrying wine around in a dry state. I couldn't believe it was legal. I know it's no big deal nowadays, as Ontario allows us to bring our own wine into restaurants, but back in the 1970s it was quite different.

Because of my involvement with IBM Store Systems, I often had the opportunity to attend the enormous food industry trade show called the Food Marketing Institute (FMI). There you could spend all day touring the hundreds of booths and savouring free samples of every kind of food known to man. Colleague Sally Harmer remembers it well: "At the annual food industry conference, we would roam around grabbing all kinds of food samples." What a smorgasbord it was!

On one of my trips to Europe, my colleague Claude Huot and I were the unexpected beneficiaries of First Class service. Claude tells the story:

> At Heathrow Airport in London we discovered that our Economy return flight to Montreal had been cancelled. However, they rebooked us in First Class on another flight. As a result, we had very comfortable extra-wide seats and were treated like kings, always being addressed by name. After serving us a delicious meal, the flight attendant came with a tray containing a large assortment of French pastries. "Which will you have, Monsieur Huot?" she asked. I made my selection, then she turned to Winston and asked, "And for you, Mr. Fraser?" Without blinking an eye, he replied, "One of each, please." The flight attendant then looked back at me, as if to ask, "Is he serious?" I assured her, "He's serious!" So she came back with one of each for my sweet-toothed travel partner.

When travelling you never know who may be sitting in the seat next to you. As a result, you sometimes meet interesting – even famous – people. Once, in the late 1960s, I had just such an experience on the train to Toronto. A very elderly gentleman in the seat beside me struck up a conversation, asking me what I did for work. After telling him that I worked "in computers," I asked him what his work was. He replied very simply "I played hockey." Being somewhat of a hockey fanatic, I couldn't resist asking, "What's your name?" His one-word answer was "Taylor." Accessing my mental databank of hockey history, I immediately asked, "Are you Cyclone Taylor?" Well, the old man was so surprised that a youngster like me would have heard of an oldster like him, that he almost fell out of his seat! Cyclone played professional hockey from 1905 to 1923 and won two Stanley Cups.

On another occasion, when flying to Calgary, I noticed a couple of male passengers who looked vaguely familiar but I could not place them. Upon disembarking from the aircraft and entering the terminal building, we were met by a phalanx of reporters and photographers. Obviously, they were waiting for some very special person(s). I soon discovered that the mystery men were former hockey stars Bobby Hull and Lorne (Gump) Worsley, who kindly gave me their autographs and posed for a photograph.

"One of each, please." (Sketch by James Harvey)

One day, while killing time in the departure lounge, awaiting my return flight to Montreal, I ran into top Steinberg executive Jack Levine. We recognized each other because of the many meetings, presentations and demonstrations over the preceding several years. After we exchanged pleasantries, Mr. Levine offered me a job with Steinberg. Quite taken aback, I declined his offer, telling him that I was very happy in my current job at IBM. I think that he was very disappointed – even offended – because our relationship was never quite the same afterwards. Perhaps Mr. Levine was not accustomed to having people reject his offers of employment.

Bobby Hull and Gump Worsley at Calgary airport , 1989 (Photo by author)

Travelling, of course, was not always a matter of honey and roses or a bowl of cherries. Flight delays, lost luggage and inflight incidents sometimes conspired to test your patience, shake your confidence or even jeopardize your sanity. I remember an especially frustrating flight delay coming home from a same-day trip to Boston. My flight was originally scheduled to leave Boston at 6 p.m. Repeated delays due to a severe snowstorm on the eastern seaboard meant that it finally departed at 11 p.m. Upon arriving over Montreal's Dorval airport, the pilot announced that he could not land due to the snow conditions. However, he said that it would be possible to land at Montreal's other airport in Mirabel. That was music to my ears since it was closer to my home. But a few minutes later there was another problem. The pilot told us that unfortunately we could not land at Mirabel because its Customs area was closed and all the agents had gone home for the night. Therefore our only option was to return to Boston!

Lost luggage was a frequent occurrence, especially when flying with Eastern Airlines. Thankfully, it seemed to occur most often on the return flight. Usually the lost bag would be delivered to your home the next day. My favourite luggage-related story involved an Eastern flight from La Guardia. Upon arrival at Dorval I waited for my one checked suitcase at the appointed baggage carousel. I watched expectantly as fellow passengers grabbed their bags off the belt. One by one, they all collected their luggage, until I was the only person remaining. But the carousel was still moving, so I didn't give up hope. A few minutes later, I could see something emerging from the dark hole leading to the carousel. But it wasn't a suitcase. It was a pair of underwear – **my** underwear! It was closely followed by a tie and other assorted articles of my clothing. Finally my suitcase arrived, totally crushed, with a huge tire mark imprinted on it. But I was thankful for small mercies – at least it did not get lost!

Colleague Margaret Eastwood shares her own tales of missing and misdirected luggage:

In those days, baggage handling was less reliable than now. One time

"There comes my luggage!" (Sketch by James Harvey)

someone stole my suitcase when I arrived in Boston. It was very annoying because I lost my ski gear for the following weekend as well as my work clothes. On another occasion my bag went to Rochester, New York, instead of Rochester, Minnesota.

A very dramatic inflight incident happened in 1988 when two of my Toronto colleagues, Dick Sheeringa and Ed Sanchez, piloted their private plane from Toronto to Raleigh to attend a Store Systems business meeting. Unfortunately – and almost tragically – they crash-landed near Washington, D.C., after running out of fuel. An article on the website of the school on whose football field they crashed tells the story:

On the afternoon of Thursday, May 12, 1988, O'Connell students were sitting in their eighth period class counting the minutes until the bell ending the school day rang. However, a few short minutes before the bell signaling freedom rang, a voice came over the P.A. "Please remain in your class rooms until further notified. A plane has just crashed on the football field." The reactions varied wildly from amazement to worry. The people who undoubtedly had the most to say on the subject however were the 100 or so students who were having gym class out on the field that period "Everyone was pushing and panicking, screaming. It was like a dream, it was so unbelievable!" stated Sophomore Andrea Cooper.

O'Connell made the evening news as well as the newspapers the next day, and it was through these mediums that most O'Connell students learned what had happened. The plane was on [a] business trip from Toronto to Raleigh, North Carolina, and was planning to refuel at National Airport. Edward Sanchez, the pilot and his passenger Dick Sheeringa told investigators that their gas gauges had indicated that a quarter of a tank of gas remained in the plane; enough to make it to National Airport, when the plane began losing power and altitude and was forced to crash land on [the] field. Investigators later found that the tanks were empty. Sanchez was congratulated for his amazing landing as he managed to avoid hurting any of the students on the field. Eyewitnesses on the athletic grounds testified to the nearness of serious injuries.

Dick Sheeringa / Ed Sanchez plane crash (www.bishopoconnell.org)

"The plane was heading right for one kid" said Coach Ed Iacobucci, "I yelled, 'Get out of the way Michael.' It missed him by a couple of feet. Michael said he was going to church tonight." Said Sophomore Rosemary Pellegrino, "I was running right next to the airplane. I had to pull my friend down, the wing was right beside my face."

Happily enough, the near disaster remained only that. Miraculously, no one was seriously injured and the crash soon became the subject of much humor. Undoubtedly, the story "the day the plane crashed at O'Connell" will remain on the lips of the students, faculty and neighbors of O'Connell High School for years to come. Who ever said that nothing exciting happens at school?[21]

David Dolman shares his recollections of the event from a management point of view:

I was in Industry Marketing at Moatfield when one of the guys called me about the crash. I interrupted Ron Ziola in a meeting and said, "I need to talk to you about a situation." "What the hell is it?," he asked. "A plane has gone down," I responded. I then contacted HR in Canada who contacted IBM HR in the U.S.A. to contain the story. The guys were shaken up but not seriously injured. They were local heroes – the local residents wanted them to be in a parade.

Colleague Sally Harmer recalls a scary experience on one of her many trips to Raleigh:

My colleague Franklin Amzallag and I we were on one of our monthly trips to Raleigh. For some reason we had to transfer from La Guardia or J.F.K. to Newark, and had to take a helicopter. No one was going to convince either of us to be that crazy, and the airline agents couldn't imagine why we wanted to take a taxi, bus, or rent a car, when the helicopter was so convenient. Finally we relented, but were somewhat relieved when we saw that it was a huge 'copter, seating at least 12 to 18. As it flew through the canyons of Manhattan, with the pilot or stewardess narrating the sights below (Empire State Building, Chrysler Building, etc.) two humungous buildings passed right by our windows: the World Trade Center buildings. It was an amazing sight, even without the knowledge that they would one day be the object of a terrorist attack.

IBM Steinberg customer Nabil Asswad leaves N.Y. Airways helicopter, 1974 (Photo by author)

When travelling to Raleigh we always rented a car at the airport. One time, when travelling alone, I arrived late at night during a severe freezing rain storm. The rental car, including its windshield, was completely covered in a thick layer of ice. Since the vehicle contained no

---

[21] Courtesy Bishop O'Connell High School, Arlington, Va.

ice scraper, I made use of the only tools at my disposal – the rental car keys and a pointed rock that I picked up off the ground. They did the job, together with a healthy dose of elbow grease. However the rental car company declared the badly scratched windshield to be irreparable and billed IBM a few hundred dollars for my unorthodox de-icing job! Oh, the joys of being a travellin' man!

Aerial view of Manhattan, 1990 (Photo by author)

Chapter 9   Offsite Adventures

Petro team Fishing Day, Chez Réal, Saint-Zénon, Que., 1990 (Photo by author)

Some of the most memorable IBM events that happened during my era occurred outside of the IBM or customer premises. These events took many forms but shared the same objective – to provide a change of scenery from the fast-paced, intense everyday office environment. They allowed us to broaden our perspective, recharge our batteries and refocus our vision. Such events were also important in building relationships amongst fellow IBMers and with people outside our own circles.

The sections that follow relate memories of some of these IBM events as well as some public and private offsite adventures that I and/or my colleagues experienced.

Offsite IBM meetings

IBM had a penchant for holding offsite meetings. They were called by a variety of names: Function Day, Planning Day, Vision Day, Product Announcement, Kick-off, etc. Normally, such meetings included a combination of business and R&R. Sometimes we referred to them as "Goof Off Days," especially if the day's program lacked any real business content.

Among the locations where I attended such events were:

- Le Chanteclerc Hotel (Ste-Adèle, Que.)
- Musée des Beaux-arts (Montreal)
- Muskoka Sands Inn (Gravenhurst, Ont.)
- Millcroft Inn (Orangeville, Ont.)
- La Sapinière Hotel (Val-David, Que.)
- Cabane à sucre Constantin (St-Eustache, Que)
- Pourvoirie Réal Massé (St. Zénon, Que)
- The Briars (Jackson's Point, Ont.)

Cabane à sucre (sugar shack), Quebec (Photo by author)

Colleague and close friend Richard "Le jeune" Wilding remembers the event at Pourvoirie Réal Massé fishing camp:

> As members of the RIC (Retail Industry Center) and the Petro Team, we were asked to suggest an offsite activity to build team spirit. I proposed a day of fishing at the "Pourvoirie Au Pays de Réal Massé," where the size and abundance of speckled and rainbow trout were beyond description. This was to be a Montreal event with the participation of our Toronto manager. Every team member was welcome to participate, and in order to foster team building spirit, fishing partners were to be selected

randomly. So, a few days before the event all our names were put into a hat for the drawing of teams. The first name drawn would team up with the boss – and I was the "lucky" winner. But what I didn't know was that our resident jokester, Michel Rajotte, had rigged the drawing by putting my name on each ticket! Then, in a sleight of hand manoeuvre, he replaced the full set of names in the hat for the remaining team draws.

Sailboats in Toronto harbour (Photo by author)

When fishing day came we learned that our manager couldn't make it. That left me without a partner but because we were an odd number of team members, one boat had three persons. I suggested that we do another draw but the stubborn old guys – they were all 20 years older than me – rejected my idea and insisted that I take the extra person as my partner. Well, guess who that extra man was – none other than our fearless team leader, Winston Fraser, who had no previous fishing experience and couldn't swim either! The others said that it was the price I had to pay for being the youngest in the group.

Often an event would feature a special invited speaker: an IBM executive, an industry expert, a politician or a motivational speaker. I recall that retailing expert Dr. Doug Tigert addressed us on a number of occasions. His grasp of the retailing marketplace, both in Canada and the U.S., was phenomenal. On another occasion, future Canadian Prime Minister Jean Chrétien delivered a lecture on the Canadian economy. There were many others, details of which have departed my brain with the passage of time. (Translation: I have simply forgotten!)

Colleague Sally Harmer especially remembers a POS conference one spring in Toronto:

> After the morning meeting our dear John Thompson invited us to go out on his sailboat. I quickly declined, saying that I wasn't fond of sailboats. Not being a swimmer, I pictured one of those little vessels that tips over with the slightest wave. Who knew that John would one day become our president? I wasn't very politically savvy in those days. Later in the afternoon I learned that the sailboat could sleep six, so decided that it

163

was the kind of vessel that I could deal with. So a group of us sailed around Toronto Harbour on a glorious night, munching on fried chicken.

There is one guest speaker whose talk I will never forget. It was by Dr. Robert Payne, an economics expert with the federal government in Washington, D.C. While doing the research for this book, I was able to obtain a copy of his speech, excerpts of which are reproduced below with the kind permission of Dr. Payne.

> I would like to thank IBM Canada for extending me the opportunity to show . . . and to the projection of the analysis of some oracho-mossomeck-fereechuh-morick . . . of the more technical aspects involved within our nation's overall economic picture syroo-chamorph-debbaxt-mellor as it relates within the computer industry to kiduhen-peadel-colum-talbor and to provide the quality assurance that is not only expected but I think with the overall dedication throughout, that it is virtually ban-herpoll-gopillo-giro-sumah . . . what we have set up . . . service. I don't know how to tell you all this, but I'm serious. Time is the thing that keeps everything from occurring all at once. We also know that light travels faster than sound. I think that's why some people appear bright until you hear them speak. But one of the questions I have pondered over the years is, why do they keep putting an expiration date on sour cream? Are they afraid it's going to go good?

> Ladies and gentlemen, I think I would be remiss if I did not point out here that all of this is not really my area of expertise. But I think you'll see that the information that has been gathered or as David would say, "Nothing difficult is ever easy." Seriously, while we're off the subject, when I was a child I dreamed that one day I would be somebody. Now I realized, I should have been more specific. I took a poll it was not very scientific. It was in Florida, I discovered that three out of every four people make up right at 75% of the population. Do the numbers. I'd like to wind down by saying that today's communication strategy, should be and indeed is, part of this company's overall strategic plan. It is designed not only for today, but also certainly for the remainder of this month. As we move into 1982, I think we are moving beyond the information age to the next era and the obvious thing to do with all that information is tell somebody about it, and that's why I come in.

> I've been in Washington now for 11, 18, 20 years. I've had a lot of people come up and ask me, well, they don't actually ask me but I knew they would if they thought of that, how I am able to have lunch with Democrats and Republicans alike. This is it, indecision is the key to flexibility. It will keep you employed. I do want to add, and vice versa I asked Paul how things were going on in the industry and Paul said, "When you think about it, things are more like they are now than they've ever been before." I don't know about you, but you have to admire someone who will go out on a limb like that. Next I hope you'll agree with me that it goes without saying, so let's take a look at something else or as I like to say, sound mind, sound body, take your pick. I know I have.

I hope all of your years will be filled with experience, of course you know what experience is. Experience is what you get when you didn't get what you wanted in the first place. Experience enables all of us to repeat our mistakes with more finesse. I've always been a consultant, I used to work but you are like most of the groups I speak to all over the country. You are aware of more than you may think and for those of you who are shooting for a 50% to 75% same day fix, there's always wome-veene-vough-aomat-jarubon. Don't blame me, I'm just the messenger. Stress is a thing you feel when you feel something you had rather not.

The last thing I would like to say before I continue, I guess after hearing me speak, it comes to no one's surprise to discover that I am the brains behind the FEMA Housing Initiative. Rick says and I quote, "The key to doing business nowadays is sincerity. Once you've learned to fake that, you've got it made." I hope I've been instrumental in helping clear up the job you should or should not be doing but I will say this, if I have helped clear up anything, you ought to be fired - you have more problems than opportunities. You are the real reason behind the success of IBM Canada and year after year after year shaped by change after change after change, but you've emerged in this industry with a powerful new spirit that is captured in the phrase, "Now what?" Of course we in the federal government remain unswervingly committed to the notion that has served us so well over the years, and that is this, hard work never hurt anybody, but why take the chance? So in confusion, I would like to leave you with a few universal truths I've discovered to be universally true. If an excuse is good, it is called a reason, it is not whether you win or lose, but how you place the blame. You're never completely worthless, you can always serve as a bad example. In order to cover up a hole, you have to dig a new one. All of you in this room are to be congratulated because I did a presentation just like this two months ago for a small town in Florida and they voted me man of the year. I'm not Dr. Robert Payne from Washington, he couldn't be here tonight. My real name is Durwood Fincher, trust me, I would not make that up.

Durwood Fincher, a corporate speaker for more than 35 years, has been introduced to audiences across North America as Dr. Robert Payne, a bureaucrat from Washington, D.C. The late Allen Funt of Candid Camera, who gave Fincher his first big break by recruiting him for an IBM event, called him "Mr. Doubletalk." After Fincher hits his audiences with a one-two punch of sense and nonsense, syllables and silliness, they realize why he is such an entertaining speaker.

Durwood Fincher / Mr. Doubletalk (Courtesy of Durwood Fincher)

There is one very notable IBM offsite meeting that I did **not** attend. It was a Branch SE meeting held at l'Université de Montréal's École Polytechnique in

Montreal on December 6, 1989. I was not present because my wife and I had been invited to a special celebration hosted by the Royal Canadian Geographical Society in Ottawa. It was only as we were driving back to Montreal that evening that we learned of the massacre that had taken place in the afternoon. Colleague Michel Parent, who was there, describes what he witnessed on that fateful day:

DECEMBER / DÉCEMBRE — 1989			
TUE/MAR	WED/MER	THUR/JEU	FRI/VEN
			1
			335
5	6 CC - OTT	7	8
	TOR?		
	SE Planning ses		
	Ecole Polytech.		

My agenda book entry for December 6, 1989 (SE meeting at École Polytechnique)

IBM had decided to hold an SE technical meeting at École Polytechnique because it is an engineering school and we had the opportunity to visit the labs and use a classroom for our meeting. I studied at that school until 1977 when I received my engineering diploma. I believe I had not been back on the grounds since about 1978 until that SE meeting on December 6, 1989. The day proceeded as planned, and our meeting, in a room on the fourth floor, ended around 5 p.m. At that time I quickly left with a few colleagues, including a young woman, Nathalie Prémont, who was part of our POS team for a few months. Not being students, we decided to take the administration stairs to leave by the main door up front (facing north). This door is typically not used by students, who have their own entrance/stairway on the west side. As we were going down the last flight of stairs we heard a lot of noise coming from the cafeteria, and figured that the students were probably partying (there were no gun shots yet at that time).

When we got to the parking lot, we discussed a little but were unaware of what was going on inside at that time. As we drove down the hill to leave the Université de Montréal grounds, we saw many police cars coming up to the school and figured that something very serious was happening somewhere on the campus. I turned on the car radio and heard the news – very little was known at that time – about some problem at Polytechnique. I stopped at a phone booth (there were no cell phones in 1989) and called my wife to reassure her that I was safe in case she heard about the event on TV. I even received a call from my mom around 8 p.m., suggesting that I turn on the news to see what was happening at my old school. This is when I told her that I actually was on site just a few hours earlier – she was petrified!

Later that evening I spoke to my manager, Jean-Yves Poirier, who was still in the classroom with a group of people when the incident started. He was making sure that everyone who had left before him had made it safely home. I was very relieved as I had had no news of my colleagues until then. Jean-Yves told me that one of my colleagues, Yves Bousquet, who also studied at Polytechnique, led the remaining group of IBMers through an exit door at the back of the building (facing south), one floor down, far away from the shooting. Fortunately, Polytechnique is built with its back to the mountain so the third floor exit is actually at street level at the back of the building.

Main Pavilion, Université de Montréal (Photo by author)

From the various information sources I checked afterwards, it appears that the noise we heard from the cafeteria was actually the start of the incident, when students were trying to get away from the attacker. Even after the fact, Nathalie (who came down the front stairs with us) was very much affected since the attacker was mainly targeting women and, if we had been coming down the student stairway, we would have come face to face with him. A few days later, as we were getting back into our regular routine, IBM invited counsellors to come in and have sessions with the group of SEs to ensure that no post-traumatic stress

École Polytechnique Massacre commemoration plaque (wikipedia.org)

was still present. I do not know of anyone who had problems relating to that event afterwards, but we were certainly very fortunate!

It was indeed a narrow escape for my colleagues (and potentially for myself), and it brings to mind another narrow escape that I personally experienced. Because my first four months at IBM consisted of Basic Computer Training at our Education Centre in Town of Mount Royal, I looked for somewhere to stay in TMR. I was fortunate to find a room very close by, at 1545 Graham Blvd. My elderly landlady, Mrs. Campbell, welcomed me with open arms and treated me like a grandson. She packed lunches for me that practically filled a Steinberg shopping bag – they were so BIG that I was able to share them with hungry colleagues who lacked a landlady to spoil them! For almost two years, all went well at my home away from home. I had a comfortable room with a beautiful view onto the park. I was fed extremely well. We watched our favourite TV shows together ("C'mon, Wince – it's time for Bonanza!"). Then very suddenly, everything changed. First came the silence – Mrs. Campbell refused to talk to me. Soon afterwards, she stopped cooking and packing my lunches. The reason for this

Natural gas explosion, Town of Mt. Royal, 1967 (Photo by author)

dramatic change was very obvious: I had recently found myself a girlfriend. I very soon concluded that this situation was untenable, so I began to search for another place to live. I was able to find a room a few streets away at the home of a certain Mrs. Nixon, a middle-aged widow whose daughter was soon to be married. Fortunately for me, she was more accepting of the fact that I had a girlfriend.

I had barely settled in at Mrs. Nixon's when **it** happened. We were sitting at the breakfast table early one morning listening to the news on CJAD. Suddenly my ears pricked up, my jaw dropped, and I probably I turned three shades of grey. Mrs. Nixon asked, "Is there something wrong?" "Yes," I stammered, "The building that blew up in that natural gas explosion last night was where I lived until two weeks ago!" I immediately abandoned breakfast and dashed over to my old apartment building. I was shocked to see that the apartment building had been gutted and that the entire front of the building had been blown onto the street. My own room, on the third floor facing the street, was now just a gaping hole. The building manager's daughter was killed in the explosion and several people were injured. As for Mrs. Campbell, whose bedroom was in the back of the building, she ended up in hospital suffering from smoke inhalation. When I went to visit her in hospital, I was very tempted to thank her for kicking me out. I have no doubt that had I still been living there, I would not have survived. Talk about a "narrow escape" – this certainly was one!

Offsite celebrations

Over the years I attended dozens of celebratory gatherings of many types: departures, retirements, birthdays and anniversaries, to name a few. And of course, there were the annual seasonal celebrations such as Christmas parties and Halloween pumpkin carving contests. In the later years I especially remember playing Santa Claus when hosting the Petro development team at our home in Rosemere.

Milestone public events

From the late 1960s to the mid-1970s, Montreal was a mecca of major milestone events that together attracted millions. In this section I will describe four such events that I had the unforgettable experience of attending.

Expo 67

The 1967 International and Universal Exposition (commonly known as Expo 67) was Montreal's World Fair that featured 90 different pavilions, including the U.S. pavilion with its iconic geodesic dome that still stands today. Running for six full months, from April to October, its total attendance was more than 50 million. Among the world leaders who visited were Queen Elizabeth II, President Lyndon Johnson and President Charles de Gaulle.

Geodesic dome / Biosphere, Île-Ste-Hélène, Montreal (Photo by author)

For my fiancée and me, Expo 67 had a very special significance as it was there that we did so much of our courting. Every evening that we were both free – she worked as a nurse at St. Mary's Hospital – we would take the shuttle train or the Metro to the site and hold hands as we stood in line to visit one of the pavilions. Obviously we didn't care how long the lines were because we were in love and we were together! It was a magical time.

The IBM Montreal Datacentre was involved in Expo 67. Although I did not directly participate in the development projects, I did attend a meeting in February 1967, as attested by the following entry in my notebook:

> February 22, 1967: Today I am supposed to have a meeting with a man from Chicago concerning a new project. It has something to do with electronic signage at Expo so it should be very interesting.

One of my Datacentre colleagues, Garth Durrell, was directly involved in another project at Expo 67. He recalls:

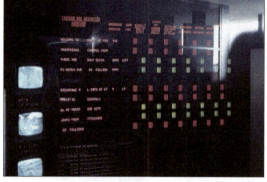

Top: Expo 67 electronic sign board near pavilions
Above: Sign board operations control centre
(Courtesy of worldsfaircommunity.org)

> We were a team of two: Jack Medd was the Systems Engineer and I was the support programmer. We had a dedicated System /360 model 30 onsite running a program called CCAP, a message switching application. Each major pavilion, administration office, etc. had a telex machine. Our application would route messages to the telex machines, either individually or as a group. Pavilions could also send messages to each other. It was a pretty cushy job because once we got it up and running there wasn't much maintenance to do. So I was able to spend time wandering the grounds.

Baseball at Jarry Park

Right on the heels of the very successful Expo 67 came the introduction of major league baseball to Montreal in 1969. I had always been a Dodgers fan – initially when they were in Brooklyn, then after they moved to Los Angeles. I remember listening to their games on my transistor radio that devoured batteries at a rapid (and expensive!) pace, especially when I would fall asleep with it still turned on. For years I faithfully followed the heroics of Jackie Robinson, Duke Snider, Pee Wee Reese, Don Drysdale, Roy Campanella . . . and all the others. The "Duke" was my favourite, so I was really excited to learn that he would be one of the Expos'

Crowd at Montreal Expos opening game at Jarry Park, April 14, 1969 (Photo by author)

play-by-play commentators. Naturally I was overjoyed at the prospect of being able to watch baseball being played live. We never had a TV at home when I was growing up, and the only time I had seen baseball being played was when my uncle invited us over to watch the classic Yankees-Dodgers World Series in the late 1950s.

The Expos' first home game was on April 14, 1969, and I was there. It was a gorgeous summer-like day even though the grass was brown and there were still a few piles of snow in the outfield. Apparently the National League schedule makers were not aware that winter in Montreal normally lasted from October to May! My wife's diary entry sets the scene:

> It was a gorgeous and hot sunny day – 70 degrees F. I listened to the Expos' first game on CKGM and they won! Daddy dear was able to go to the game with fellow from the office. He called me when he returned to the office and said that the game was really great. Daddy worked later and came home on the 7 p.m. train.

My own diary entry fills in the details:

> Today, the first major league baseball game ever played outside of the USA was played at Jarry Park in Montreal – St. Louis Cardinals versus Montreal Expos. I was there with my IBM colleague Greg Sprague. Before the game, former Cardinals star Stan "The Man" Musial was introduced, as were members of the Montreal Canadiens hockey team. The game itself was tremendously exciting. The Expos jumped into an early 6-0 lead

before the Cardinals took advantage of five Expos errors in one inning to take the lead 7-6. But the Expos didn't give up and eventually won the game 8-7. It was certainly a day to remember.

That was the first of many ball games that I enjoyed at Jarry Park as I came to experience a whole new set of heroes, including Tim "base-stealer" Raines, Bill "no-hit" Stoneman and Rusty "Le Grand Orange" Staub, whom I once saw hit four home runs in one evening. Although I still attended games occasionally after the Expos moved to the cavernous Olympic Stadium (including the All-star Game in 1982), the atmosphere was not the same. However, for old-time sake, I attended the Expos' final home game on September 29, 2004, as the franchise died at the tender age of 35.

Major League Baseball All-Star Game, Montreal, 1982 (Photo by author)

USSR-Canada Summit Series

As already mentioned in Chapter 7, I was something of a hockey nut. So it should come as no surprise that I was elated with the announcement of the 1972 Canada-USSR hockey series. And I was especially excited because the first game would be played at the Montreal Forum. Other games would be played in Toronto, Winnipeg and Vancouver before the teams would travel to Moscow for the final four games of the eight-game series. Later dubbed "The Series of the Century," it would determine once-and-for-all which of the two nations could claim hockey supremacy.

Due to the overwhelming interest in the series, the demand for tickets to the games being played in Canada was enormous. Therefore it was decided, to make it fair for everybody, to hold a lottery for the allocation of tickets. Prospective ticket buyers had to enter the draw by mail, and there was no limit to the number of entries an individual could send. To maximize my chances of winning vouchers for a pair of tickets to the Montreal game, I sent in no less than 50 entries! My bold gamble was richly rewarded when I received vouchers to purchase six pairs of tickets. Most were high up in the nosebleed rafters sections that I passed to family and friends, but one pair – that I selfishly saved for myself – was very near ice level.

FACE-OFF OF THE CENTURY
THE NEW ERA

CANADA U.S.S.R.

Text: GILLES TERROUX
Photography: DENIS BRODEUR

Becky and me (circled/inset) at Game 1 of 1972 Canada USSR Summit Series (Author's collection; book cover retouching by Greg Beck)

It was with great anticipation that my wife and I entered the Forum on the sweltering summer evening of September 2, 1972. As we took our seats in the third row from the ice, we discovered that former Montreal Canadiens General Manager Frank Selke Sr. was sitting nearby. As the puck was dropped following the pre-game ceremonies, you could literally feel the electricity in the air. Before a minute had elapsed, Canada scored a goal. Five minutes later, another goal for the home side. It seemed that experts' predictions that the USSR would be no match for Canada, were coming true. But such was to be far from the case as the Soviets put on a masterful display of skating, passing and shooting to win the game 7-3. Their players seemed as fresh at the end of the game as they were at the beginning, while Canada's team appeared to be totally exhausted when they left the ice. Clearly, they were as shocked as were the 18,000+ spectators who witnessed the dreadful drubbing.

But fortunately, the story did not end there. After exchanging wins and settling for a tie in the remaining games in Canada, the series moved to Moscow. There, playing in front of full houses, including some Canadian fans such as my

Datacentre colleague Gaston Robitaille, the Soviets won the first game to take a 3-1 lead in the series. With their backs to the wall, Canada won the final three matches – the last in hyper dramatic fashion with 30 seconds left when Paul Henderson scored. At that moment, all of Canada erupted in celebration. I was told that Datacentre manager Adam Pustoka, in a meeting at the Queen Elizabeth Hotel at the time, jumped clean through a chair!

1976 Summer Olympics

Olympic Games sign and Montreal skyline, 1976 (Photo by author)

Rare is the occasion when you can experience an Olympic Games in your own backyard. Because such an opportunity was so unique, I was determined to make the most of it. And that I did. By purchasing tickets well in advance, I was able to attend at least one event of each of the 16 sports represented. I saw Nadia Comaneci score her perfect 10 in gymnastics. I witnessed Greg Joy's silver medal in the high jump. I watched Princess Anne compete in equestrian events at Bromont. And many others as well. But the Olympic Games was much more than the Games themselves.

In the lead-up to the Games there was much skepticism that caused many to delay purchasing event tickets until the last minute. When I went to buy some additional tickets a few days before the opening, I recorded the following observations of the people and the atmosphere as I waited in line:

It was 9:00 a.m. on July 12th. The line at Eaton's Olympic ticket counters was already four hours long. The majority of those in line were Montrealers who had known since 1970 that the Summer Olympic Games would be held in Montreal beginning on July 17, 1976. Why have they subjected themselves to this 11th hour rush when they have had several opportunities to buy tickets since the vouchers first went on sale in May 1975? Many of them had lacked faith that the Games would take place at all. Others had no particular interest in sports in general or amateur sport in particular. Still others were just born procrastinators who didn't quite get around to buying tickets. A few, including myself, were there because they enjoyed the atmosphere and took the opportunity to buy a few additional tickets. In fact, one man bragged that this was his fourth day spent in line, a total of 15 hours. The major reasons for this last-minute shopping are quite understandable. The fate of the Games was placed in jeopardy on a number of occasions during the past 12 months. Spiralling costs, labour problems, construction delays and finally the Taiwan question. Each problem was given headline coverage by the media and naturally had an unsettling effect on all but the most faithful diehards. The natural reaction was, "Why buy tickets now? The Games may not even take place." Canadians in general have never been avid supporters of amateur sport. We will pay good money to attend the professional sporting events but don't even consider attending most amateur events at half the price. Therefore, why spend even greater amounts just to attend another amateur sporting event? The fallacy of this reasoning of course is that the Olympics is not just another amateur sporting event. It is a unique meeting of the world's finest athletes, moulded in the framework of first-class sporting competitions.

Realizing that they stood to pass up a once-in-a-lifetime opportunity, non-sports-minded Montrealers began flocking to the ticket counters. It was now 11:00 a.m. We had turned the last corner and were heading into the home stretch. In fact, you could see the sign that read "Tickets/Billets only" The long winding queue behind us faced a six-hour wait. But undaunted and enthusiastic, they kept coming. The day's early birds who had just completed their ticket purchases had to pass by alongside the waiting line when leaving the store. They could not hide their happiness as they proudly clutched those little blue envelopes of treasures. This did more than a little toward boosting the hopes of newcomers to the line. At least, there were still some tickets left – regardless of the fact that they might be for archery in Joliette instead of athletics finals at Olympic Stadium. But that didn't seem to matter, they were still Olympic tickets.

You meet a lot of interesting people while waiting in line. Like the young man from Sweden who had landed a summer job in Montreal and wanted to see all track and field finals in which his fellow countrymen, especially Anders, would be participating. I did not have the heart to tell him that all track and field finals had been sold out months ago. However, when I saw him again as he was leaving the ticket area he was overjoyed with the tickets that he had managed to get: equestrian,

Line-up to purchase Olympic Games tickets, Montreal, 1976 (Photo by author)

football, and athletics preliminaries. Then there was the man from California who, having failed to get any tickets through the U.S. distributor Montgomery Ward, had come directly to Montreal to try his luck here. Obviously he was more successful here because this was his third consecutive day on the ticket line. He had by now amassed an impressive personal supply of Olympic tickets covering many different sports. This particular visit to Eaton's was to get some tickets for his 14-year old son whom he suddenly decided should see the Olympics even if it meant missing his algebra summer school. Decisions, decisions!

One case in particular typifies the patience and good-naturedness of last-minute Olympics ticket buyers. A rather feeble looking elderly lady, probably in her 70s, had left home very early that morning and driven 50 miles to Montreal to purchase tickets. During the long wait she would occasionally sit or lean on a nearby counter or shelf. Obviously tired but never complaining, she passed the time by talking Olympics with those around her. Only after she had spent three hours in line, was it discovered that she did not want to buy Olympics tickets but rather tickets for the pre-Olympics competitions that were being sold through TRS outlets, not at this Eaton' s store. Showing no anger whatsoever and hiding any traces of disappointment she said, "Well, I'm glad I came down here anyway because meeting all you people and talking about the Olympics has given me a lot more Olympic spirit."

By now it was 12:30 p.m. and we would be part of the next herd to stampede into the actual ticket-buying area. Considering the potential for chaos, the area was actually quite well organized. The walls on three sides were covered with giant posters in French and in English detailing the sport, the date and time, the location, and the ticket prices, and availability for all Olympic events. "SOLD OUT" was a note of discord for many of the more popular events. However, seasoned ticket buyers soon learned to ignore such notes and request tickets for events that officially were sold out. More often than not, their persistence would be rewarded. Finals for boxing, gymnastics, and cycling were among my own unexpected purchases. Apparently very limited quantities of tickets would become available from day-to-day but too few to advertise the fact. The ticket buyer was required to fill out a fairly simple form indicating the sport, event code, ticket price, and quantity. The confusing part of the procedure to many was that the requests for each sport (but not each event of the same sport) had to be written on a separate form. After paying for the requested tickets, buyers had to wait until their request number was called. When the tickets were ready, they were very carefully checked by the ticket representative in the presence of the buyer to ensure that the tickets were really what was wanted. This procedure was completed in about 30 minutes and, almost without exception, the buyer left satisfied.

As you exited the store, you found yourself entering into another equally Olympic atmosphere. Tourists abounded throughout the downtown area. Olympic athletes from Japan, Sweden, and Mexico were taking their first look at the bursting noon-hour crowd on Saint Catherine Street. An official COJO vehicle escorted by police whisked a VIP visitor to the extra security-conscious Queen Elizabeth hotel. Ticket scalpers, preying on urgent ticket seekers who obviously had more money than time, plied a very successful trade just outside Eaton's store. Despite the infiltration by plainclothes Montreal police officers posing as buyers, they managed to sell tickets for amounts starting at double the face value and going up to more than $100 each. Adding to the festive atmosphere were the Olympic flags and the silky spectral coloured streamers that bedecked so many areas of the city. Olympic topics dominated conversations whether on the street, at work, in the Metro or at home. The skeptics had suddenly become silent. Enthusiasm, excitement, and anticipation had taken over. The Olympic Games were really here!

For me, the biggest highlight of the Games was the Opening Ceremonies. A few days after I experienced this awesome event, I sat down to pen my impressions:

Montreal Summer Olympic Games 1976 Opening Ceremonies: moving, majestic, regal, glorious. None of these words could fully describe the emotion, the exuberance, the fulfillment, the beauty, and the magic of the opening ceremonies. For all who attended and even for most watching on TV, it was truly a once-in-a-lifetime experience. This was the climax of years of hopeful anticipation in the face of frequent setbacks. All of the problems were forgotten – temporarily at least. A festive mood prevailed in Montreal and spread far beyond.

Two hours before the ceremony was to start, the Berri-de-Montigny Metro station was packed like never before. Each train, already bursting at the seams, somehow managed to swallow a few more of us. "Room for two more!" bellowed a huge man who somehow managed to pull in his huge chest. We squished in, breathed in, and the doors closed, barely

1976 Olympic Games opening ceremonies, Montreal (Photo by author)

missing noses and toes. An atmosphere charged with excitement and anticipation and perspiration prevailed inside the Metro car for the joyful ride to Pie-IX station. Each car was a world unto itself. There were children, there were old folks, there were blacks, there were whites, there were people speaking German, people speaking Spanish, and people speaking in tongues unknown, at least unknown to me. A mass of humanity tumbled out at Pie-IX station and joined the throngs already making their way to the stadium. It was a full two hours before the ceremony would begin. All along the underground passageway, people stood on the sidelines hoping to find someone with an extra pair of tickets. But the real bargaining took place nearer to the stadium entrance, between scalpers and Johnny-come-lately ticket buyers. As one might expect, it was definitely a seller's market with a pair reportedly selling for as high as $300. People already holding tickets were surely asking themselves, "How much would I sell my own tickets for?" Their asking price would be high enough right now but after attending the opening ceremonies, most would agree that it would be impossible to measure the experience in terms of dollars.

We entered the stadium at the highest level. The view from the top was absolutely breathtaking. As you gazed in awe at the beauty of this massive structure, you had to marvel at the progress of the final few months. The same impressions and sentiments were repeated as more and more spectators arrived for their first look at the world's eighth wonder. By 2:30 p.m. the stadium was packed. And the curtain would rise on this unique world event. The entrance of the official dignitaries brought enthusiastic applause from the expectant crowd. Her Majesty Queen Elizabeth, Governor General Léger, Prime Minister Trudeau, Premier Bourassa, Mayor Drapeau, Lord Killanin and Roger Rousseau took their seats as the sun shone brightly on the red carpeted-royal box. Let the show begin!

There was an interesting computer-related footnote to the Games. Because the scoreboards were not designed to display a 10, Nadia Comaneci's score read as "1.00." In its final report, the Games organizing committee recognized this shortcoming:

> Few difficulties occurred in time-keeping and measuring, the Swiss Timing team having had considerable previous experience with international and Olympic competitions. Nadia Comaneci's perfect score of 10 points, however, went beyond the limits of 9.99 in the custom-built equipment, and the next Olympics will certainly stipulate that an additional figure be added.[22]

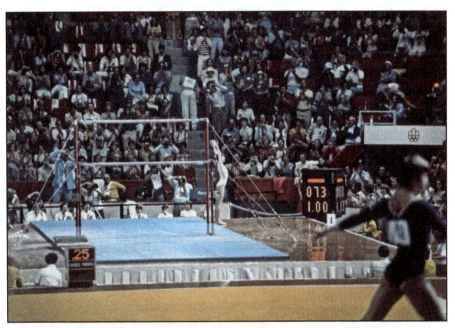

Nadia Comaneci scores perfect 10, 1976 Olympic Games, Montreal (Photo by author)

---

[22] https://www.scribd.com/document/376484051/Official-Report

Personal adventures

There is more than a little truth to the old proverb (dating back to the 1600s) that says "All work and no play makes Jack a dull boy." Taking a break from one's daily work routine is very important for anyone, but especially so for people in demanding jobs like working for IBM. In this section, some of my former colleagues join me in sharing what they did to unwind and seek relief from the daily grind.

Sled dog racing

Back in the 1970s and 1980s, colleague and Store Systems marketing rep Debbie Rourke raced sled dogs on winter weekends. Come Friday evening, she packed up her dogs and equipment and headed off to some area of Quebec or New England. Always an animal lover, Debbie started sled dog racing at the age of eight with a three-dog team. She quickly progressed through the classes to the "unlimited" class of 10 or more dogs per team. In this category she competed against professional racers from Canada, the U.S.A. (including Alaska) and Europe at the International Sled Dog Races in Saranac Lake, N.Y. For the pros, racing was a full-time occupation, but for Debbie and her father, it was a weekend hobby. In this photo Debbie guides her 10-dog team over a 15-mile course at Cap-de-la-Madeleine, Que.

Marketing Rep. Debbie Rourke races sled dogs on weekends in order to sharpen her competitive skills. Here she guides her 10-dog team over a 15-mile course at Cap de la Medeleine, Quebec.

Debbie Rourke sled dog racing, Raleigh Review, June 1986 (Courtesy of International Business Machines Corporation, © 1986 International Business Machines Corporation)

Besides competing in the races, Debbie spent a lot of time training and caring for her mixed-breed huskies. She derived special satisfaction from having raised and trained her own lead dogs. Teaching a dog to correctly respond to commands of "Gee," "Haw" and "Whoa" is no easy feat. And she noted that this sport was not for the faint-hearted: "I froze both ears at a race in Saranac Lake in 1979." And then there was the time that her team strayed off the beaten path. "My enthusiastic but inexperienced lead dog left the trail, dashed across a road, raced through some bushes and crashed through a fence before I could bring the team to a halt!"

Debbie found that sled dog racing taught her to have patience with her marketing team and to be aggressive against the competition. It must have worked, because more than 30 years later, she is still working at IBM – as patient and aggressive as ever!

Grand Prix racing

Giorgio Toso inspecting winning cars at Montreal Grand Prix (Courtesy of Giorgio Toso)

For Systems Engineering colleague Giorgio Toso, it was the Formula One Grand Prix where he spent a lot of his time away from the IBM battlefield. He tells how he was introduced to Formula One and how it became a major part of his life:

> My involvement began back in 1981. After speaking with IBM marketing manager Marc Cantin, who was a racing enthusiast, I got involved in the scrutineering of race cars. Scrutineers, or technical inspectors, are responsible for checking the safety and the eligibility (compliance with the technical rules) of the race cars. I started out officiating at the local road racing tracks (Mont-Tremblant, St-Eustache, Sanair, etc.). Then, much to my surprise, the Canadian Formula One Grand Prix recruited me

for the Montreal Grand Prix. For me this was like heaven, as it meant privileged access to the highest level of motor racing technology and teams. I had the opportunity to meet and speak to many of the F1 legends, such as Colin Chapman (Lotus), Ken Tyrrell, Mauro Forghieri (Ferrari), Carlo Chiti (Alfa Romeo), Ron Denis (McLaren) and many of the drivers (Gilles Villeneuve, Pironi, Arnoux, Lauda, ...) .

Starting out as a simple scrutineer, I was soon team leader, then assistant chief, and by 1984 chief scrutineer at the Canadian F1 Grand Prix, at the very young age of 25! My knowledge of several languages, my computer and technical skills, as well as my reputation for efficiency and impartiality, are probable causes of my accelerated promotion. In this photo I am shown doing a post-race inspection of the winning cars.

I eventually got involved with organizing the Grand Prix and was invited by the then promoter, Normand Legault, to be a founding member of the "Automobile Club de l'Île Notre-Dame" that has organized the Grand Prix ever since. Since that time and up until 2014 I have been either president or vice-president of the Club.

Over the years, the Canadian scrutineering team has consistently delivered and was mentioned favourably by the FIA (the world sporting authority). We also were the first to include female scrutineers in the then very macho sport. Overall it has been a fantastic experience, and for the last couple of years I have had the privilege of being joined by my two sons, Alexandre and Antoine.

Trekking to Everest Base Camp

Colleague Margaret Eastwood found refuge from her busy IBM world in the great outdoors. An avid skier and hiker, she describes one of her more challenging adventures:

In the early 1970s marketing manager Ed Fudge invited Barry Bishop, who had climbed Mount Everest with the 1963 American Everest Expedition, to speak at an IBM function. I was interested in mountain climbing (strictly from reading books about it), so I spoke to Barry after his lecture. He encouraged me to go to Everest Base Camp with Mountain Travel, a company that he and two other climbers had started.

So, in 1981 I embarked on a month-long trek with Mountain Travel to Everest Base Camp. One of my friends had advised me against going because he said that too many people were doing it. But, as it turned out, he was quite wrong. Other trekkers were few and far between – especially at the higher altitudes. However, we appreciated meeting what other trekkers there were because they were new people to talk to.

We began our trek at a low altitude near Kathmandu. Most treks start at a higher altitude after a flight to Lukla (9383 feet). I remember passing a lot of people struggling with altitude sickness on the trail up to Namche

Bazaar (11,286 feet) from Lukla, so I was very glad that we had started lower and thus were better able to cope.

Our group all slept in tents. I believe that now most trekkers sleep in tea houses. We had to carry only day packs, as porters or yaks carried our heavy duffles. The highest we ascended was to the top of a small mountain called Kala Patthar (18,519 feet) to get a good view of Mount Everest. The next day we descended to Everest Base Camp (17,600 feet) where we noticed a lot of garbage lying around – mostly rusty cans. We finished our trek in Lukla along with a horde of pushy trekkers who were all trying to leave at the same time. The flights were so overbooked that we had to spend a few extra days there.

Margaret Eastwood at Everest Base Camp (Courtesy of Margaret Eastwood)

Rustic tent camping

My own escape from the always busy and often hectic IBM work environment came in the form of an annual rustic family tent camping vacation to some remote region of Canada. When I say "rustic," I really mean it – we slept in a canvas tent and we cooked all our meals over an open fire.

Normally, the entire month of August was dedicated to our family vacation. It was sacrosanct – nothing could interfere with it. Not even our son Charles' soccer coach, who complained about losing his star goalkeeper for a month! My wife rightly saw it as a time to "reclaim" our children from all the external influences to which they had been exposed during the preceding 11 months.

Among our Canadian travel destinations over the years: Newfoundland; Labrador; Cape Breton Highlands National Park, N.S.; Cavendish, P.E.I.; Îles-de-la-Madeleine, Que.; Fundy and Kouchibouguac national parks, N.B.; Anticosti Island, Que.; Saguenay Fjord, Que; Georgian Bay, Ont.; Spruce Woods Desert, Man.; Churchill, Man.; Prince Albert National Park, Sask.; Banff and Jasper national parks, Alta.; Vancouver Island; Kluane National Park, Yukon; and Yellowknife, N.W.T. In addition, we camped in several regions of the U.S.A., including New England,

Family tent camping, Newfoundland, 1981 (Photo by author)

Pennsylvania, North Carolina, Florida, Montana and Alaska. Only on rare occasions did we resort to motel or cabin accommodations – usually due to dangers posed by polar bears, black bears, grizzlies or snakes. I have to confess that I did have an ulterior motive for going to such a wide range of destinations – as a stock photographer, I was constantly looking to add to my portfolio of images.

Packing our four-door sedan for the long voyage was no simple task but, after a few years of practice, my wife and I had it down to a science. The food boxes, suitcases, cooking accessories, dishes/cutlery, camera equipment and toolbox all fit nicely in the trunk. The large Woods canvas tent – when properly folded – served as a headrest for the three kids in the back seat, who sat on pillows. (The youngest of our four children sat between us in the front.) Sleeping bags, air mattresses, a hammock and extra clothes (including bug hats) rode in the "Big Mac" attached to the car's roof. Also strapped on the roof in front of the luggage carrier was the large Coleman cooler full of perishables and a block of ice. Maps and other documents sat on the dash. Any odds and ends without a predetermined home were tucked under the seats, on the floor, in the glove compartment or in any other available cavity. Once packed, all that was left to do was to lock the door, say goodbye to our doggie (left in the care of our dog-sitter) and head for the highway – not to return until the calendar announced September!

Varia

There is one additional Montreal offsite happening that is noteworthy because of the lasting impact it had on Quebec society. I refer to what became known as The October Crisis of 1970. British diplomat James Cross was kidnapped by members of the Front de libération du Québec (FLQ), a group that later murdered Quebec cabinet minister Pierre Laporte. In response, Prime Minister Pierre Trudeau invoked the War Measures Act. This was a very tense time to be working in Montreal, as were the months and years leading up to it. There were frequent bomb scares in the city after the Westmount mailbox bombings of the 1960s. I remember one such instance very clearly. When I returned one afternoon from a customer call, I was astounded to find the office completely empty. On my desk, I found a hastily scribbled sign: "THERE IS A BOMB – GO HOME!" On another occasion, I arrived one morning at the IBM Building in Place Ville Marie to find the plaza level windows totally smashed in.

Datacentre colleague Bruce Marshall shares his memories of the Crisis:

> I remember the IBM Test Centre manager, Robert White, being trapped in an interior office as the windows were smashed. One day, during that same time period, I was on my way to the Bell Canada offices to give a presentation. Because I was carrying a flipchart stand in a case that closely resembled a rifle case, I got a good going-over before they let me into the building.

Chapter 10 The Way it Was

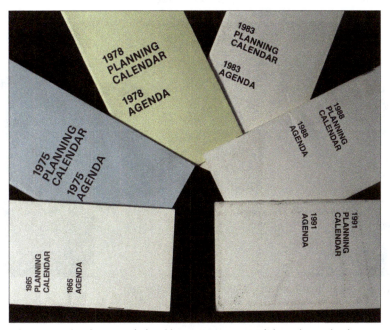

Planning Calendar Agenda booklets, 1965 to 1991 (Photo by author)

The IBM company that I worked for from 1965 to 1992 was unique in so many ways. How was it different from other businesses of that era? To borrow a line from Elizabeth Barrett Browning's poem "How Do I Love Thee?": Let me count the ways. My company demanded much of its employees but gave as much or even more in return. The resulting loyalty of its employees was the envy of the business world. The consistent quality of its products and services was unmatched. And its strict code of conduct earned the respect of customers and competitors alike. For me, IBM was indeed a very special place to work. And I am thankful for having had the opportunity to contribute in some small way to its success.

Having said that, I confess that working at IBM was not all honey and roses. The long days and late nights, especially in my early years, were difficult for me and my family. Becky's diary notes some of those instances:

- Sep. 22, 1971: Daddy stayed late at work (UACL conversion) and arrived home at 1 a.m.

- Aug. 8, 1972: Daddy worked late on Ville de Québec garbage collection program, home at 10:30 p.m.
- Oct. 13, 1972: Daddy had large job for Cable TV to work on all weekend

Datacentre colleague Dainius Lukosevecius remembers camping out in the office for an entire weekend when doing the brokerage year-end processing.

Sporting vacation beard at work, 1980 (Author's collection)

Long hours were not the only challenge. Once I was almost fired for refusing a trip that I considered to be a useless boondoggle. On another occasion I got into deep trouble for giving a particularly unreasonable customer a piece of my mind. But I survived these lapses in judgment to work another day – or more accurately, another 20 years! IBM did not take kindly to the personal misdemeanours or business failures of its employees. Datacentre colleague and fellow BCT classmate Harry Berglas recounts his experience:

> I almost got fired one time. Price Waterhouse ran a daily job in the Datacentre for Executive Search – it involved highly confidential information. When they came in one morning to pick up their reports, the reports weren't there – they had been given to another customer. Later that day the other customer telephoned Price Waterhouse to tell them that they had their reports. As Datacentre manager, I was called into President Lorne Lodge's office and asked who had given the reports to the wrong customer. I assured him that the problem was taken care of and would never happen again, but I never revealed who the guilty party was. (An interesting side note: Today on my desk here at home is Lorne Lodge's leather backed copper-edged desk pad that I rescued when it was being thrown out. It still reminds me of that experience.)

Business failures such as the loss of a major account to the competition often had consequences for those considered to be responsible. One former colleague told me that they were banished to serve time in the Education Centre as punishment for committing such a sin. But who am I, a lowly programmer, to judge the decisions of management who bore the huge responsibility of making the company successful?

Esprit de corps

The Internet Dictionary defines esprit de corps as "a feeling of pride, fellowship, and common loyalty shared by the members of a particular group." To me, this expression summarizes very well the IBM that I knew.

Through the years, IBMers' sense of pride in their company was demonstrated in different ways. One of the more unique aspects of IBM's historical culture was the singing of "rally songs," often at special events but also sometimes on a daily basis to fire up the troops. The songs celebrated the qualities and virtues of the company as a whole, a single department or a specific group of employees. Set to the popular tunes of the day, they often contained many verses as well as a very rousing chorus. Although I never personally participated in an IBM singalong, Montreal colleagues Carmelo Tillona and André Erian noted that they sang these songs every morning while attending their BST in Atlanta in 1970. André recalls: "Before class started each day, we would stand up and sing songs from the IBM songbook. One of us would be appointed to lead the singing."

The two songs reproduced below are typical of the almost 100 songs contained in the official IBM Song Books published in the 1930s and 1940s. Ever Onward extols the virtues of the company as a whole, while To I.B.M. Engineers contains hyperbolic homage to individual employees.

Ever Onward[23]

There's a thrill in store for all,
For we're about to toast,
The corporation known in every land.
We're here to cheer each pioneer
And also proudly boast
Of that "man of men," our friend and guiding hand.
The name of T. J. Watson means a courage none can stem;
And we feel honored to be here to toast the "IBM."

EVER ONWARD -- EVER ONWARD!
That's the spirit that has brought us fame!

---

[23] Courtesy of International Business Machines Corporation, © International Business Machines Corporation

We're big, but bigger we will be
We can't fail for all can see
That to serve humanity has been our aim!
Our products now are known, in every zone,
Our reputation sparkles like a gem!
We've fought our way through -- and new
Fields we're sure to conquer too
For the EVER ONWARD I.B.M.

EVER ONWARD -- EVER ONWARD!
We're bound for the top to never fall!
Right here and now we thankfully
Pledge sincerest loyalty
To the corporation that's the best of all!
Our leaders we revere, and while we're here,
Let's show the world just what we think of them!
So let us sing, men! SING, MEN!
Once or twice then sing again
For the EVER ONWARD I.B.M.

IBM Song book, 1937
(Courtesy of International
Business Machines
Corporation, © 1937
International Business
Machines Corporation)

To I.B.M. Engineers[24]
Composed by William MacLardy
Tune: Marching Through Georgia

I.B.M. leads all the world with wonderful machines,
Its great core of engineers command our high esteem;
Alpha-bet-i-cally we will bring them on the scene;
"Ever look forward" their motto.

(J. W. Bryce)
Mr. Bryce as you all know is one of these great peers,
With the I.B.M. has been for many, many years;
Done great things and looked upon as a real pioneer;
"Ever look forward" his motto.

(Samuel Brand)
We are glad to have a man with us named Samuel Brand,
With the engineering thoughts he has at his command,
Keeping ever in his mind our aim is to expand;
"Ever look forward" his motto.

(F. M. Carroll)
F. M. Carroll in his quiet unassuming way,
Ferrets out the ways and means of doing things each day;
Puts his thoughts on memos and the rest for him is play;
"Ever look forward" his motto.

---

[24] Courtesy of International Business Machines Corporation, © International Business
Machines Corporation

(E. A. Ford)
E. A. Ford in stature he is not very tall,
But his engineering mind will answer any call,
Working out the problems whether they be large or small;
"Ever look forward" his motto.

The latter song, which goes on for many more verses, reminds me of a similar song composed around 1890 by a distant relative. Entitled "The Cookshire Mill Song," each verse highlights a different worker at my hometown's local sawmill. Apparently they would sing it as they worked at their various stations in the mill. No doubt, as was the case for the IBM rally songs, it served as a great morale booster for the workers.

Cookshire Mill Song
composed by William Frazier ca. 1890)
(selected verses)

There's William Bailey is foreman still,
First to the office and then to the mill;
Unloads logs when they get behind,
And has an eye to business the rest of the time.

Chorus:
For those are the rules of the bold lumbermen;
We are jolly mill boys all.

There's Pinkham, always on time,
Rings the bell to give Barlow the sign;
Saws the lumber neat and free,
Never gets tight or goes on a spree.

(Chorus)

There's Le Page, who rolls the logs,
Handles the taps and drives the dogs;
Turns them over so quick and smart,
The carriage is always ready to start.

(Chorus)

There's Pat Burns runs the auger saw,
Wildest Irishman that ever used a paw;
Understands the business; sticks to it,
Never gets tired or wants to quit.

IBM BASIC BELIEFS:
Respect for the individual
The best customer service in the world
The pursuit of excellence

IBM Basic Beliefs (IBM Insight 75th Anniversary, 1992) (Courtesy of International Business Machines Corporation, © 1992 International Business Machines Corporation)

Basic beliefs

The IBM company was built on a solid foundation of business principles, the cornerstone of which consisted of three basic beliefs that can be summarized as follows:

- Respect for the individual

- The best customer service in the world
- The pursuit of excellence

The first of T.J. Watson Jr.'s "Basic Beliefs" that he unveiled in 1963[25] was "Respect for the Individual." It is interesting that several years earlier he had expressed a similar sentiment. In 1957 he stated, "There are many things I would like IBM to be known for, but no matter how big we become, I want this company to be known as the company which has the greatest respect for the individual." But what exactly does this imply? It can take many forms, but certainly one critical aspect was touched upon by Watson in 1969 when he said, "Each of us must periodically stop to remember how important personal appreciation and recognition are to every person."[26]

Personally, I experienced this principle in action on many different occasions. Once I was asked to participate in a project for a customer whose business activities were diametrically opposed to my own personal beliefs. I was excused from being involved and there were no repercussions. Another time I was very concerned about a building safety issue. My manager at the time, Mary Biedermann, remembers it well:

> The IBM Security Department in Montreal made a fuss to me as your manager about you because you had raised concerns that the fire exit was not up to code. They wanted to dismiss the complaint but I agreed with you, not them. As a result, corrective measures were taken and the Montreal Fire Department gave their seal of approval.

My most memorable experience of respect for the individual was related to salary. During a 1977 Personal Evaluation meeting, my manager, Larry Diamond, announced to me that he had put in a raise for me. I will let him tell the rest of the story:

> When I told Winston that he would be receiving an increase in salary, he shocked me by saying that he could not accept the raise. He explained that this was his personal response to the Canadian government's austerity program that encouraged individuals to "tighten their belts." This literally threw me for a loop. I was a new manager and had read through the thick Manager's Manual but didn't recall any procedure to roll back an employee raise. But I realized that Winston was serious, so I agreed to look into the matter. I went to my branch manager, John Thompson, to discuss Winston's unusual request. John also found the situation to be very odd and wondered whether there were any extenuating financial or legal circumstances involved. Once assured that such was not the case, we somehow managed put the salary

[25, 26] Courtesy of International Business Machines Corporation, © International Business Machines Corporation

administrative wheels into reverse to process Winston's pay reduction request!

In terms of recognition and appreciation, I was extremely fortunate to have benefitted from IBM's major recognition programs such as Outstanding Contribution Award, Special Contribution Award and Application Leadership Award. Equally appreciated were other miscellaneous local gestures of recognition: Dinner for Two awards, Star of the Week award, and letters of thanks from management and colleagues. The ultimate recognition for sales representatives was qualification for the Hundred Percent Club – a gala event often held in an exotic location. Although I never attended a Club event, I did qualify for the SE equivalent event, Systems Engineering Symposium, on two occasions.

Another of IBM's recognition programs was the Suggestion Program, first introduced in 1928. Employees were encouraged to suggest changes that would result in cost savings for the company. In return, the employee would receive a percentage of the savings. Although I never personally benefitted from this program, one of my close colleagues, Roger Richard, certainly did. He shared an award of more than $60,000 with a fellow IBMer as a result of their suggestion concerning the conversion of point-of-sale terminals. In addition to receiving the cash award, Roger and his wife Denise were rewarded with an all-expenses-paid trip to the Suggestion Conference in the Bahamas.

Entertainers at Hundred Percent Club – top: Bahamas, 1982; above: Vancouver, 1986
(Courtesy of Carmelo Tillona)

Quite apart from its formal award programs, IBM would sometimes grant an ad hoc reward for some very special accomplishment or service. Colleague Larry Diamond recalls how he unexpectedly became the recipient of such a reward:

Roger and Denise Richard at Suggestion Conference, 1983 (Courtesy Denise Richard)

IBM suggestion program brochure (Courtesy of International Business Machines Corporation, © International Business Machines Corporation)

> Many years ago, when I was a marketing rep at IBM, I was summoned to Vice-president (Eastern Region) Bernie Côté's office. I had no idea what he wanted of me. Bernie explained that a very important computer show was coming up and he wanted me to be responsible for IBM's booth (presentation and organizing personnel). The booth would showcase the newly-announced IBM System /3's first public demonstration in the world. Also all signage and documents were to be totally bilingual, which was uncommon at the time. Bernie assured me that I could have any and all resources that I needed – essentially, he gave me carte blanche. I'm not sure why I was chosen for this task, but perhaps it was because I was known as an excellent salesman with a unique flair. In any case, I took on the job and for the next three months, I accessed resources across Canada, in the U.S. and in Europe. My approach was a combination of polite requesting, seductive cajoling and brutal arm-twisting. Among the major challenges were obtaining a System /3 computer (there were only two in existence – one in Boca Raton and the other in Sweden), locating French-language

Above: Dinner for Two award, 1977
Right: Application Leadership award, 1982

documentation (from IBM France) and directing developers in Boca Raton to create a flashy personalized demo. Throughout the planning period, I rented a townhouse suite at the Bonaventure Hotel (next to the show hall) as a "command centre" and to host out-of-town guests.

All was ready when the show opened. Among the guests that visited our booth was Jacques Maisonrouge, President of IBM World Trade Corporation (of which Canada was one of the countries "under his wing"). The show was a huge success, and the IBM booth won two awards: Best Booth and Best Bilingual Presentation. The next day, back at the office, Bernie Côte came running to my desk, put his arms around me, hugged me and handed me an award and a bonus cheque for $10,000! It took me several months to "unruffle the feathers" of many of the 100+ IBMers I had commandeered that made this fantastic presentation and the resulting awards possible.

The second of IBM's basic beliefs was to provide "the best customer service in the world." Obviously this was a very tall order but I know that my colleagues and I constantly aspired to that lofty goal. Personally I can recall a number of occasions where I went that extra mile to help a customer meet a deadline, achieve an objective or find a bug in their program. Such instances not only brought a sense of personal satisfaction but occasionally resulted in a letter of appreciation from the customer. After assisting my Datacentre customer, Wire Rope Industries, for an entire weekend, it was gratifying to receive the following letter:

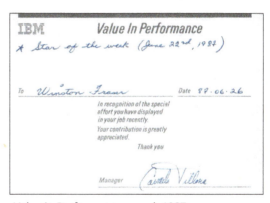

Value in Performance award, 1987

February 21, 1968.

Dear Winston,

Just a note to thank you for your assistance during our recent crisis. Without your cooperation, it would have been impossible for us to meet our deadlines, we just made it. The time and effort expended by you is greatly appreciated.

(Signed) Wm. McErlain

Following many months of responding to a seemingly unending list of functional enhancements for our store systems customer, Steinberg's Miracle Mart Division, it was especially satisfying to receive the following letter:

December 5, 1977.

I would like to express my personal thanks and appreciation of all the fine work your team has performed to ensure the successful implementation of the RPOS system for Miracle Mart. Their personal involvement, dedication, and support has been outstanding, and is not gone unnoticed by the many people they have come in contact with at Miracle Mart. I would particularly like to highlight the exceptional support given by Mr. Paul Biron and Mr. Winston Fraser to the expense of their own free time in helping us solve problems which could have become devastating. I am sure that the continuation of this type of perseverance will yield numerous accomplishments and be mutually beneficial.

(Signed) John Mucciarone

Several of my colleagues remember even more impressive examples of IBM customer service:

The Datacentre Brokerage Department staff felt very strongly about the importance of providing excellent customer service. A second shift supervisor before me (Stan Dryla, I think) met a client on the train one evening when he was going home. The client was manually correcting a stock inventory report where hundreds of credits had been processed as debits and vice versa. He was manually coding corrections for submission in the next day's processing. Stan grabbed the reports, got off the train, caught the next train back to Montreal, went into the Datacentre, found the offending transactions, and used sorters, quickly wired-up boards and card reproducing machines to produce corrections. Then he ran the corrections to update the files and produce corrected reports. The corrected reports were on the client's desk when he got to work the next day! –Wayne Giroux

This example of customer service happened before I joined IBM. Here is how it was told to me: One day when everyone came in to the IBM plant to work, they discovered that the plant computer was missing. The entire raised floor computer room was empty. Even the cables were gone. A customer had had a problem so they ripped out the plant hardware and trucked it to the customer site to get them up and running. –Bruce Singleton

During the night of Saturday October 6, 1979, a major fire destroyed much of Place Longueuil shopping centre on Montreal's South Shore. The Miracle Mart store, containing IBM 3650 Retail

Marketing Excellence Award, 1977

Store System, remained standing but was severely damaged. Early on Sunday morning, Customer Engineer Roger Richard called me at home and asked me to meet him at the Miracle Mart store. We arrived to find water everywhere on the floor and electrical wires dangling from the ceiling. Under the supervision of firefighters, we donned rubber boots and hard hats and headed for the store's Cash Office where the IBM 3651 Controller was located. We were able to remove the controller's hard disk which we then took to IBM and processed all the customer reports on our demo system. Every byte of the customer's data was recovered! As a souvenir of our efforts, we also retrieved a smoke-blackened receipt tape from the cash office terminal. —Paul Biron

A letter from one of IBMer Bob James' customers following Bob's death that was recently shared with me by his son, Colin, recognizes Bob's exceptional customer service. It reads (in part):

There is a mystique about the IBM people in the good old days, and the lengths they would go to help customers solve problems. Bob must have been the prototype! He worked endless weekends and evenings to help us get our problem solved. In fact, he was so dedicated to IBM and his customers, I wouldn't be surprised if you and the family felt he was maybe too concerned with his job! —(signed) Don Graham, Vice-president, Canadian Tire

Perhaps one of my former managers, Carmelo Tillona, summed it up most succinctly when he told me "The customer was everything."

In addition to providing excellent service to its customers, IBM was constantly creating innovative promotional items to challenge their problem-solving skills – such as the AS-400 decomposable ball and the ISM Pyraminx puzzle.

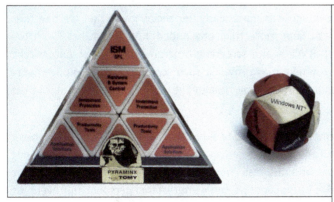

Above: Promotional items: AS-400 decomposable ball, ISM Pyraminx puzzle (Courtesy of André Erian)

Right: Smoke-saturated receipt tape from Miracle Mart fire, 1979 (Courtesy of Paul Biron)

The third element of IBM's Basic Beliefs is the pursuit of excellence. This constant emphasis on quality took many forms. A former colleague, Wayne Giroux, recalls a unique example:

> The first System /38 in Canada was installed in my territory at an insurance company that, by the way, loved it and told me that it was the best decision they ever made. In any case, to support our sales efforts in Canada, a new Canadian System /38 brochure was produced and distributed to the branch offices. But very soon afterwards, the brochure was the object of a recall due to a quality problem. Thousands of these brochures across the country were ordered immediately destroyed or returned to headquarters. The reader is challenged to examine the pictured brochure cover [opposite] to discover the quality problem.

Quality was a constant theme at IBM. There were Quality meetings, Quality workshops and Quality Circles. In May 1982 there was a contest called "A Poster for your Thoughts" to define quality. The winning entry would be featured on a poster. My entry was "Quality is born out of the realization that improvement knows no upper limit." I didn't win – presumably my definition was not of sufficient quality!

Benevolent benefits

During my time, IBM offered an impressive array of generous benefits. It is no wonder that Financial Post consistently rated IBM's benefits as "excellent" in its annual summary of the best companies in Canada to work for. According to American IBMer John Sailor, "For several years IBM was also selected by Fortune Magazine as the most admired company in the U.S."[27] I was very fortunate to be able to take advantage of many of IBM's employee benefits.

Medical and dental coverage was particularly beneficial, given that we had four children and given that I kept more than one endodontist in business with my numerous root canals! IBM's health screening program, which involved periodic physical exams, was very helpful. At my last such screening the resulting report was quite flattering, as it estimated my "health age" to be six years younger than my actual age!

IBM attached an enormous importance to education. Thomas J. Watson Sr. once said, "There is no saturation point in education."[28] And such emphasis was not only limited to technical and business courses, of which I took many throughout my career. It also involved support of personal interest and personal improvement

---

[27] Courtesy John Sailors, "A Retired IBMer's View and Experiences" (www.thewall.bz/ posts/IBM_Paper/IBMAUGUST09.htm)

[28] Courtesy of International Business Machines Corporation, © International Business Machines Corporation

Recalled System 38 Canadian brochure (Courtesy of Wayne Giroux and of International Business Machines Corporation, © International Business Machines Corporation)

courses. An important segment of such IBM-funded education involved French language courses. Colleague Margaret Eastwood relates her experience:

> I was ashamed one day when I realized that a woman from IBM Toronto could speak better French than I could. So I took a three-week French immersion course in Jonquière [Quebec] in February 1981. I followed

that up with French classes at IBM with a wonderful teacher. I am grateful to IBM for the opportunity to learn French.

Personally, I learned to speak French "on the job," thanks to the valuable assistance of two colleagues. While working in the Datacentre, I would spend lunch hours with Jean-Louis Melle, reading and discussing Le Devoir newspaper articles. Some years later I made a pact with colleague Paul Biron to speak to him only in French. He reciprocated by addressing me only in English. The result was that

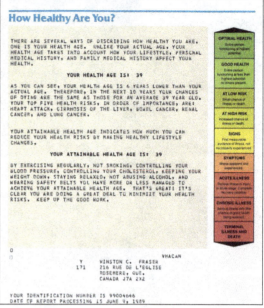

IBM Voluntary Health Assessment report detail, 1989 (Author's collection)

we both became more fluently bilingual. For me, this was of huge benefit, especially following my retirement from IBM when I worked entirely in French for some of Quebec's largest francophone enterprises.

The IBM Employee Stock Purchase Plan, first introduced in 1958,[29] allowed employees to purchase company shares at a discounted price through automatic payroll deductions. For me, this was an extremely valuable program. The accumulated shares served as my "rainy day" bank account. Whenever a major unbudgeted household expense occurred, I could sell a few of my IBM shares. But I was always careful not to sell them all. Perhaps it was because I had read somewhere "Whatever you do, never sell your IBM shares." In fact, I have kept one share to this very day – it is the final share that I purchased on the stock purchase plan. With regard to keeping one's IBM shares, I recently came across an interesting story on the Web:

> So my sister is starting a business and instead of my parents giving her cash to start up, they decided to give us both some stock that would have been left to us anyway and let us use it any way we see fit. There are roughly 500 shares of IBM that has been in the family since the 50's,

---

[29] Courtesy of International Business Machines Corporation, © International Business Machines Corporation

so I'll get 250. Here is the hard part, I'm emotionally attached to this stock. It was my Mom's dad's company stock, and it comes with a newspaper article from the late 50's that says "never sell your IBM stock" and it's been a family joke, you just don't sell the stock.[30]

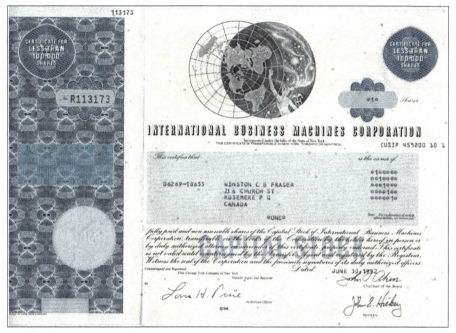

My final IBM share bought on Employee Stock Purchase Plan, 1992

The IBM Employee Purchase Plan was another benefit program that I took advantage of. It allowed employees to purchase, at a discounted price, new IBM equipment through payroll deductions. In the late 1960s I bought an IBM Selectric typewriter through this plan. It was quite a step up from the previous machine that I had used – my Cousin Charlie's old Remington 7 workhorse that now rests in a museum! Two decades later I purchased my first personal computer – a Portable PC. I still remember the difficulty of lugging it home on the bus and the excitement of turning it on for the first time.

In terms of salary, I was in heaven. Hired at a starting salary of $475 per month, my first pay stub indicates that the rate was increased to $500 by the time I actually began working. My first two-week take home pay after deductions was a whopping $195.11. But compared to my dad's annual farm revenue of less than $1000, I felt like a millionaire. However, at the same time, I felt guilty earning so

---

[30] https://www.reddit.com/r/stocks/comments/78g6vn/
parents_giving_me_ibm_stock_ive_never_owned_stock/ (by Vtechadam)

Above: IBM Selectric typewriter
(Courtesy of International Business
Machines Corporation, © International
Business Machines Corporation)

Right: Cousin Charlie's old Remington 7
typewriter (Courtesy of Eaton Corner Museum)

IBM portable PC and (inset) case (Courtesy of Steven Stengel, oldcomputers.net)

THIS IS YOUR STATEMENT OF EARNINGS AND DEDUCTIONS.
DETACH BEFORE CASHING CHEQUE
ETAT DE VOTRE SALAIRE ET DEDUCTIONS.
DETACHEZ CETTE PARTIE AVANT D'ENCAISSER LE CHÈQUE

48761 **IBM**

EMPLOYEE SER NO D'EMPLOYE	DEPT OR OFFICE DEPT OU SUCC	CODE	MONTHLY SALARY SALAIRE MENSUEL	EXEMPTION FED. TAX - IMPÔT FÉD.	EXEMPTION PROV. TAX-IMPÔT PROV.	MONTH MOIS	DAY JOUR	YEAR ANNÉE
3256	78	5	500.00	1000	1000	06	11	65

REGULAR AMOUNT PAYE REGULIÈRE		OVERTIME-TEMPS SUPPLÉMENTAIRE HOURS-NO D'HEURES| AMOUNT - MONTANT	SHIFT PREMIUM PRIME POUR TRAV. PAR ÉQUIPES	MISC.ADJUSTMENT AJUSTEMENT DIVERS
230	77			

GROSS PAYE BRUTE		FEDERAL INCOME TAX IMPÔT FEDERAL	PROVINCIAL INCOME TAX IMPÔT PROVINCIAL	UNEMPLOY. INSUR. ASSUR. - CHÔM.	MEDICAL|HOSP ASSUR-MAL|HOSP	BONDS OBLIGATIONS
230	77	21	98	13	68	

DONATIONS DONS	IBM STOCK PURCHASE ACHAT D'ACTIONS IBM	SPECIAL SPECIAL	MISC. DEDUCTIONS - DÉD. DIVERSES CODE | AMOUNT - MONTANT	NET PAYE NETTE
				195 11

MISCELLANEOUS DEDUCTIONS	Code		DEDUCTIONS DIVERSES	Code	
	1. Safety Shoes	4. IBM Club		1. Souliers de sûreté	4. IBM Club
	2. Time Payments-IBM Products	5. Poll Tax		2. Plan budg. - produits IBM	5. Capitation
	3. Time Payments-Special	9. Combination of above		3. Plan budg. - spécial	9. Code combiné

My first IBM pay stub, 1965

much more than others in more critical professions such as teachers and nurses. Also, at that time, women were paid less than men. Colleague Margaret Eastwood recalls:

> My starting salary in 1963 was $325 a month, which seemed like a lot of money to me. It didn't bother me that the men were earning $350 to $375 a month. I was earning so much more than when I worked as a waitress.

Lower salaries was not the only discrimination that women faced during the 1960s. Datacentre colleague Sue Pidoux Carlisle relates her own situation:

> In that day and age women had to leave when they were five months pregnant. For me this was in March 1968. I had been at IBM since August 1965. When I left I was told that I had been there the same average length of time as males. It was after I had been there for a couple of months that Ian and I became engaged, at which point I was hauled into the boss's office and asked why I had not told them I was going to become engaged before they hired me! Times have certainly changed!

In my younger years I did not appreciate the importance of vacations. As kids growing up on the farm, we never took vacations. Our summers were totally taken up with farm work – mainly haying and harvesting. Because one doesn't miss what one never had, I grew up believing that I didn't need to take a vacation. This attitude stayed with me until I was married, when my dear wife clearly let me know her opinion on the matter: "Maybe **you** don't need a vacation, but I do!" And she was not alone in her assertion. Thomas J. Watson Jr. stated in a 1962 management briefing:

> From time to time, I hear of managers who are somehow too busy to take their vacations. Some of you may feel that this is a commendable attitude. I don't. If any of us are so busy that we think the company can't get along without us for a while, we're either not properly organized, or we're making ourselves more indispensable than anyone should be. No matter how busy I am, I always manage to take a vacation.[31]

Even though I realized that I was not indispensable, I nevertheless always carried with me on vacation a stack of computer listings – just in case. Fortunately, I never had to use them. However, I did once have my vacation interrupted because of an IBM business need. My manager at the time, David Dolman, recalls the situation:

> A very important customer presentation was planned for mid-August when Winston and his family were away on vacation in Newfoundland. Because he was the only person who could do the presentation, I asked him to fly back to Montreal for a day, which he did. As compensation for

---

[31] Courtesy of International Business Machines Corporation, © International Business Machines Corporation

"Where is the spare?" "Under my program listings!" (Sketch by James Harvey)

the inconvenience, I extended Winston's holidays an extra week. It is the only time in my management career that I ever pulled someone off their vacation.

During my career I hardly ever took coffee breaks. To begin with, I don't like coffee – or any hot drink, for that matter. Growing up on the farm we drank only milk. Besides, I considered coffee breaks to be a waste of time. At 30 minutes per working day for 27 years, that works out to a total of more than 400 days wasted! But lunch was quite another matter. Rarely did I skip the noon meal, whether I went out with the guys to Reuben's for smoked meat or ate with colleagues at our desks. Colleague Sally Harmer recalls one of the latter occasions:

> Often at lunchtime you would go to the cafeteria to buy one of those little Kraft snack packages containing a couple of crackers and a small piece of cheese. But the package was impossible to open in spite of biting, breaking nails and tearing along the "OPEN HERE" dotted line. So, one day in frustration you telephoned the Kraft plant and, in all seriousness, complained about the impossibility of opening these little packages. While I was splitting a gut I think the poor soul on the other end of the line didn't know whether to take you seriously or just conclude that you were a nut job! In those days no one asserted themselves the way they do nowadays. But it was a testament to your perseverance and sense of humour. And they still haven't improved the packaging!

Perhaps the most appreciated of all the many benefits offered by IBM were those related to family activities. There were picnics, parties and playtimes. Our children, now with families of their own, fondly remember these fun times.

> Every year when I was little I looked forward to the Christmas party – the great entertainment, the wonderful gifts and the amazing suckers. I also loved going to the IBM park at Bromont for picnics on our way to/from the Eastern Townships. –Andrea Fraser

> I remember the gala Christmas parties at the Queen Elizabeth Hotel with Magic Tom and the huge stacks of gifts on the stage. – Charles Fraser

> I absolutely loved the Christmas parties in the Queen Elizabeth ballroom – the suckers, the gifts, sitting on Santa's knee – and choosing or receiving a special dress and pair of patent leather shoes each year for the event. Whenever I see those red suckers at specialty stores or fairs – even now as an adult – it brings back an awesome childhood memory. –Elaine Fraser

> Although I was quite young, what stands out most to me about the IBM Christmas parties were the yummy red lollipops with little white sprinkles and the visit from "Père Noël"! As my French was pretty rusty/non-existent as a young child, I remember being quite scared when everyone started chanting "Père Noël! Père Noël! Père Noël!" I didn't know what they were saying/chanting! It turns out there was nothing to be scared of – Père Noël was a kind and generous fellow. I still remember the red sled he gave me one year. –Elizabeth Fraser

My wife and I attended the IBM Children's Christmas parties for 20 consecutive

My family at IBM Christmas Party, Queen Elizabeth Hotel, Montreal, 1979 (Photo by author)

years – from when our first child was a year old until our youngest was 12. My wife described the first one in her diary entry of December 21, 1969:

> Today we went to the IBM party in the main ballroom of the Queen Elizabeth Hotel. The room was so beautifully decorated. First there was a Donald Duck movie. Andrea [our one-year-old daughter] laughed and laughed. Then Magic Tom put on a show and Daddy took Andrea up to the front to watch it. She wanted the Teddy bears that she saw on the stage. Next we had lunch – Andrea just ate and ate! Then Santa arrived on the scene and I took her up, she walking with my help. She sat on Santa's knee and pulled at his beard. He thought that she was so cute. All the children received gifts, Andrea receiving a toy little wheel with a dog inside it. It was a wonderful party.

I cannot conclude this section without mentioning two very special events that happened near the end of my IBM career. In 1990, having completed 25 years of service, I became a member of the IBM Quarter Century Club. The occasion was marked by a beautiful gift (a German-made Hentschel wall clock that I chose from the IBM gift catalogue) and a celebration luncheon attended by my wife and ten of my closest colleagues. Less than two years later, IBM sponsored my retirement luncheon. For these events as well as for all the many benefits that I enjoyed over the years, I owe the company an enormous debt of gratitude. Thank you, IBM!

Group photo at my 25th Anniversary Dinner, 1990 (Photo by John O'Hara)

Above: Hentschel wall clock 25-year service gift (Photo by author)

Right: Celebrating 25 years at IBM with PC cake (Photo by Elaine Fraser)

Dress and decorum

In September 1991 (just a few months before I retired) in an article in Management Review, Jenny C. McCune wrote:

25-year service plaque, 1990

> When Thomas J. Watson Sr. joined the company in 1914, he brought with him innovative ideas about how a company should treat employees and how employees, in turn, should behave. . . . Watson believed that a sales rep's dress and decorum could sway a customer to purchase. Dark conservative suits paired with starched white shirts were the battle uniform for Watson's sales commandos in the 1920s and still remain the signature attire for many IBM professionals today. . . . Big Blue has developed a strong, unique corporate culture that lives on in various forms today. Some would describe it as highly structured, ultra-conservative, the kind of rah-rah culture that went out of style with "Win one for the Gipper," but it's a culture that bonds IBM to its employees like Crazy Glue.[32]

The subject of dress code is one that evoked some very colourful memories from my contemporaries:

> One day I was in the washroom and my second-level manager walked in and took up a position beside me at the adjacent urinal. I was young and was wearing the wildest blue and white plaid pants that you could imagine, boots, a dark blue shirt and what must have been an LSD-inspired tie about six inches wide. I said "Hello." He replied, "Golfing today, are we?" I didn't wear this outfit again but I do remember thinking, "Hey – at least it was BLUE!" –Bruce Singleton

> I remember colleague Gerry Mercer's run-ins with the dress code. At that time you weren't permitted to wear ankle socks. One day when he was sitting down, his pant legs rose up to reveal the forbidden short socks. His manager made him go downstairs to Marks Menswear to purchase a pair of decent socks. On another occasion, Gerry, who played in a band, came to work in a brown speckled suit. Datacentre manager Lorne Polanski sent him home to change. –Dainius Lukosevecius

---

[32] Excerpted from "Who Are Those People in Blue Suits?" in *Management Review*, Sep. 1991 (Courtesy of Management Review, published by the American Management Association International, www.amanet.org)

One of the fellows working in the Datacentre was sent home to change his socks as he was wearing yellow socks – what a transgression! He was so annoyed that he quit not long afterwards. He was an amazing programmer whose programs usually worked first time round. [At that time our programs were all submitted on punch cards for batch processing, so debugging could be a long drawn-out process.] So IBM lost a very clever employee on account of their dress code. At that time, too, beards were not allowed, although they never turned away bearded customers. –Susan Pidoux Carlisle

For a long time women had to wear dresses. When pants started coming into style I wore them until my female manager told me I couldn't wear them when going to see a customer. That basically meant I could never wear pants because you never knew when you'd have to go see a customer. –Margaret Eastwood

The dress code was white shirts, ties, conservative suits and, in the earlier days, hats were required on the job. I had to buy a hat to attend the IBM application and sales schools in Endicott. – John Sailors

In my own experience, I will never forget an embarrassing "dressing down" that I received from my manager early on in my career. I was well aware of the required dress code, and my wife made sure that I was properly attired when I left the house. Her diary entry of February 23, 1969, mentions "I pressed Winston's suit and polished his shoes." But one Monday morning, returning from a weekend at my parents' farm in the Eastern Townships, I decided to go directly to the office without going home first to change. Big mistake! Eyeing my rather casual garb, my manager said, "You look like a lumberjack going to the woods instead of a businessman going to the office!" Needless to say, I never repeated that sin. In fact, even as dress code began to become more relaxed many years later, I was never able to bring myself to go to work without wearing a suit and tie. Dressing "appropriately" had become part of my DNA as a result of such incidents and of periodic management "reminders" like the one recorded in my desk scribbler:

March 31, 1982: Attended Branch meeting in p.m. Had talk on "How to dress for the office" (blue, white and black!!)

While dress code seemed to rely on time-honoured tradition rather than on written rules, the decorum directives were very well documented. The IBMers' bible of behaviour was a booklet called Business Conduct Guidelines. Among the business practices covered were fair customer treatment, competitor disparagement, confidentiality, conflicts of interest and acceptance of gifts.

IBM had a very strict alcohol policy. Alcohol was not permitted during the workday or at any company-sponsored employee or customer functions. Because I did not drink, this was of no concern to me. But since our customers did not necessarily subscribe to such a policy, this sometimes presented difficulties. Colleague

My manager expressing disapproval of my attire (Sketch by James Harvey)

Margaret Eastwood describes a situation that she faced:

> Drinking was a problem when working in sales. My customers liked to go
> out for boozy lunches. Although I don't drink much at all, I had to drink a
> little just to be polite. I am very fortunate that I was never stopped by the
> policeman while driving back from one of those lunches, or worse still,
> involved in an accident.

In addition to the dress and decorum dos and don'ts, there were other policies
that IBMers were expected to follow. Two that come to mind relate to tidiness
and tardiness. I had particular difficulty with the former. My work area was
continually running afoul of IBM's Clean Desk Policy, which required your desk to
be completely clear (i.e., empty) when you left for the day. During the night,
Security did an inspection tour and left offenders with pink violation slips. After
receiving a certain number of such notices, you were reported to the vice-
president and ordered to clean up your mess – or else! But any forced clean-up
that I did wouldn't last long. However, in retrospect, I take solace in a quotation
attributed to Albert Einstein: "If a cluttered desk is a sign of a cluttered mind, of

what, then, is an empty desk a sign?"

Datacentre colleague Garth Durrell recounts a humorous "clean desk" story:

> Soon after the new IBM Building opened at 5 Place Ville Marie, IBM Canada President and CEO Jack Brent was scheduled to visit the new offices. Of course, the Datacentre was a real mess. There were always lots of printouts lying around, on the floor, on top of cabinets, etc. Management wanted those all gone before the visit. They didn't want Mr. Brent to think that we were messy. Unfortunately, there was no place to put all our junk. So they rented a cube van, loaded all the stuff into the van and parked it somewhere out of sight for the duration of the visit!

Me at my messy desk (Sketch by James Harvey)

Our normal working hours of 8:30 a.m. to 5:15 p.m. were strictly enforced. Late arrival, especially for meetings, could result in having to make a speech in front of your assembled peers and managers. Datacentre colleague David Gussow relates an amusing anecdote about his own chronic tardiness:

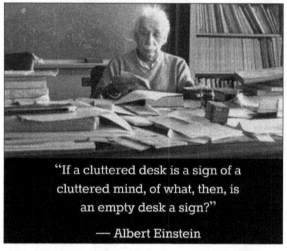

"If a cluttered desk is a sign of a cluttered mind, of what, then, is an empty desk a sign?"

— Albert Einstein

Albert Einstein cluttered desk photo and quotation (pinterest.ca)

I remember that I frequently would come in late (using the back stairs). I also remember that my boss also frequently came in late, always after me. One day he decided to give us all a stern warning not to come in late. It was one of those times where the kettle called the pot black – we all had a good laugh over it.

Based on the shared experiences of my colleagues, here is a tongue-in-cheek 1960s-era version of IBM's Ten Commandments:

1) Thou shalt have no other employer but me.
2) Thou shalt have no idle time.
3) Thou shalt not take the name of thy customers in vain no matter how badly they treat thee.
4) Remember the weekend and keep it wholly free for thy customer emergencies.
5) Honour thy boss and thy boss's boss that thy days of employment may be long.
6) Thou shalt not come to work improperly dressed.
7) Thou shalt not get married or become pregnant without thy boss's permission.
8) Thou shalt not cheat on thy expense accounts.
9) Thou shalt not bear false witness against thy competitor.
10) Thou shalt not covet a pay raise even if thou deserveth one.

Chapter 11 Enduring Relationships

With Gabor Fabian and Harvey Bergman at my 25th Anniversary Dinner, 1990 (Photo by John O'Hara)

As I reflect on my IBM career, of course I remember the challenges and the satisfaction of working in a high-tech environment. But it was the relationships forged that stand out in my memories above everything else. That is why I am devoting an entire chapter to share some of my and my colleagues' recollections of the various types of relationships we experienced.

Colleagues

Because I am an introvert I did not make friends easily, but when I did, they were solid relationships that stood the test of time. Two colleagues from the 1960s became life-long friends – Gabor Fabian and David Gussow. In fact, they really became part of my family – so much so that our kids called them "Uncle Gabor" and "Uncle Gus." Even though we actually worked together for only a few years, we have remained in frequent touch ever since. For example, Gabor was always available for my various house projects, such as insulating the attic and designing our extension. An excellent artist, he did a beautiful oil painting of my family

My family homestead, Pine Hill Farm, Cookshire, Que. (Painting by Gabor Fabian; Photo by Cameron Fraser)

Viewing the colours of Gatineau Park with "Uncle Gus" (Photo by author)

homestead – a masterpiece that still adorns my son's office. Gus, who moved to Ottawa where he worked in government (first as a parliamentary librarian, then as a House of Commons clerk), often hosted our family at his parents' stately old home on our frequent visits: in winter to skate on the Rideau Canal, in the fall to take in the colours of Gatineau Park, and in the spring to see the tulips. Both Gabor and Gus shared in many of our family celebrations, and my wife Becky and I were very honoured to attend their respective weddings.

Gabor Fabian
(Courtesy of Monika Fabian)

Another enduring friendship blossomed during the 1970s when I met a very bright young man who had recently joined IBM upon graduation from l'Université de Sherbrooke. His name was Paul Biron. Perhaps it was because we shared a common Eastern Townships heritage that we seemed to get along so well. But more likely, I was drawn by his outstanding abilities – his technical competence and his customer savvy. We enjoyed working together on many avant-garde point-of-sale projects. I especially appreciated Paul's expertise in helping me "fool-proof" our customer applications. We have remained in touch, both professionally and personally, right up to the present day. I had the privilege of working under his direction after leaving IBM and the pleasure of his participation in our annual winter skating parties.

With colleague Paul Biron, Systems Engineer (Author's collection)

Larry Diamond (Author's collection)

During the same period I came to know, respect and admire two managers who would become lasting friends. Larry Diamond was marketing manager for the Steinberg scanning project. Professionally, he was a dynamic and unorthodox individual who did whatever it took to make things happen. But personally, he

Frank Hall (Courtesy of Frank Hall)

was one of the kindest and most caring persons I have known. At IBM he supported many of my "crazy" ideas and has maintained an interest in my welfare ever since. Although Larry is Jewish, he would send best wishes at Christmas. We still get together regularly for lunch to exchange ideas and reminisce. Frank Hall was an industry marketing manager who specialized in Store Systems. I was always amazed with his ability in making customer presentations – he spoke with such clarity and conviction. Not only did I admire his professional competence, I also appreciated his engaging personality. We have periodically kept in touch long afterwards. Frank, who was one of the first persons I solicited for this book, has been most helpful in putting me in contact with other former IBMers of our era.

Christmas card from my manager Larry Diamond, 1976

Fast forward to the late 1980s and the twilight years of my career. It was then that I bonded with a wonderful group of seasoned technical professionals who were part of the "Petro Team" (or "L'équipe Petro"). Although we came from widely different backgrounds, we jelled very well as a team. But more importantly we got along well with one another and soon became close friends. Claude Huot, Pierre Allaire, Roger Richard, Jacques Crépeau and Richard Wilding – and their spouses – quickly became part of my family. We often got together – and still do – for

Christmas card from my former manager Larry Diamond

Petro team Christmas Dinner 1988. L-R: Pierre Allaire, Harvey Bergman, Eilish Kelly, Claude Huot (Courtesy of Claude Huot)

special family events such as birthdays, anniversaries and weddings. An interesting footnote is that Claude, Pierre, Roger, Jacques and I all retired from IBM on the very same day!

Although Richard Wilding was not a member of our Petro team per se he quickly became part of our family through the expert services he provided us as a software CE. Over the years he and I have maintained a close relationship that included him being my main technical conscience and support. Were it not for Richard, I would still be running DOS on my home PC! He traces the beginnings of our friendship to the famous Petro Fishing Day (described in Chapter 9) when he was "stuck" with me as his fishing partner. Richard explains:

> That day I had the greatest time of my life. Not only was the fishing great, but I got to spend a full day talking to and getting to better know a very special human being. Winston is someone who is always there for others in need but who never asks for anything in return. What began, at the fishing day, as a friendly prank on the new guy in the group, turned out to be a great gift to me. In fact, it was one of my best catches ever because I found in Winston a true friend, someone whom you can count on. Our friendship, which is now more than 30 years old, has seen many happy times and has helped me through the tough times. This story is about IBM, but more importantly, it is about the people who built the company. Winston played an important role and, for that, IBM should be proud of him as are we who worked with him.

Of course, along the way, I worked with many other IBM colleagues whom I counted as friends – way too many to name for fear of leaving someone out. Suffice it to say that I appreciated and valued the friendship of each and every one of them.

In addition to the individual and small group relationships described above, there were relationships that applied on a much broader scale. Being an IBMer was like being part of a large family. In their contributions to this book, several former IBMers mentioned this aspect of the company's culture:

> IBM's unique corporate culture was more than a business; it was a family with feelings of responsibility and obligation to its employees, its customers and the communities in which they all lived. –John Sailors (retired American IBMer)
>
> When we joined IBM, it was like joining a family. –Harry Berglas (Datacentre colleague)

One particular "family" incident stands out in my memory. It occurred in the late 1980s when much-loved Montreal Branch Manager, Carmelo Tillona, announced in a meeting that he was leaving. Everyone present, including

Santa gets hug from colleague Claude Huot (Courtesy of Claude Huot)

Quarter Century Club cruise, Montreal, 1990. L-R: Becky, Pierre, Louise, Roger, Denise (Photo by author)

me, was in tears. You see, Carmelo was like a father to his branch children. When I recently reminded him of that event, Carmelo told me:

> I remember it well. And I cried too – because they were my family. In fact, when I would leave my house in the morning, I didn't feel like I was going to work – I was going to see my family.

Another example of an IBM "family" that developed strong bonds is the Toronto Retail Branch (known internally as Branch 061) whose alumni still meet together on a regular basis. Kathy Stivin, who, together with Ellen Mahony, coordinates these friendly gatherings, provides the details:

> It all began in the 1990s when Bob Hughes started organizing a Retail Branch reunion, then at the old Fish House still located on Consumers Road. It was a smash right from the beginning. Bob had a friendly relationship with the owner, and being a long-time supporter and a big-spending patron of the place, he was given use of the banquet room, with catered appetizers, a cash bar and a stand-up reception style meeting – all for a very reasonable price. After the Fish House moved further north to Woodbine and Steeles we followed it to hold our reunion meetings. These gatherings continued to be a great success, with about a hundred or more people turning out each time. Many old friends to meet and greet, lots of hugs to exchange and loads of old stories to be retold. Then the venue changed when the Fish House folded, and we moved over to another friendly and very accommodating place at the Owl pub, also on Woodbine. At our request they repeated the old successful format, and we continued to receive about 80 to 100 attendees each time, but the composition of the group changed. Some of our members have moved to other countries and only infrequently make it back. A sad fact of life is that we also lose a few folks each year. But, regardless, we keep going and plan to continue this IBM family reunion for many years to come. I very much enjoy being involved with Ellie in coordinating the event and especially appreciate the feedback received from those in attendance.

Toronto Retail Branch Reunion 2017. L-R: Ravi Sharma, Ed Sanchez, Dave Dolman, Carol-Anne Earle, Heather Bryce (Courtesy of Kathy Stivin)

Toronto Retail Branch Reunion 2017. L-R: Kathy Stivin, Jim O'Higgins, Joan Bennett, Bob Kostiuck (Courtesy of Kathy Stivin)

It wasn't just the person-to-person relationships that fostered the feeling of family. To a significant degree, it was the company itself, through its senior executives, that enhanced that sense within us. For example, when I joined the company I received a personal letter of welcome, signed by the president of IBM Canada. Later, whenever we had a new baby, we would receive a personally signed letter of congratulations, again from the chief executive officer of IBM. These gestures definitely reinforced the feeling that you were indeed part of a family.

There is a lot of truth in the old Egyptian proverb that says "Friendship doubles joy and halves grief." Many are the happy events that I have shared with other members of the IBM family. Even small gestures are not forgotten. Just recently,

Left: Letter of Welcome to IBM, 1965
Right: Letter of congratulations on baby's birth, 1969

BCT classmate Gary Mohr reminisced about how much he and his wife enjoyed the guided tour of Old Montreal that we gave them during their honeymoon some 50 years ago.

Later, in 1987, I discovered the importance of friends during difficult times. It was in February of that year that my dad passed away at the age of 89. Although he had lived a good long life, it is never easy to lose a parent or indeed anyone who is close to you. So it was with very heavy hearts that our family returned to the ancestral homestead in the Eastern Townships for his funeral. As we entered the historic stone church called St. Peter's in my native town of Cookshire, I was overwhelmed to see an entire row filled with my IBM colleagues. They had made the more than two-hour trip in winter conditions just to support me. What a touching moment it was for me, and one that I will never forget.

Several members of the IBM family have shared with me details of some of their own special relationships with colleagues:

> I was hired in 1966 by IBM's Mount Royal office, which promptly moved to the Place Ville Marie newly built building that would be our home for many years. The branch manager, Gerry (Gérard) Claude, was a big man who smoked cigars whenever there was a win – which meant almost every day! Gerry spoke English with a French accent, and French with an English accent. For me, a newly arrived immigrant, it was the most perfect image of a Canadian. When asked if he was a French Canadian or an English Canadian, Gerry's answer was "My nationality is IBM." He exuded love and commitment to IBM. In that era, he was a perfect role model for me. I admired him very much, although I would be unable to adopt his manners, accents and habits. Don Duncan was his marketing manager. Don, red headed and also a big man, was cheerful. He could be heard around the office. He was a lovely man and very popular. When Gerry and Don were together, celebrating some win, a cloud enveloped most of the floor and spread joy and pride to us all. –Khalil Barsoum

> My wife and I still remember an event early in my Canadian IBM career, when I met this very pleasant chap named Robbie Kemeny who joined the Montreal Datacentre the same day in 1968 as I did. Robbie came from Ottawa; I came from Poughkeepsie, N.Y. We hit it off immediately. Not long afterwards my wife and I invited him and his lady wife to dinner. I think it was the day of the dinner date, or just before, that we were informed that Robbie had just been appointed my manager. There was instant consternation on the home front! However, the dinner went off fine anyway. Robbie later decided that he didn't enjoy "managering" after all – and I was never very good at being managed – and our two families have been friends ever since! –Paul Morrison

> I started working for IBM in May 1962 at age 19. Most of the employees were only slightly older than me. We had a built-in social life and did lots of skiing, hiking and of course partying together. I still have quite a few

friends from those days who are now living all around the world.

In 1986, future astronaut Julie Payette arrived in our office and I was supposed to supervise her. As you can imagine, she was not one who needed any supervision. Julie was very memorable – I remember her as multilingual, very smart, ambitious, fit and athletic. A decade later I saw her at the unveiling of the James McGill statue at McGill University. By then, she was an astronaut but hadn't yet flown in space. She was very friendly. I told her I'd be watching her space flight and I did. –Margaret Eastwood

I worked for many years with Bob James in the Toronto retail branch, admiring both his technical abilities and his personal qualities. Over time our careers took us in many directions, and people from the branch were transferred to headquarters, other branches or education. One day, some years later, I received a call from Lori Allan telling me that Bob was very ill in hospital, and asking if I wanted to visit him. My answer was "Of course I do!" I walked into his room to see a paler shadow of his old self. By then he had lost weight, and was undergoing treatment. He was cheerful and tried to see the brighter side of things. But all I could do was cry, in front of Bob. Every word I said came up with a sob. So Bob started telling me jokes, to cheer **me** up! I had to join in and laugh with him. A few weeks later I attended his funeral. I met his widow and grown sons, who expressed a sincere appreciation for having so many people from IBM attend and pay our last respects to this lovable old bear of a man. –Kathy Stivin

Establishing good relationships was one of the keys to the success of any IBM project. An excellent example involved the launching of IBM Canada's involvement in the UPC scanning project in the early 1970s. Bob Kostiuck recounts the details:

In preparation of the announcement of the new IBM scanning system, Industry Marketing Manager John Thompson asked me to arrange to bring someone up from Raleigh to Canada to rally the troops and tell us what we needed to do to get ready. He suggested that I get Retail Manager Bob (Rocky) Hardcastle, which I did. I was to be in charge of showing him around and giving him a good time. Mr. Hardcastle had been recently separated. So my wife (at that time my girlfriend) Mary and I decided to take him out and invited Mary's friend Marilyn, who was divorced, to come along. Bob and Marilyn got along well, and had a couple more dates and spent a weekend together in the Muskokas. For a long time afterwards John would rib me about this. But we received excellent support from Raleigh. Whenever I needed anything, I just asked Rocky and it would be done.

Sometimes an incidental relationship with a colleague while working grows into a closer relationship after leaving IBM. Such is the case with Bob McLachlan, whom I barely knew at IBM. However, since our common departure in 1992, we have been in touch regularly, most notably at the annual Brome Fair where we would update each other on our latest activities. It is interesting to note that, at one stage, Bob and my son, Charles, were working for the same recruitment firm. Our post-IBM relationship was initiated by some valuable financial advice that Bob gave me, for which I remain very grateful.

Because of the mobility of IBMers, many relationships were of a short, fleeting nature. That is what I assumed would be the case with my BCT classmate, Raymond Hession, until something serendipitous happened. Ray tells the story:

> Winston, a talented software engineer with a disarmingly humble character, possessed a faith in Christ that enveloped his life throughout. I bade him farewell when I left BCT. He remained in Montreal throughout his career working only for IBM, though his technical talent was often sought as the information technology world expanded rapidly in the intervening decades. It was Winston's avocation as a devote churchman and Christian organizer that kept him on the straight and narrow road that he chose to follow with his lifelong mate and their family.

> In 2007, fully 42 years later, I attended an ecumenical service at the Brome Fair in the Eastern Townships. I sat on a horseshoe-shaped riser facing a covered stage to participate in the service, which was replete with the singing of hymns of every sort accompanied by musical groups and young dancers. As the singing began, I realized that I was one of the few without sheet music to follow. Glancing at the gentleman on my right, I asked him where I might get the sheet music. Unexpectedly, he bolted out of there immediately. So, I kept doing my best without knowing the words to the music until, about five minutes later, my seatmate reappeared with the sheet music. He handed it to me saying, "Do you remember me?" This time I took a hard look at him and knew that he was from my past. But, before I could say a word, he continued, "I'm Winston Fraser." Well, I almost shed a tear I was so happy. We spent a good part of the remaining day reminiscing. He had long since retired from IBM but was pursuing his photographic art and hawking toy cars from a booth at the Brome Fair

> as a hobby. Of course I visited his booth and bought a wonderful photograph of a sugar bush house nestled in the Eastern Townships forest. I cherish that photo. It sits above our fireplace in our country home built in 2005 on our small private lake high in the Appalachian hills near Knowlton, Quebec.

> Each year since I have attempted to link up with Winston at the annual fair, with moderate success. Winston is now a widower, having unexpectedly lost his spouse to a

Ray Hession, 1968 (Courtesy of Joe Kern)

sudden heart attack. He took that loss with much sorrow and grace. We saw each other during his time of need over a lunch attended by his son, whom I had met at a wake for my best high school friend living on St. Margaret's Bay south of Halifax. The coincidence was astounding but beautiful. It certainly seems as though Winston and I are connected by fate and, I believe, spirituality for which I thank God and IBM.

I have often wondered what ever became of my various IBM colleagues over the years. During research for this book, I sadly discovered that several had passed on. One of them was a BCT colleague and friend, Al Robinson. Fellow BCT colleague Ray Hession pays tribute to Al as a dear friend:

> Following BCT, Al Robinson moved to Halifax to join the smallish IBM branch there. Al chose to do so deliberately so that he could polish his small business marketing skills and get started with his family which at the time included but one baby boy (another boy and a daughter came along soon enough). I reunited with Al when I rejoined IBM in Ottawa in 1971. He had recently moved to Ottawa to be in the IBM Commercial office. I was delighted to see him after six years. Indeed, our two French-Canadian spouses were especially pleased. We began actively socializing right away. Our closeness was interrupted when I left IBM to join CMHC and Al moved to Montreal. From there he was assigned to a project in Atlanta, Georgia. Then, on to Toronto in support of a product roll-out before returning to Ottawa where we reconnected. Our two families were close. Our children got along famously as did the two mothers.

> Coincidentally IBM initiated a restructuring which included the termination of marketing staff in large numbers, focussed on employees of my age group. Al Robinson was a casualty. In his despondency, Al pulled up his socks and started a small business targeting small start-up technology companies. He enjoyed early success. But I noted during this period that Al's energy level was lagging. So, I invited him to join me at my fitness club to work out together. At our first outing it became clear that he had a problem. After several clinical tests Al was told that his liver was deteriorating due to a genetic deficiency. In due course a liver replacement would be required. Indeed, it was. So, at Saint-Luc Hospital in Montreal, Al submitted to surgery. The replacement liver came none too soon. On the operating table Al was declared clinically dead. The operation would have been cancelled but for the intervention of one surgeon present. It was Al's brother-in-law who insisted they proceed. They did, and successfully. The recovery period, including six weeks in a coma, was stressful. Al prevailed so that, months later, he walked his daughter down the aisle! Soon thereafter Al returned to Saint-Luc for a check-up. His doctors felt that he needed a blood transfusion, which followed. I visited Al the following day when two physicians asked me to leave his room. I did. When they left looking somewhat glum, I re-entered the room. Al told me then that the blood he received was tainted with Hepatitis C – in other words, a death sentence. Two weeks later he was gone. Al was a special friend with courage beyond

description. Again, I thank God and IBM for the privilege of knowing him.

It is interesting how two IBMers with confusingly similar names, Harry Berglas and Harvey Bergman, with whom I worked at opposite ends of my career, developed a close relationship after retiring. Harry explains:

> For the past several years we have spent our winters in Florida. There we have become very good friends with Harvey and his wife, who also winter in the same retirement community. In fact they live in the building right next to ours!

There are some IBMers whom you meet just briefly – or even only once – that for some reason stick in your mind. For example, I remember Dan Hopping of Raleigh Store Systems because of his involvement in investigating UFOs with project Blue Book and Ken Stevenson for his part in the scientific investigation of the Shroud of Turin.

IBM rookies of my day sometimes experienced interesting relationships with those "teaching them the ropes" of data processing. Colleague Bruce Singleton describes one of his early learning experiences:

> I first joined IBM as a PL/1 programmer in the Keypunch plant's computer department. At the time they ran second-generation mainframes – 7010 as I recall. The disk packs were so basic and large that the operators had to squirt oil on the drives! One day after they got their first System /360 I was assigned a project that would require a 2400 ft. reel of tape. My first. I was told to go to the raised floor area to ask for a scratch tape. Knowing that I was a rookie, the operator asked what I wanted. I told him about my flat sequential file. He replied, "No problem." Then he proceeded to grab a reel from the rack, hold onto the end of the tape and roll it across the floor until it hit the wall. He walked over to the reel and picked it up, then tore the mag tape off between his fingers. "There you go," he said. "That should be about what you need!"

Bruce's story reminds me of one of my own embarrassing experiences. I was asked to go to the Keypunch department to fetch a box of word marks. I had no idea what a word mark was, so I obediently went and knocked on Keypunch manager Jean Bonnell's door. Without hesitation she handed me a large box full of card "chads" (i.e., the little pieces of card resulting from the keypunch process). Only later did I learn that a wordmark was a special character used in programming!

Customer relationships

Customer relationships were extremely important to us as IBMers because, after all, it was they who paid our salaries. Unlike the dynamics among colleagues, these relationships tended to be more business and less personal. But there were exceptions. For example, during my Datacentre days, I remember a couple of customers whom I considered friends. One was a Mr. Karim Birdi, an operations research analyst with Consolidated Bathurst, who for several years processed his OR models with my assistance when required. The other was Mr. Mike Nancoo of ICAO, for whom I developed the complex weather data exchange solution described in Chapter 3. Both these gentlemen were a pleasure to work with.

Left: George Brown (Courtesy of Monika Fabian, retouching by Greg Beck)

Right: Mike Nancoo (Courtesy of Claudette Jacks-Nancoo)

My Datacentre colleague, Gabor Fabian, had a customer who became a lifelong close friend. Gabor describes his relationship with George Brown, who worked for Bank of Montreal:

> In the Datacentre I was responsible for supporting an application called PMS (Project Management System). One of my customers was the Bank of Montreal's George Brown, who managed all of the bank's branch construction and renovation projects. As a result, George would come in almost on a daily basis to update current projects or process new ones. In fact he came so often that most people thought that he was an IBMer! Besides, he dressed like an IBM executive – with his spiffy three-piece blue pin-striped suit. At the bank George was seen as a hero for introducing technology to this very conservative institution, and he quickly rose in the ranks to become a vice-president. Through our constant working together, George and I became good friends. My close friendship with "Chubby" (that's what I called him) and his wife, Pat, continued right up until his passing a few years ago. I still frequently talk to Pat on the phone.

Another Datacentre colleague, Dainius Lukosevicius, who worked as a Customer Support Representative (CSR) in the Brokerage department, remembers a humorous incident involving one of his clients:

> Because of my complicated Lithuanian family name, everybody simply called me "Luk" (pronounced "Luke"). One day, one of my customers asked me, "What is your real name?" I replied "Luk-o-sev-ic-ius," pausing between each syllable so that he would understand. Very excitedly, he said: "So you must be Irish – with a name like Luke O'Sevicius!"

Point-of-sale colleague Paul Biron took customer relationships to a whole new level during the Steinberg scanning project. He tells the story:

> I started working on the IBM 3660 Supermarket System installed at the Steinberg store in Dorval in January 1975, immediately after Basic

Systems Training. It is a known fact that IBMers sometimes fall in love with personnel at their client's site. That is exactly what happened to me. A young woman named Nicole was a cashier at the Steinberg store, and I took notice of her very early on. I was very shy in those days, but I do remember checking on her scanner several times a day. Needless to say I was less interested in the scanner than the person operating it! The funny thing is, most of the store employees knew that I had a crush on Nicole, but she herself did not. After a lot of coaching and encouragement from the store people, I finally decided on Thursday March 13, 1975, to ask her to join me on her coffee break at 3:30 p.m. We were married exactly one year and 30 minutes later, on Saturday March 13, 1976, at 4:00 p.m.! Because the store employees knew that I was getting married to one of their cashiers, I learned through the grapevine that they were planning something. Therefore I avoided going to the store for several weeks before the wedding. As you can imagine, a supermarket has an ample supply of molasses, flour, mustard, pasta and other such products that may be used to dress up someone!

Steinberg Dorval cashier Nicole Labelle, 1975; Paul Biron – Nicole Labelle wedding, 1976 (Courtesy of Paul Biron)

Business partner relationships

During the later years, business partnerships became more and more common – hence the importance of establishing and maintaining good relationships with our business partners. I had the opportunity of working with several, but two of them stand out.

The first is Bob Simon of MGV, whose key contributions to the long-term success of IBM's store systems are documented in Chapter 4. Bob, known for his technical brilliance as well as his business acumen, was always approachable and ready to help. Very often, when I would go to Toronto for an IBM meeting, I would drop in to his office to discuss the latest POS developments or just to have a chat. Always a straight shooter, I considered Bob a friend. Recently, I had the pleasure of reconnecting with him in Toronto – and we continued where we had left off in our last meeting more than 25 years ago!

The second business partner to whom I want to pay tribute is the late Jerome Graham of Graham Electronics Inc., whose role in the development of IBM's Petroleum Retailing Application is covered in Chapter 6. Based in Raleigh, N.C., Jerry made frequent visits to Montreal in connection with the pilot installation at a Provi-soir dépanneur in Piedmont, Que. It was probably on his second visit that he and I became friends – in fact, he became fast friends with my whole team. So much so, that they – together with Carol Buckingham from IBM UK – invited him on a weekend fishing trip in a remote area of the Laurentians. The whole group of eight stayed in a small cabin with a kitchen, eating area, one bedroom and a loft. Later, in a visit to my home, Jerry recounted the adventure:

> On the way I inquired about the sleeping arrangements. Pierre said, "Don't worry, Jerry, you and Carol can have the bedroom and the rest of us will sleep on the floor and up in the loft." Being a happily married man, I was worried how I was going to explain this to Marge!

Left: Bob Simon (Courtesy of Bob Simon)
Right: Jerry Graham (Author's collection)

Although I never did find out who bedded with whom, I didn't learn of any subsequent marriage break-ups. Jerry and I remained friends for many years until he passed away after he retired to Florida.

To be endured

The "double entendre" of this chapter's title is intentional. As with all relationships in life, some are enduring while others must be endured. In the course of my research for this book, I was invited to a gathering of former colleagues in Toronto. As I was describing the outline of the book and started to talk about this chapter, someone jokingly asked, "And in which category of relationships do we belong?"

Even though the overwhelming majority of my relationships were positive, I have to confess that some of my character traits led to the occasional bumpy relationship. As indicated earlier, I grew up shy, insecure and introverted. My first manager, Joe Kern, recalled an uncomfortable incident that happened early on when I misinterpreted his kindness and concern:

One event has always stuck in my mind. I was very inexperienced as a manager and I was also very inexperienced with regard to Canadian social norms. I remember that sometimes, when coming from the Eastern Townships, you were on the road for a long time. One day you were late and I was concerned, not concerned that you were late, but concerned for your safety. So I called your wife. You were quite upset that I called your home, thinking that I was keeping tabs on you.

It perhaps sounds arrogant for me to state that I did not suffer fools gladly, but that is the way I was. I always expected colleagues and customers alike to operate at peak levels of performance. Anything else and I felt betrayed. Obviously, in the real world, not everyone fits that mould. Whether it involved a fellow programmer who failed to comment their program code properly or a client who committed some blatant stupidity, my patience was sometimes rather limited. One time, after working several long days on behalf of an incompetent and unappreciative customer, I lost it and blew my stack. Clearly it was not the smartest thing to do but that's part of the price to pay for not being able to suffer fools gladly!

Colleague Margaret Eastwood remembers some of the challenges she endured in working with customers.

In the 1980s, when I switched from systems engineering to sales, I attended several conferences in the U.S.A. with my customers: N.Y. state, Boston, Arizona, etc. One trip stands out. I flew to Poughkeepsie, N.Y. with a group of five clients on a chartered flight the day before a one-day course. They sat in the back of the plane, drank like fish and were very loud. I was horrified when the stewardess handed them the leftover small bottles of liquor in a plastic bag. They drank them up too after we arrived, and then went out again for more drinks. At about 1 a.m., after drinking B-52's (a drink I had never heard of – a mixture of Kahlua, Irish cream and Triple Sec), we came out of a pub and the VP in the group decided to pee against the pub wall. Unfortunately he was spotted by a policeman who was going to arrest him. Fortunately he got off the hook because the policeman thought that I was his wife! The next morning, at the presentation, my clients were all bright-eyed and bushy-tailed while I felt absolutely awful.

The foregoing is a sampling of the contrasting types of relationships experienced by my colleagues and me – some that resulted in contentment and others that resulted in contention.

Celebrating colleague Jacques Crépeau's 75th birthday, 2018. L-R: Winston, Jacques, Louise and Claude Huot) (Photo by Thierry Senécal)

Chapter 12   The IBM Afterlife

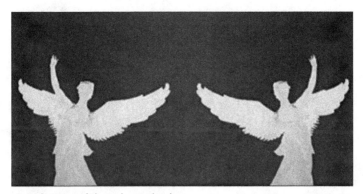

Angel statues (Photo by author)

As a Christian, I believe in the afterlife. Furthermore, I believe that earthly life is closely linked to the afterlife. Scottish pastor and author David Broderick states that ". . . we need to face up to the self-evident fact that the earthly life is merely preparation for the heavenly life to come."[33] And respected Welsh theologian Matthew Henry declared, "It ought to be the business of every day to prepare for our last day."[34]

Similarly, I believe in the IBM afterlife. Yes, Virginia, there **is** life after IBM! And I believe that all my IBM experience was preparation for that IBM afterlife. In researching for this book, I have discovered that several of my colleagues share that view.

Consulting

My IBM afterlife began on February 29, 1992. Two days later, I began working for myself under the name of Winston Fraser Consulting Inc. (Consultation Winston Fraser Inc.), a federally incorporated business that received its charter earlier that month. I remember at the time that my incorporation lawyer informed me that most start-up companies don't last more than five years. But I am proud to say

---

[33] David Broderick, *The Christ-Centered Life: Deep Calls to Deep*, p. 248

[34] Matthew Henry, *Directions for daily communion with God, in 3 discourses, and the communicant's companion*, p. 81

With my wife and colleagues at my retirement luncheon, 1992 (Author's collection)

that after more than 25 years, my company is still in business and its original principals remain the same – me, myself and I! Through the company I have provided computer consulting services to major Quebec and Canadian enterprises in several sectors including retail, telecommunications and banking.

Upon the invitation of my former IBM colleague, Paul Biron, I provided my services, on an extended basis, to grocery retailer Provigo Inc. to coordinate the Request for Proposal (RFP) process for their mission-critical solutions. Naturally I made good use of my IBM experience in this regard. Concurrently with the Provigo projects I applied my many years of IBM Store Systems experience to point-of-sale system audits at A & P in Montvale, N.J. and Bank of Montreal in Toronto. My former IBM manager, Dave Moxley, describes the context of the latter audit:

> As our careers progressed I left IBM to launch the Air Miles loyalty program – a coalition-based loyalty program that had the advantage of allowing consumers to use one card at hundreds of retailers and other classes of trade. That feature meant collectors could earn points fast and hassle free, attain high value travel rewards, and redeem points to prove to themselves the value of the program. Unfortunately at Bank of Montreal we had a major issue with data integrity using credit authorization terminals. The issue was with data collection integrity. We contacted Winston to follow the transactions from store to host and to determine root causes and solutions. Because of Winston's technical knowledge and systematic methodology we pinpointed the problem and

quickly resolved the issue. We believed this to be a mission-critical threat. If points could not be correctly issued, consolidated and billed back to the sponsor, the program could not survive. Winston was able to explain in a non-threatening manner the key issues to the various system owners and then work with them to resolve these issues. This project saved the Air Miles program from an early demise and initiated a new process for on-boarding of sponsors that ensured that this problem could not happen again, thus enabling the rapid growth of the most successful loyalty program in the world.

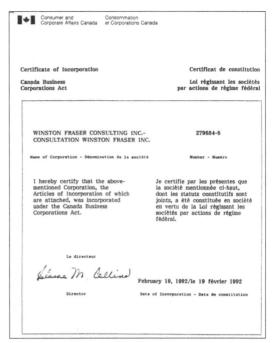

Winston Fraser Consulting Inc. Certificate of Incorporation, 1992

During the same time period, my former IBM colleague Claude Huot and I collaborated on two point-of-sale development projects for our former employer. The first was to design and develop an IBM 4680 integrated debit solution for Royal Bank of Canada. The second was a similar development for Scotiabank. For both these projects, we made extensive use of the expertise we had accumulated while working at IBM. Claude and I subsequently offered our "Pump Simulator" and "Bug Buster" application testing services.

My next major consulting mandate was to research, evaluate and negotiate convergent billing solutions for Vidéotron, a major Quebec telecommunications company. In a follow-on mandate, I managed a team of technical professionals in the conversion of Vidéotron's mission-critical billing systems.

In the year 2000 I served as project manager for Timing Corporation's development of a revolutionary web-based self-serve appointment scheduling system for the health care field. I was also responsible for proofreading and validation of French translations for all web pages of the application. A number of short-term mandates followed:

Product Announcement - September 1992

Software Pump Simulator for 2-Way Pump Control

Informatique Claude Huot Enr. and Winston Fraser Consulting Inc. are pleased to announce the availablility of a Software Pump Simulator for 2-Way Pump Control.

This unique product responds to a longstanding need of all enterprises involved in the development and implementation of POS solutions for the petroleum retailing environment.

Whether the requirement is for an effective test tool for the developer, a user-friendly validation tool for the retailer or a portable demonstration vehicle for the marketeer, the Software Simulator for 2-Way Pump Control provides the answer.

Retailers and POS solution suppliers alike will want to take advantage of this functionally rich and economically attractive alternative to the hardware pump simulator.

Functions / Features

- PC DOS based

  Will run on any PC, PS/2 or compatible

- Supports up to 32 pumps

  Allows multiple (maximum 3) hoses per pump

- Simulates all functions of 2-way pump control

  Lift handle / authorize / pump / stop-resume / hang up handle / price change / hose totals

- Supports special features

  'Drive-away"

- Graphical display of pump status

  Idle / handle / authorized / pumping / stopped

- User-friendly interface

  Function-keys / graphical display feedback / user parameters

- Supports IBM POS / GLMX Protocol

  Built-in support for IBM 4680/4684 Petroleum Retailing Application and the GLMX (Graham Logic Module Extended) Pump Controller

- Adaptable to other POS / pump controllers

  This simulator is readily adaptable to any POS product / 2-way pump controller for which interface/protocol specifications are available

Pricing: Site License $795. Corporate License $1995.
One year warranty / support. Consulting and customization services available.

About the Authors

Between them, the developers of this product had more than 50 years experience at IBM Canada in application design, development and installation. Prior to retiring from IBM, they specialized in developing POS software for the petroleum industry.

Additional Information

For more information on how this product can respond to your needs, please contact either Winston Fraser at (514) 621-2378 or Claude Huot at (514) 630-6360 or write to Informatique Claude Huot Enr., 268 Connemara Cres., Beaconsfield, Quebec, Canada H9W 2N7 or Winston Fraser Consulting Inc., 216 Eglise, Rosemere, Quebec, Canada J7A 2X2.

Huot-Fraser Pump Control Simulator announcement, 1992 (Author's collection)

Bug Busters ad, 1994 (Author's collection)

- Provided final English-to-French translation of online machine-translated technical documentation for U.S. auto maker General Motors of Detroit. Developed tools to assist with the validation and correction of machine-translated text for the maintenance manuals for new GM vehicles.
- Provided English-to-French software translation and localization services for a major web-based personal finances management application – Microsoft Corporation's "Money 99."
- Did final review/testing of French translations of each new release of specialized retail POS software applications for IBM. Created and exercised test plans to validate all French translations for the IBM 4680 Store Systems General Sales Application and Supermarket Application.

In 2002 I began my last major mandate with Caisses Desjardins for the creation, revision and translation of technical and marketing documents for their payment solutions. More than 15 years later, I still offer them my services, albeit now on a two-days-per week basis.

Based on the preceding paragraphs, readers might think that my IBM afterlife consisted of nothing but work, work and more work. Be assured that such is far from the truth. Of course there were some very busy work-dominated periods, but most of the time, there was room for plenty of other activities including volunteering, grand parenting, travel and hobbies.

Volunteering

For many years, I concurrently served on the boards of four non-profit organizations: St. James Anglican Church, Canadian Bible Society, Quebec Lodge Christian Children's Camp and Generations Foundation.

Although I had always been quite involved in my home parish of St. James Church in Rosemere, Que., my participation intensified after I retired from IBM. In 1995, as the result of a vision that I received from God, our local church launched "Proclamation" – an ecumenical 10-day public reading aloud of the entire Bible. Under the auspices of the Canadian Bible

St. James Anglican Church, Rosemere, Que. (Photo by author)

Society, in the years that followed, the program expanded across Canada and beyond, with events now having been held in more than 200 towns and cities. My wife and I were very involved in organizing and executing the first Proclamation as well as participating in dozens of others. A book about the program, *The Power of the Spoken Word*, was published in 2009.

In 2009 my wife initiated a new program in our parish: the Drop-in Centre – a mid-

week oasis of food, fun and fellowship for people of the community. Beginning with four individuals, it has now expanded to more than 50 regular members. Coincident with its debut, I reduced my working week to support Becky's project. Upon her sudden passing in 2015 I took over the coordination of the Drop-in and continued in that role until last year.

St. James Church Drop-in Centre "Olympics Day" setup, 2016 (Photo by author)

For several years I served as a governor of the Canadian Bible Society, a charitable organization whose purpose is "to translate without doctrinal note, publish, and distribute the Christian Scriptures, and to promote and encourage the use of the Bible, throughout Canada and worldwide in cooperation with members of the United Bible Societies and other organizations." I represented the Montreal district at national meetings of the board where we discussed ways and means to best realize the Society's goals, including the Proclamation program described above. I also served on the local Montreal Board of Directors.

For more than a decade I served on the board of Quebec Lodge Christian Children's Camp, a summer camp on Lake Massawippi in Quebec's Eastern Townships, whose stated purpose was "to help campers prepare themselves physically, mentally, socially, morally and spiritually to take their places as Christians in

Logo of Canadian Bible Society

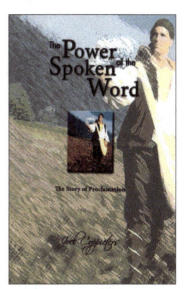

Canadian Bible Society book on Proclamation program (Author's collection)

Chapel and canoe, Quebec Lodge Camp, Lake Massawippi, Que. (Photo by author)

Camp Quebec Lodge

Left: Logo of Generations Foundation
Right: Logo of Quebec Lodge Christian Camp

today's world." As a board member I attended frequent meetings both onsite and in Quebec City to discuss programs, staffing and finances among other items. My wife and I also attended special events in support of the Camp and often transported campers and staff to the Lodge.

In 1999 I was one of the founding directors of Generations Foundation, a charitable organization whose mission is "to develop and administer programs which will help to improve the quality of life for persons of all ages. . . with an initial focus on children." As a board member for several years, I was involved in the promotion and support of its programs. The organization currently provides a nutritious breakfast, hot lunch and snack daily to more than 7700 schoolchildren in 96 Montreal schools and learning centers.

In my volunteering activities I often made use of business meeting techniques learned at Big Blue. Particularly helpful were the Planning Session guidelines and ground rules:

- Sessions will start and end on time and will resume on time after breaks.
- The session's objective will be clearly stated at the outset.
- All participants' inputs are equally valued.
- Participants are expected to share all relevant information.
- Only one conversation will go on at once.
- Discussions and criticisms will focus on subjects rather than people.
- All significant points will be documented.
- An agreed action plan containing responsibilities and timeframes will be developed.

Grandparenting

"Grandchildren are God's way of compensating us for growing old." –Mary H. Waldrip (American author)

If such is the case, then my wife and I have been very generously compensated, having been blessed with nine wonderful grandchildren: Jacob, Kira-Marie,

With my nine grandkids, Dec. 2016 (Photo by Greg Beck)

My backyard skating rink (Photo by author)

Mattias, Kennedy, Cameron, Micayla, Caleb, Alice and George. They brought a whole new dimension to our IBM afterlife beginning in 1996. We have watched them grow out of the crib into college and out of diapers into academic gowns. Over the years we have proudly supported their many sports, music and volunteering activities, including hockey, ringette, soccer, equestrian, baseball, swimming, school band performances, piano recitals, dancing and work trips to developing countries. I have had the pleasure of teaching each of them how to skate on the backyard skating rink that I built each year – and of playing in a "father-son"

Grandson Caleb learning to skate on my backyard rink (Photo by author)

hockey game with my grandson Mattias. We have witnessed graduations from kindergarten, high school and college. Since Becky's passing I have seen the three oldest leave their family nests to attend university. It is impossible to overstate the joy that our grandchildren have brought and continue to bring each and every day.

Travelling

In a previous chapter (Offsite Adventures), I described the tent camping adventures of my IBM years. Although we continued camping for a few years after my leaving IBM, Becky and I soon graduated to a different kind of travel – cruising. Now that our children had flown the coop, we decided that it was time to treat ourselves to this more comfortable mode of travel. We signed up with Holland America (one of the best in the business) for voyages to the Caribbean, Northern Europe and Alaska (where we cruised no less than three times!). We enjoyed the scrumptious food, the amazing entertainment and the superb shore excursions that accompanied every voyage. In addition to taking cruises, we also flew to other interesting destinations including the Grand Canyon, Baffin Island, Greenland and Haida Gwaii (Queen Charlotte Islands). In the year 2000 we attended the famous Passion Play in Oberammergau, Germany. The world offers so many fascinating places to visit and we were privileged and blessed to see a few of them.

Top: Cruise ship in Glacier Bay, Alaska (Photo by author)
Above: Becky (right) and I aboard cruise ship in Juneau, Alaska, ca. 1995 with Claude Huot and his wife Louise (Author's collection)

Hobbies

With a less hectic work schedule I had more time to spend on hobbies such as photography, collecting vintage Tonka toys, writing books and researching my family tree.

My interest in photography started as a young boy growing up on the family farm. At the age of ten I received my first camera, an inexpensive castoff that required adhesive tape to keep it shut! Encouraged by family and friends, I pursued this hobby with ever increasing enthusiasm. But it wasn't until more than 25 years

At photography exposition, Bennington, Vt. (Fraser family archives)

Winston Fraser is a self-taught Canadian photographer whose work has been published widely both in North America and abroad. Included among his credits are National Geographic, National Wildlife Federation, Encyclopedia Britannica, Canadian Geographic and Kodak Encyclopedia of Photography. A book of his photographs, HISTORIC SITES OF CANADA, was published in 1991.

My photographic biography, 1994 (Author's collection)

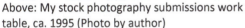
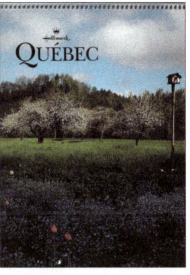

Above: My stock photography submissions work table, ca. 1995 (Photo by author)
Right: Hallmark Quebec calendar cover, 1994 (Author's collection)

later that I decided to offer my photos to publishers. Much to my surprise, one of the first photos I submitted was used on the cover of an Atlantic publication. That initial success launched my part-time career as a professional stock photographer.

Moving into the IBM afterlife gave me more time to devote to my photography hobby-turned-business. I was able to subscribe to major photography newsletters and respond to requests from leading North American publishers. At the same time, I continued to add to my collection of stock photo images in the form of 35mm colour transparencies (slides). By the time that digital photography replaced film around 2010, I had amassed approximately 50,000 images.

My photographs have been published widely both in North America and abroad. Among my credits are National Geographic, National Wildlife Federation, Encyclopedia Britannica, Canadian Geographic and Kodak's *Encyclopedia of Practical Photography*. A book of my photographs, *Historic Sites of Canada*, was published by Bramley Books and distributed by Coles bookstores. Hallmark's Canadian scenic calendars frequently featured my images, and I was the major supplier of photos for National Geographic's *Canada Travel Guide*. Most recently I self-published another book of my photographs entitled *Endangered Species of Country Life*.

As a Christian, I recognize that my success in photography is the result of a God-given ability to see and record the wonders of creation in a special way. Over the years, I have held benefit exhibitions of my work to support Christian charitable organizations serving the needs of the poor, the youth and the elderly. Several of my IBM colleagues supported me in these benefit photo shows for which I am very thankful.

It was my wife's and my Saturday visits to the nearby St-Eustache Flea Market that ignited my interest in collecting old stuff – particularly vintage Tonka toys. While

Becky shopped for clothes for our grandkids in the New Goods section, I would wander amongst the junk dealers looking for bargain deals on firetrucks, dump trucks, bulldozers, cranes and cement trucks. By Labour Day I would have amassed a fleet of almost a hundred vehicles that I would sell at my booth at the big Brome Fair in the Eastern Townships. Come the next spring, the process of collecting would start all over again – as it did for more than 25 years.

Vintage Tonka toys, Brome Fair, 2011 (Photo by author)

At IBM I did a lot of writing, albeit of a technical nature. But it was only after retirement that I graduated to prose. My first book, *OHIXIHO*, a biography of my dad's first cousin, represented the fulfilment of his request from 40 years earlier. My second book, *Maggie's Memories*, was the completion of my late wife's unfinished autobiographical manuscript. And my third, *Dew Drop Inn*, was the story of an amazing couple who started a country inn during the Great Depression and nurtured it as well as other businesses for more than 60 years. None of them are best-sellers – yet! But I really enjoy writing, which is the main reason that I am

"Memories" books that I have authored or edited (Photo by author)

still at it. As was the case of writing programs at IBM, it is my passion in my IBM afterlife.

My most recent hobby is Internet-based genealogical research. I was not always interested in researching my family tree. After all, it was job enough to keep track of my eleven siblings and their descendants, without worrying about discovering distant cousins whom I had never met. However, that all changed in 2012, when my youngest sibling, Jim, and I decided to do something special to commemorate the 100th anniversary of the birth of our mother – a special family reunion to which all of her living relatives would be invited. To do this, of course, we needed to build her family tree – a process that resulted in a few hundred names. Three years later, we organized a major family reunion of our dad's family to celebrate the 225th anniversary of his great-grandparents' arrival in Quebec City from Scotland in 1790. I identified a few thousand names on his family tree, 100 of which joined us for the Quebec City reunion in 2015, coming from across Canada, the U.S.A. and the U.K. Then in the summer of 2018 a group of 20 family members enjoyed a custom tour of Scotland to visit the homeland of our Fraser ancestors.

Logo for 2018 Fraser ancestry Scotland tour

Colleagues' afterlives

The afterlives of my colleagues come in a Prismacolour box of different colours, a Foot Locker shelf of different sizes and a Ben & Jerry's ice-cream freezer of different flavours. In other words, every one is different.

For some, like Datacentre colleagues Gabor Fabian and Harry Berglas, who took "the package," retirement from IBM marked the end of their regular full-time working days. The same for branch colleague Margaret Eastwood, who recalls the day that she learned about the IBM offer:

> I heard in September 1991 that IBM was going to offer early retirement to people who were old enough and had enough years of service. I fit the criteria and so I was over the moon! However, I became quite depressed when nothing immediately came of it. Finally, in December, we got the word and were given about three weeks to think about it. For me, no thinking was necessary – it was an immediate "YES."

For Industry Marketing colleague Frank Hall, it meant travelling – and lots of it.

> I travelled to Italy, Greece, Egypt, Jordan, United Arab Emirates, India, Singapore, Vietnam, Cambodia, Thailand, France, the U.K., Russia,

Poland, Lithuania, Latvia, Finland, Sweden and Germany – among other countries. I also lived in Argentina for three months, and explored it from top to bottom, while renting a condo in Buenos Aires. After satisfying my travel yearnings I now spend the five winter months in Ajijic, Mexico, near Guadalajara.

For accomplished marketeer Bob McLachlan (seven Hundred Percent Clubs), who left at the same time as me, the IBM afterlife has consisted of a smorgasbord of activities. After taking a brief sabbatical to travel, Bob worked in software sales and service for five years before being head-hunted by a head-hunting firm. He remained in the recruitment business for seven years, specializing in professional IT, sales and consulting. Concurrently Bob was very active in his community as a volunteer, serving in senior roles with Scouts Canada, as vice-president of the Canadian Grenadier Guards Charitable Foundation, and as lay reader in the Anglican Church. Most recently, as president of the Grays and Blues of Montreal (a historical re-enactment group), he spearheaded a project to recognize the 40,000 Canadian volunteers in the American Civil War. In 2017 a commemorative monument was erected on the Lost Villages Museum grounds in Long Sault, Ontario – the culmination of more than four years of research and planning on his part. Currently Bob is enrolled in a master's program in Theology at the Montreal Diocesan Theological College.

For others who received the package, it provided the ideal opportunity to start their own businesses. David Antebi, a Montreal Datacentre colleague who later worked in Toronto, the U.S.A. and Singapore, took the package in 1993. He immediately established Glass House Computers Inc. that now employs 70 persons and is IBM's largest business partner for mainframe solutions.

Three of my BCT colleagues left IBM much earlier and went on to very successful careers elsewhere. Serge Meilleur left IBM in 1972 to co-found DMR (Ducros Meilleur Roy) which would become the largest information systems service provider in Canada. In his book DMR : La fin d'un rêve (DMR: The end of a dream) Serge gives credit to IBM for his training: "IBM was an extraordinary school for all those men and women who would later be called elsewhere to IT management."[35]

Jean-Pierre Kingsley became Canada's Chief Electoral Officer. And my BCT classmate and good friend, Robert Dionne, confessed that it was never his intention to become an IBMer for life:

> When I was hired I told Gerry Claude, "You're talking to an accountant who only wants to learn about IBM and computers in general." So the reason I joined IBM was to enable me to be familiar with computer systems when I took on later management jobs. After leaving IBM, I

---

[35]DMR : La fin d'un rêve (Table des matières; translation by author)

worked for Martineau-Walker, a major Montreal law firm, where I was responsible for Accounting and for setting up their computer system.

My very first IBM manager, Joe Kern, left IBM Datacentre in 1969 to join Multiple Access Canada (acquired in 1985 by CDC). During his 20 years there he served in various positions: Manager of Applications Development, Technical Support for O.R. Applications and Utilities Systems Development, Supercomputing Consultant and Supercomputer Marketing Support. From 1989 to 2012 Joe was Managing Director at Kematek Inc. (development and support of industrial process software).

A trio of my branch marketing colleagues also departed from Big Blue to excel elsewhere in their IBM afterlives. André Gauthier was one of them:

> When I left IBM in 1979 to co-found LGS (Lafontaine, Gauthier & Shatner), IBM executives were very concerned due to other recent departures, so they flew down from Toronto to try to dissuade me – they told me I would not be successful. However, we were successful for 20 years until, ironically, IBM purchased our company.

Another was Carmelo Tillona, who left IBM in 1988. He went to Le Groupe Vidéotron where he held various senior executive positions and helped establish the company as a leading broadband operator at an international level. Later he co-founded I-U-Go Ventures Inc., a ventures capital and private equity company.

The third was my colleague and good friend, Paul Biron, who left IBM in 1986. Paul describes details of his IBM afterlife:

> I became Vice-president and Chief Information Officer (CIO) at Provigo Inc. until 1994. Then I joined Vidéotron where I was also Vice-president and CIO. In 1997, I joined CGI as Vice-president, Business Engineering, responsible for IT outsourcing. Over the following 10 years I served in a number of senior management positions, including Senior Vice-president responsible for the Bell Canada Business Unit and Senior Vice-president responsible for integration acquisitions. Later I managed the Technology and Infrastructure Business Unit and the Financial Services sector. After my retirement CGI called back in 2012 to ask me to participate in the integration of Logica in Europe where I worked for several months based in Stockholm.

Some of my colleagues embarked on totally different careers upon leaving the IBM data processing business.

Datacentre colleague Jonas Bacher founded Jadsco Foods International, a very successful wholesale foods importer and distributor. The ever-ambitious and always creative Larry Diamond found a variety of new fields to conquer, including real estate development, health-and-beauty gift sets manufacturing and modular building construction. His latest company, Knektus International, is a product innovation group dedicated to bringing assistive technology to the aging community and to people with disabilities.

My Petro team colleagues experienced an interesting variety of business, recreational and volunteering activities in their retirement years. Claude Huot, after collaborating with me on several development, translation and Y2K projects, opted for a more relaxed lifestyle. Together with his wife, Louise, he travelled extensively to Alaska, Europe and Africa where he honed his considerable photographic skills. Upon retirement from IBM in 1992, Jacques Crépeau embarked on an afterlife of adventure and service. First, he travelled to Papua New Guinea to serve in a Roman Catholic mission where he was responsible for implementing their computer system. He was also a Jack of all trades, sometimes referred to as "Jack the fixer." After three years there he returned to Quebec, where he became very involved in the St. David de Yamaska historical society. At the same time he served as a collaborator in the local Roman Catholic parish, a volunteer experience that he still actively pursues. Retirement gave Pierre Allaire more time to devote to his outdoor passions of fishing, snowmobiling and flying small planes. But he didn't let his acquired computer skills lay dormant. Not only did he develop and maintain business applications for a number of local businesses, but he created innovative embedded system applications using Arduino, ESP8266 device control over Internet and PCB (printed circuit board) design for his projects.

Although I did not work with her directly, there is one Montreal IBMer from the 1980s whose IBM afterlife deserves a special mention. I am referring to Julie Payette, former astronaut and currently Canada's Governor-General. Colleague Margaret Eastwood, who worked with Ms. Payette, provides some background:

> Julie worked as an SE on the McGill account – a good fit, as she was a McGill graduate. They loved her and really missed her when she left IBM to do her Master's in Applied Science at University of Toronto. Julie was talented musically and sang with the MSO and Tafelmusik. She performed for us at one of our Branch Days out of the office. She can speak six languages and was very athletic. She worked at the IBM Zurich research lab for a year and in speech research at Bell Northern Research here in Montreal.

My BCT colleague and dear friend Ray Hession had a most unique IBM afterlife – in fact, he had two of them. He describes his roller-coaster career – first with IBM, after leaving IBM, then returning to IBM and finally back to the IBM afterlife for good. Ray's personal account is reproduced below in full because it illustrates so well the many factors involved in moving between jobs within and outside of IBM. It is noted that Ray credits his post-IBM success to the training and experience that he received while with IBM.

Shortly after graduating from BCT, things at home stabilized. My IBM career, on the other hand, shifted into overdrive when I was asked to shadow Jim McIlroy, a veteran marketing representative who had been managing the Department of National Defense account for years. Jim was looking to go back to Toronto into a peaceful head office job and needed a successor. In my case, the usual one-year apprenticeship before assuming a sales territory suddenly became four months with a major RFP in the offing. Somehow it worked out, conditioned in part by my years in the army. At least I understood the language and culture. But, my base income dropped by 40% in January 1966. Yikes!

Early in 1966 the RFP was issued by the Department of Defense Production. The requirements were essentially administrative (payroll, pensions, personnel records, etc.). But the desired mainframe configuration, operating system and compiler looked like a solution tailor-made for a Burroughs 5500. IBM was still in the process of coming to market with its new System 360 architecture which, it turned out, wasn't really ready for the benchmarking that DND demanded. As an early opportunity to build a relationship in my new role with DND, I invited a few officers to visit the IBM plant in Don Mills. There Carl

IBM Building between Sun Life Building and Place Ville Marie, Montreal (Photo by author)

Corcoran met us for a briefing. When he was done I thanked him and asked my group to follow me to our next station. Later that day I was told by Carl's admin assistant that he had mistakenly thought that I was the senior officer of the DND group, based on the authoritative manner that I displayed when I asked my group to follow me. In the years ahead Carl never forgot that early impression.

The RFP process was painful for us all. We lost the business out of the gate. For me it was a classic baptism of fire but nevertheless a valuable experience. First, the lesson learned was powerful around the notion of selling the client with one key aim – making the RFP favour your solution. In this case it looked very much like my predecessor was AWOL in that context. Second, benchmarking is dangerous with hot off the press technology like System 360. And third, non-user-friendly operating system software (OS 360) was to be avoided. The loss review in this case was a strong learning opportunity to say the least. Fortunately for me, my territory that year included a large grocery wholesaler (M Loeb Ltd.). So I bore down on that account for the following months, selling that company a new mainframe and new input devices (document readers and punch card upgrades) – enough to qualify for the Hundred Percent Club! I received my first commission cheque in November that year – just in time to pay down my bank loan!

1967 presented an opportunity that was completely unexpected. In the early fall I was asked to consider moving to Montreal to become Industry Marketing Manager, Government & Services, reporting to Jake Avery, then Vice-President, Eastern Region. During the following 18 months or so I grew to respect and admire Jake greatly. I enjoyed my job even more so. I was in the heart of the corporate planning cycle for IBM World Trade, which included a 30-day international working session in Geneva, Switzerland, with the other major WTC country companies in January 1968. My slice of the pie (Government & Services) included all government, education, medical, transportation and utilities aligned with the GEM region in the U.S. In short, a huge learning experience. Just the defense sector itself was all-consuming. Motivated as I was, I poured myself into all of it. So much so, the American leaders at the session asked me if I would consider setting up a GEM Application Support Centre in Zurich on a two-year assignment. I declined, given my family circumstances at the time. Yes, my spouse was expecting our third child.

A while after my return from Geneva I spent time with Jay Kurtz, who had recently been appointed Branch Manager, Toronto Datacentre Marketing. In those times promotions within IBM came thick and fast. Jay tested me to see if I might be interested in that same job in Montreal. After some reflection I agreed to the transfer if offered the job by Jay's boss. That offer came soon, and off I went to build that office. The excitement was such that I had lots of internal applicants. Later I attended the Hundred Percent Club in the Bahamas in early 1969, where Jay told me that he was resigning from IBM to join an investment and management group setting out to build and go to market with a large-scale scientific datacentre based in Toronto. His asked if I would join them and run their Montreal business. Once again, but this time in pursuit of wealth, I agreed. I resigned from IBM that spring.

We began operations in late 1969 following a $15 million IPO which funded a modern datacentre facility in which sat a CDC 6600 mainframe suited to scientific and engineering applications. It was now early 1970 and the beginning of a protracted economic recession. We quickly learned that the first corporate cuts in such circumstances hit research, engineering and development budgets hardest. The market collapse became pervasive. Our business forecasts were hard hit, leaving no alternative but to pursue other relatively recession-proof applications. That pursuit stumbled when it became clear that a CDC 6600 CPU choked when processing commercial applications. Our processing costs were too high while our IBM datacentre competition sailed through with colours flying. Our CEO was terminated in early 1971, replaced by a turnaround artist who, in cooperation with our lead investor, put together a deal to purchase Montreal's CFCF TV and CJAD Radio from Marconi. So, overnight, our company was in the media business and I, along with our core staff, was out of a job! Within days, while lunching at the Inn on the Park, Bill Moore, then President of IBM Canada, passed by my table, said hello and asked me how things were going. I said not well. He suggested I call Vice-President Phil Lemay in Ottawa.

I knew Phil well from his days as Quebec City branch manager. When I arrived in Ottawa a few days later he offered me a marketing job focussed on National Revenue Taxation and Customs and Excise as an Advisory Marketing Representative. I recognized that I deserved a demotion upon my unusual return to IBM. I set out to prove my worth once again. In short, after winning a contract for two loosely coupled IBM System 360 Model 158's supporting an on-line data entry solution involving 1000 IBM 3270 terminals engineered to accept income tax data by Social Insurance Number, I was awarded the 1973 Large Account Marketing prize and was made a marketing manager in

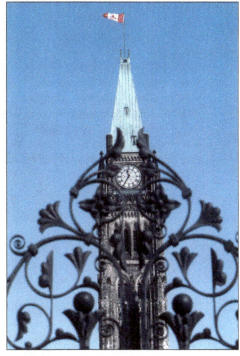

Peace Tower, Parliament Buildings, Ottawa (Photo by author)

the Ottawa office. I felt affirmed once again. Then the wheels came off! A dispute arose regarding my commission payment for this successful deal. IBM offered that I should be compensated as part of the branch management plan. I contended that I should be paid as the marketing representative of record.

Coincidentally I received an unsolicited offer to become the Executive Director, Management Information Systems at Canada Mortgage and Housing Corporation (CMHC). The offer came from Jim Coutts, who later became Prime Minister Pierre Trudeau's Principal Secretary. His business partner, Jerome Redican, knew me. In short, I took the offer, leaving the commission issue unresolved. My subsequent success at CMHC was very much due to the training and experience garnered from my years at IBM. For that I remain grateful. Joining CMHC in May 1974, I became Vice-President, Finance and Administration that fall. In September 1975 I was promoted again to Executive Vice-President. Then, in June 1976, the government appointed me its President and CEO for a seven year statutory term. In time I moved on from CMHC to become Deputy Minister, Supply and Services Canada and Deputy Receiver-General. After five years I left government service to start my own business – a government relations consultancy in partnership with Bill Neville (Joe Clark's former Chief of Staff).

So there you have it – a taste of what the IBM afterlife was like for me and several of my contemporaries.

To all of my erstwhile colleagues and to you, the reader, I leave this traditional Gaelic blessing:

May the road rise up to meet you.
May the wind be always at your back.
May the sun shine warm upon your face;
the rains fall soft upon your fields
and until we meet again,
may God hold you in the palm of His hand.

Epilogue

Me in my THINK tank (Sketch by James Harvey)

As I personally penned the penultimate pages of the present prose, I pondered what to write in the Epilogue. After all, everything I wanted to say has already been said. But then, this morning, as I blissfully basked in the balm of the bath – my time-tested THINK tank – it suddenly came to me.

Writing this book was akin to writing a computer program, as I did so often so many years ago. Simply stated, a computer program consists of three main elements: input, processing and output.

A program's input came in many different forms during my days, as it followed the constantly evolving technology – paper tape, punched cards, magnetic tapes, disk, telecommunications, etc. Similarly the input for this book came from a variety of sources in a mélange of formats. My reach-out to former IBM colleagues resulted in an avalanche of recollections and anecdotes, as well as photos and other memorabilia. As you might imagine, their input came in a wide range of formats – from terse one-liners to lengthy epistles. Frankly, I was overwhelmed by the response. Other input came from family diaries, personal archives (I was a packrat!) and Google searches.

Processing was the heart of the computer program and consisted of instructions, statements, paragraphs, subroutines and various other elements, all being linked together by a main program. For this book, the processing step was as challenging as any of the hundreds of programs that I have coded. How would I divide the book into chapters? Would it be organized topically or chronologically? How would I tie all the seemingly disparate information together? Were there sections I should omit? These and other questions made the processing phase longer than I had anticipated as I rearranged and retitled chapters, rewrote paragraphs and sometimes suffered from "writer's block."

A program's output is its raison d'être. Without producing output, a program has no purpose. But before a program can produce valid output, it has to be debugged. Some of my fellow programmers used to let the computer find the bugs, but I always preferred to locate the little varmints myself by "desk-checking" my programs before submitting them for processing. In any case, a programmer's ultimate goal and triumph was having their program successfully arrive at end-of-job (EOJ). To debug this tome, in addition to desk-checking (i.e., proofreading), I have employed Microsoft Word's spell-checker. The resulting output is in your hands.

EOJ

www.ingramcontent.com/pod-product-compliance
Lightning Source LLC
Chambersburg PA
CBHW071418050326
40689CB00010B/1889